Jim Gilbert's
Minnesota Nature Notes

Jim Gilbert's
Minnesota Nature Notes

Exploring the changes in our
backyards, fields, lakes and woods—
week by week, season by season

NODIN PRESS

ISBN 978-1-932472-68-4

Library of Congress Control Number: 2008907660

Second printing, 2009

Front cover photos:
Wood ducks: U.S. Department of Fish and Wildlife
Sunflowers: mrspants / dreamstime.com
Winter cardinal: Claudine Bessel / Dreamstime.com
Fall leaves: Aaron Moen

Design and layout: John Toren
Printed at Bang Printing: Brainerd, Minnesota

Nodin Press, LLC
530 North Third Street
Suite 120
Minneapolis, MN
55401

To Norton Stillman, for his determined efforts to get me to gather some of my nature notes into a book as a way of encouraging others to see, value, and help preserve Minnesota's natural wonders.

Acknowledgements

For more than two decades it has been my privilege to gather and then share nature notes with WCCO Radio listeners, and most of that time has been on Denny Long's show, Sunday mornings starting at 7:15, 830 on the AM dial. Denny is always upbeat and is truly an outstanding communicator.

There is a group of people from around the state that regularly share their nature observations with me, and I use this information to keep up to date for teaching, writing and broadcasting. My sincere thanks to these people: David and Mary Brislance from Lutsen, Julie Brophy and Bill Lutz from Victoria, Naturalist Beth Conant from the Minnesota Zoo, Terry and Kathryn Frazee who live on the shore of Green Lake at Spicer, Rick Haley (science teacher) from Delano, Naturalist Peter Harris at Wolf Ridge Environmental Learning Center, Richard and Marlys Hjort from Chisago City, Jim Hovda from Rice, master birder Oscar Johnson from Brooklyn Park, Marge Kellor from Pierson Lake in Carver County, Tim Kornder from Brewery Creek Farm on the edge of Belle Plaine, Eric Luetgers from Timberlake Orchard located 9 miles south of Fairmont, Russ and Sandy Rippberger who live on the edge of Bass Creek in Brooklyn Park and have 40 wood duck nesting boxes in a half-acre yard, Naturalist Orwin Rustad from Faribault, Kevin Schramm who farms near Plato, Matt Schuth (wildlife manager) from the University of Minnesota Landscape Arboretum, and Walter Thomas from Hastings, who travels the state.

Gloria Benson, Dick Gray, Derald Johnson, Jim Wyer and many more help me gather ice-out and freeze-up dates for Minnesota lakes. Clark Machtemes, and Ed and Mary Zieroth from the Lake Waconia area, Don and Mary Somers from Minnetrista, and Bev Gustafson from St. Peter help me keep track of spring maple sap runs. I truly appreciate all these nature observers and their reports, plus the first-hand sightings called in or sent by hundreds of others each year. It's wonderful to know that so many people find the natural world fascinating and are interested in sharing what they notice.

I continue to be thankful for all who have helped me along my journey to become and then to serve as a naturalist, phenologist and educator. My parents, Gil and Marge, got me started. In the early 1960s professors at Gustavus Adolphus College helped launch me into a career. Three of the many fine teachers included Charles Hamrum who introduced me to the world of insects, Geologist Chester Johnson who first taught me to read the landscape, and Bob Moline who helped me understand meteorology.

The thousands of students from Hopkins Public Schools and hundreds of Gusties I have taught have helped me become a better observer and learner. My thanks to them.

I am grateful to John Toren for his masterful work in editing and designing the book, and to a talented group of photographers—including Anders Bjorling from St. Peter and David Brislance from Lutsen—whose works enhance this book. If one could tell the story of nature's beauty in words, there wouldn't be a need to carry around a camera.

A special thanks to staff members of the Andersen Horticultural Library at the University of Minnesota Landscape Arboretum. Librarian Richard T. lsaacson; and library assistants Christine Aho, Susan Cross, Renee Jensen and Susan Moe provided invaluable research materials and a quiet study environment for me as I wrote day after day.

I express appreciation and love to my wife Sandra. It's a joy to share life, including long walks with our dog Gilbey, and a multitude of outdoor observations with her and our three sons Andrew, Christian and John, and Andrew's wife Liisa and their children Lukas, Ailsa, Anja and Lonne. The family pontoon boat outings on Lake Waconia are especially memorable.

Jim Gilbert
Waconia, Minnesota
July 30, 2008

Table of Contents

Introduction

This book is not a plant and animal identification volume or a novel with a good plot, but a collection of outdoor observations put together to highlight the subtle changes that take place in the course of a Minnesota year. Each week is different, and has much to offer even the casual observer. My hope is that the reader will also gain a better understanding of the broader canvas within which we live, catching glimpses of the arrivals and departures, births and transformations that mark the four seasons, with detailed explanations here and there of a few of nature's events and organisms to help give the observations greater meaning.

There is awesome beauty to be observed every day of the year. We just have to be aware and keep looking for it. It's interesting to follow the path solar energy takes as it flows through both the living and nonliving parts of our forests, prairies, meadows, lakes, streams, and wetlands. Even tiny and seemingly insignificant things deserve our

attention, and help us to appreciate how the earth works.

This book is organized in such a way that you can pick it up at any time and spend a few minutes pondering the question, What's happening outdoors *right now*? The text for any given week offer clues as to what things to look for, and also includes a series of "scattered events" that will suggest how variable and interesting any given day or week can be. Soon you'll be creating your own nature log to mark the weather, bird activity, and plant development you notice during a specific time of the year.

Many of the entries are based on observations made in the Minneapolis/ St. Paul and Waconia areas, which is where I live, but every effort has been made to include events from throughout the state. Minnesota is a big state, after all—about 360 miles north to south and 250 miles east to west. Northeastern and north-central Minnesota can be characterized as coniferous forest interspaced with aspen, birch and sugar maple, plus lakes and wetlands. Southern and western Minnesota is now predominantly agricultural land. Less that one percent of the original tall-grass prairie remains and most of the prairie wetlands have been drained. But this part of the state also has lakes, and there are still wetlands and deciduous forests left to enjoy and preserve.

Jim Gilbert's Minnesota Nature Notes will serve beginners who are just starting to discover their natural heritage, but will also be useful to amateur and professional naturalists and to those interested in the science of phenology.

Phenology

Phenology is simply observing the natural world and keeping a record of it. But it is also the science that studies the timing of natural events—for example, lake ice-out dates or the blooming dates of spring wildflowers—that mark seasonal (and sometimes climatic) changes to the environment. The Swedish botanist Carolus Linnaeus (1707–1778) is considered the father of modern phenology. In *Philosophia Botanica* (1751) he clearly described phases of plant development and outlined purpose and methodology of observations that are still valid today. He established the first network of observation stations in Sweden—eighteen in all—and stipulated that the main purpose of these study stations was to compile annual "plant calendars" of leaf opening, flowering, fruiting, and leaf fall, together with climatological observations "so as to show how areas differ."

The study of phenological data helps us establish the patterns of interdependency of all things. In this beautiful world of ours, nothing exists on its own. Most events in the annual cycle recur in regular order on or near the same date for any certain location. In the last 20 years or so we have noticed that lake ice is leaving the lakes earlier, and that common purple lilac shrubs bloom earlier. These are just two indications of climatic change. Will these early springs continue? Have humans upset the scheme of things? Phenological observations may help us find answers to these questions.

January

January is the coldest month of the year here in Minnesota, on average, yet fleeting signs of spring are already in the air, most noticably the songs of white-breasted nuthatches, northern cardinals, and black-capped chickadees. The tracks of deer, coyote, fox, squirrel, and other creatures are interesting to observe and follow. Our daylight hours increase almost an hour this month, and during January we often have a warm period—the "January thaw"—marked by melting temperatures, sunshine, and south to westerly winds. Enjoy this crisp time of the year. Go outside where you can feel the crunch of the snow, look for animal tracks, and listen for quiet sounds.

READING THE LANDSCAPE

Week one (January 1–7)

Earth is Closest to the Sun
Whistling Chickadees
Evergreens
Red-breasted Nuthatches

Week two (January 8–15)

Gray Jays
Fish Under the Ice
Common Mullein
White Cedar Trees

Week three (January 16–23)

Seasonal Affective Disorder
The First Northern Cardinal Sings
Common Goldeneye
Shivering Chickadees

Week four (January 24–31)

How Cold Has it Been?
Red Foxes
Gray Foxes
January: Coldest *and* Snowiest
Great Gray Owls

first week in january

To many people, winter is the season of anticipation and joy, and also, here in temperate Minnesota, the season of survival and frozen beauty. Already by January 1 we have gained 4 minutes of daylight since the winter solstice, a welcome gift. On New Year's Day the normal high and low temperatures for Minneapolis/St. Paul are 22° and 5°F. The record high is 48° set in 1897; the record low of -40° was recorded in 1860.

Lake ice is often heard cracking and thundering as it contracts with the cold temperatures. The loud, long sounds do not necessarily mean that the ice is unsafe for fishing or skating, but when one is out on the ice those roars and rolls are eerie indeed. Seed and plant catalogs are arriving in mailboxes, and many Minnesotans relish the opportunity to begin planning for the upcoming gardening season.

Eastern cottontail rabbits feed on the bark of sumac shrubs and other woody plants sticking up above the snow. A gray squirrel can eat up to forty pounds of acorns in one winter. The acorns are found in the ground by odor alone. Flying squirrels sometimes use wood duck nesting boxes as winter homes; several can be found in one box, each rolled up like a ball.

House finches feed on green ash seeds and European starlings relish crabapples. On bitterly cold days birds puff out their feathers for more insulation. Great horned owls can be heard hooting to one another as they set up nesting territories. Discarded Christmas trees put outside next to birdfeeders give chickadees and other visitors a safe place to perch and offer some protection from the winds.

In some parts of northern Minnesota, ruffed grouse dive into powdery snow to keep warm at night. Timber wolves travel on the wind-packed snow of the northern lakes.

scattered events

- **January 1, 2006** - Close to 30 inches of snow covers the BWCAW near the Sawbill Trail, where tracks in the snow from red squirrels, snowshoe hares, and timber wolves are easy to find, and the chattering of the red squirrels and croaking sounds of common ravens break the quiet air.

- **January 2, 2005** - Ice thickness on Lake Waconia averages 14 inches. The Twin Cities continues to be mostly brown with only traces of snow seen, and a total of only 2.8 inches recorded for the season so far. At Lutsen a foot of new snow covers the ground, making a total of 60 inches of snow for the season. Pine siskins, common redpolls, and black-capped chickadees are the most numerous of the Lutsen/Tofte area birdfeeder birds. Sightings of

great gray owls make birding interesting along the North Shore.

- **January 4, 2006** - Many flocks of up to 30 ring-necked pheasants can be seen gleaning in corn-stubble fields on Buffalo Ridge in the Lake Benton area within sight of hundreds of tall wind turbines.

- **January 4, 2007** - The string of warm winter days continues with a high of 41° in the Twin Cities, tying the modern record from 1898. Outdoor skating rinks have closed. We are quickly losing the small amount of snow cover, but it's good to hear the first spring songs of the black-capped chickadees and blue jays. The big tom wild turkeys fanned their tails in the warm sunlight.

- **January 5, 2007** - High temperature of 37° F. Lake Minnetonka, which froze over December 5, now has large areas of open water, and Lake Calhoun in Minneapolis has opened again with about 50 percent being ice free. A moderate El Nino, enhanced by global warming, plays a part in our weird weather. A great blue heron was seen at Minnehaha Creek in Minnetonka. Raccoons were out and about this warm evening.

- **January 6, 2006** - Three snowy owls were spotted at Minneapolis/St. Paul International Airport; these visitors from the far north don't come into Minnesota every year.

A Closer Look:
Earth is Closest to the Sun

Each year, sometime between January 1 and 4, the earth reaches its closest approach to the sun. At that moment (called perihelion) it is 3.1 million miles closer to the sun than on July 4. This is because our planet's orbit is not perfectly round but elliptical. Astronomers tell us that on January 2, 2008, at 5:35 p.m. CST, the earth was only 91,401,595 miles from the sun, while the previous summer, on Independence Day, we were at the point of aphelion—94.5 million miles away.

In spite of Minnesota being closest to the sun in January, it is nevertheless the coldest month of the year. During January in the Northern Hemisphere, the sun is low in the sky. Days are warmer in the spring, summer, and fall in Minnesota because the sun is higher in the sky, concentrating more heat on each acre of land or water. Also, the days are longer, giving the sun more time to heat the land and water, which then heat the atmosphere.

A Closer Look:
Whistling Chickadees

Even on these cold January mornings we sometimes hear the black-capped chickadees whistling "fee-bee" over and over

© Bruce Macqueen | Dreamstime.com

near our feeding stations. This sound lifts our spirits and is considered one of the earliest spring signs. Some people even interpret the two-noted call as "spring-soon." It is a matter of speculation whether the "fee-bee" call is the true song of the chickadee. It is heard most often in early spring, but we hear it throughout the winter also, many times on cold, cloudy days. We even hear chickadees whistling in the heat of summer and on crisp autumn days.

In a clear sweet whistle, the chickadee sounds two notes of equal length, the second tone lower in pitch than the first, making the whistled "fee-bee" sound. Frequently the second note has a slight waver in the middle as if the bird sang a "fee-beyee" rather than "fee-bee."

Those who confuse this song of the black-capped chickadee with the well-enunciated but rather coarse "pheo-be" or "fi-bree" of the eastern phoebe might be interested to know that this call is not whistled like the "fee-bee" song of the chickadee. Since the eastern phoebe is a summer resident, usually arriving in April and leaving in September, its song is only heard in the spring and summer.

A Closer Look:
Evergreens

Many of us agree that new snow on evergreen boughs is one of the most beautiful sights in nature. These trees and shrubs have special adaptations. The needles of evergreens have waxy coatings that protect them from the cold dry winter air. Also, evergreen branches bend down under the weight of heavy snow and cast it off, reducing the chance that they will break.

In the southern part of the United States, broad-leaved evergreens such as the live oak, southern magnolia, rhododendrons, and box-woods add a green look to the landscape in winter. However, here in Minnesota we have native spruces, pines, junipers, an arborvitae, and the balsam fir, to all of which the term "narrow-leaved evergreens" is applied. All these leaf-retaining plants belong to a great group of plants that botanists call gymnosperms—plants that have no flowers in the ordinary garden

sense of the word, but bear seeds on the surface of the scales of cones. It's the narrow-leaved evergreens, both native and those brought here from other parts of the country or world, that are especially appreciated in winter, when leaf-losing broad-leaved trees are without their green foliage.

The native Minnesota evergreens play a major role in the ecology of our northern forests, and to a lesser extent in forest areas to the south. However, all across the state, evergreens of many species and cultivars make our cities and individual yards more livable in the winter by protecting us from cold winds and helping us feel sheltered as they add their shades of green to the white or brown winter

Photo: John Toren

scene. They fill in for the deciduous trees and shrubs that are bare and cold in the winter. A big specimen pine or spruce can add dignity to your house, and a row of spreading junipers, a narrow-leaved evergreen favorite, can be used effectively along a boundary wall.

Photo: David Brislance

A Closer Look:
Red-breasted Nuthatches

We observe two species of nuthatches in Minnesota. The white-breasted nuthatch is a common non-migrator found throughout the state except in the north-central. Its smaller cousin, the red-breasted nuthatch, has a rusty-red belly, a black cap, and a distinctive black stripe through the eye. (The female has a gray cap and pale undersides.) Both species are tree-trunk foraging birds that regularly climb down trees head-first. "Hatch" is a corruption of the word "hack," and "nuthatch" refers to the bird's preferred method of hacking open seeds and nuts with its bill.

The red-breasted nuthatch is a permanent resident across much of the northeastern and north-central regions of Minnesota, and are often seen at seed and suet feeders. Starting in mid-August and going through early November, some red-breasted nuthatches migrate into the central and eastern regions of the state. This winter visitant can occur anywhere in the state, though it's fairly rare over most of the western regions. Its range includes southern Alaska, much of Canada, the Rocky Mountains, the fir forests of the Pacific coast, and parts of the northeast United States.

Red-breasted nuthatch habitat is the coniferous forests, where the birds are fond of the seeds of pines, spruces, and firs. They can deftly pry open cone scales with their bills and extract the seeds. Insects are also important food items.

Many of us enjoy seeing a red-breasted nuthatch visit a seed feeder, quickly grabbing a sunflower seed and flying off to a nearby tree to wedge the seed into a bark crevice before hacking it open.

Wildlife photographer Dave Brislance has actually befriended a red-breasted nuthatch who follows him on short trail hikes near his home on the forested ridge above Lake Superior at Lutsen. Dave has named the 4½-inch, ⅓-ounce bird Norris, and he meets up with him in a grove of cedars near his house, feeding him black oil sunflower seeds or sunflower kernels from his hand, even on windy winter days when wind chills drop to the -50 to -55 degree range. When it's a bit warmer, or at least not windy, a small flock of usually six to ten black-capped chickadees follow along with Dave and Norris. They too will take sunflower seeds from Dave's hand.

Over time Dave has noticed that these cordial encounters with the tiny wisps of northern forest life seem to have made other wildlife less wary of him, and this has made it easier for Dave to get fantastic photos of nesting warblers, a Cooper's hawk, a saw-whet owl, pine martins, white-tailed deer, timber wolves, and other elusive species.

On March 25, 2008, Norris's newly-acquired mate came and ate from Dave's hand for the first time. What trust!

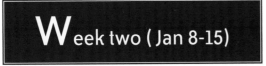

Week two (Jan 8-15)

In years when there is a lack of snow, ice boaters and ice skaters can enjoy good conditions on the frozen lakes. Icicles will grow on cold, sunny days.

We can now hear early spring bird music, largely as a result of increased daylight. Listen for black-capped chickadees singing "fee-bee" over and over, the nasal "whi, whi, whi" song of the white-breasted nuthatch, and blue jays in small noisy flocks giving "pumphandle" spring calls.

The land-hibernating frogs—wood frogs, chorus frogs, spring peepers, and gray tree frogs—lie frozen but will survive.

White-tailed deer bucks continue to lose their antlers. Deer are browsing twigs from sugar maples, basswoods, red cedars, both smooth and staghorn sumacs, and more. About six to ten pounds of twigs are eaten daily by healthy deer. Flying squirrels visit feeding stations after dark, where they relish corn, sunflower seeds, and suet.

Those brown-colored leaves from red oak trees that have been clinging to their branches since last growing season are starting to fall—a very subtle spring sign.

In the Lutsen/Tofte area, timber wolves can be heard howling, and at feeding stations Canada jays, blue jays, black-capped chickadees and red-breasted nuthatches are commonly seen.

scattered events

- **January 8, 2003** - Record high of 54° F in the Twin Cities on this 31st straight day with above normal temperatures. There were six grassfires reported in the metro area. Mosses in forests looked lush green and they were photosynthesizing. Runners ran in shorts and T-shirts; other outdoor enthusiasts flew kites, golfed, and picnicked. There is no snow on the ground in the southern half of Minnesota, and just a few inches of snowcover in the northern part of the state. Most southern Minnesota rivers are open or just partly ice covered.

- **January 9, 1998** - At the Wilderness Canoe Base, located at the upper end of the Gunflint Trail, black-capped chickadees, gray jays, blue jays, downy and hairy woodpeckers, red squirrels, and a pine martin come to the feeding station. Redpolls, pine grosbeaks, and a flock of about forty snow buntings feed on cracked corn and oats at a Grygla area feeding station. Steam fog rises from Lake Superior which is still wide open.

- **January 10, 2007** - In Victoria, a flock of at least 30 American robins feeds on crabapple fruit.

- **January 11, 1999** - More than 300 horned larks appear along the road between Cologne and Belle Plaine. About 50 bald eagles perch in trees of Colville Park at Red Wing.

- **January 13, 2006** - Due to the warm winter being experienced all over the Upper Midwest, the Rainy River east of Baudette is now open. Local people don't ever remember the river being open before in January.

Alexander Kolomietz | Dreamstime.com

A Closer Look:

Gray Jays

I met my first gray jay many years ago while on a camping trip in northeastern Minnesota, the year-round home of this species. A bird silently swooped down and snatched a hotdog, or part of one, out of a frying pan on a fire. Wow! We could hardly believe what we saw. Later we found out that gray jays are fond of baked beans, oatmeal, and other camp grub, and that campfire smoke and the sound of an ax brings them in close. Hunters know that the sound of a gun will bring the gray jays, eager for moose or deer meat.

A fluffy gray bird a bit larger than an American robin, the gray jay has a white throat and forehead, a black patch on the back of its head, a short black bill, and dark eyes. Coloration suggests a huge overgrown chickadee.

The gray jay, also called Canada jay, has been given the nickname "camp robber" because it rummages through camps looking for food scraps. Native Americans called it "wiskedjak" from which "whiskey jack," another of its common names, is taken. This bird is easily tamed, as Dave and Mary Brislance, who live on the wooded ridge above Lutsen, found out soon after becoming residents in 2003. Five years later, two gray jays often fly out of the woods to their hands if offered pieces of bread or hotdog bits.

Gray jays will eat just about anything, but are listed as insect, fruit, and seed eaters. The bird's opportunistic behavior is not purposeless. It's storing food and fattening itself against the long northern winter, when it may have to eat lichens or balsam fir needles, and when its biological clock will urge it to begin nesting in late February or early March, and sometimes as late as April. Balls of chewed food are stuck in trees with a sticky fluid secreted by glands in the jay's mouth, when food is plentiful in summer and fall. With snow and subzero temperatures keeping a gray jay close to its eggs in a feather-lined nest four to thirty feet above ground in a tree, it will need these near-by secret stores.

Found in Alaska, across Canada, the northern tier of forty-eight states, and down into the Rocky Mountains, the gray jay's habitat is the coniferous forest to the tree line. Stands of white cedar in Minnesota and Wisconsin seem to be promising sites to look for them. They usually are found in pairs or in small family groups. Gray jays are primarily permanent residents but in some years wandering individuals have been observed in central and southern Minnesota in October through December. Banding records show that these birds can live at least ten years.

A Closer Look:
Fish Under the Ice

Ice covers all Minnesota lakes except Lake Superior at this time. On most of the state's fifteen thousand lakes the ice is now from one to two feet thick. Under this concealment, fish and other animals are sealed off from their replenishing supply of oxygen. Without the mixing of air and water by waves, and with photosynthesis at low ebb, very little oxygen is introduced into the water.

To survive under all the ice and snow, fish moderate their eating, growth, movement, and reproductive patterns. As winter progresses, oxygen first disappears from the bottom of lakes, because bacteria is using it to decompose leaves and other organic matter in the sediment. Consequently, sunfishes, northern pike, and other species move up the water column. Lakes that are very shallow, quite small, or that have high decomposition rates, eventually run out of oxygen entirely. The result is what is known as "winterkill," which may kill all the fish in a lake.

A Closer Look:
Common Mullein

A native of Europe, common mullein (*Verbascum Thapsus L.*) is widely naturalized in America, and many of my field biology students over the years have found it the easiest winter weed to recognize. Mullein is quite a strange form in the winter landscape. It may grow to a height of seven feet or more, and is found in some of the poorest soils. We often see mullein growing along roadsides, even in gravel by the sides of highways.

In winter the leaves are gone, but each stem stands straight, holding its spiked flowerheads of seed capsules throughout the winter. Most of these giants have just one spike, but a few branch on top to look like roadside candelabra. A multi-spiked mullein in silhouette reminds me of a small saguaro cactus. Up to three feet long, the spikes are filled with round pods containing large numbers of small black seeds. Though the plants remain standing through the winter, winds and sometimes animals will shake the stems, causing seeds to fall on the snow, where they will be eaten by small birds and mammals. These dried plants were once used as torches in Europe. Dipped in tallow, they burned for quite a long time, each empty flowerhead holding the solidified fat.

During its first year, the common mullein produces a large rosette of big, grayish-green leaves up to a foot long and velvet to the touch, which are conspicuous in fields and so-called waste places. Being biennials, these rosettes of woolly leaves give rise to the tall flower stalks the next summer. The yellow flowers are 5-lobed, ¾-inch across, and are open a few at a time between June and September.

A Closer Look:
White Cedar Trees

The white cedar is an evergreen tree of the colder regions of eastern North America. It is native from Nova Scotia to Manitoba and south to Minnesota and the mountains of North Carolina. In Minnesota we see white cedars along the edges of swamps, lakes and streams of the northeast and north-central regions. They form almost impenetrable pure stands in poorly drained swamps with a neutral or basic substrate of organic matter, and groves can be found on upland sites of dry alkaline soils over limestone bedrock. They are not found in acid bogs where black spruce dominates.

Stands of white cedar trees provide sheltered food yards for deer during the winter, while birds and other animals find safety within the thick boughs. The tiny half-inch long cones supply seeds for pine siskins. Red squirrels eat the buds in spring and cut small, cone-laden branchlets in the fall for their winter caches. Snowshoe hares, white-tailed deer and moose browse the trees.

Pines, spruces and balsam fIrs have long thin leaves, but the white cedar copes with the dry cold of winter in its own way. Its needles form as tightly overlapping scales covering the stems, making flat fan-shaped sprays. Shorter than one-fourth inch, these tightly locked leaves do what thin needles do for other conifers—keep them from drying out and limit snow build up. The needles, when crushed, give off a strong pungent odor.

Names can always be confusing. The white cedar (*Thuja occidentalis L.)* is also known as eastern white cedar, northern white cedar and arborvitae. The common name "arborvitae" translated from Latin means "tree of life" and can refer to it being green in the winter, or to the idea that Native Americans used parts of this tree to treat scurvy.

The flat-growing twigs and branches make white cedar a favorite ornamental evergreen in southern Minnesota as well as over the Upper Midwest and beyond. It's a stately ornamental and can be used as a foundation planting, or for hedges and windbreaks, and even in lower wet situations. There are few evergreens that tolerate shade, but white cedar is one to consider. This species has been cultivated since 1536 and now there are cultivars available with many shapes and sizes to fulfill landscape needs.

Week three (Jan 16-23)

Lakes can be heard cracking, groaning and booming. This happens because once ice forms it expands when warmed and contracts when cooled. With a January thaw look for some mosses that will be lush green and growing, honey bees out on cleansing flights, snowfleas jumping on the surface of the snow, and the first few striped skunks and raccoons out of their winter sleeping quarters.

A beaver lodge is a communal home, and because several animals are in it, the inside of the lodge may be 60 degrees warmer than the outside temperature. Eastern chipmunks may wake up on cold days but will stay inside and eat from the supply of food they stored in their underground burrows.

Wintering-over mourning doves, commonly seen at feeding stations in the last 20 years, prefer to eat cracked corn and other seeds scattered on the ground in protected spots. A spectacular behavior of American crows in winter is their communal roosting. They roost in huge flocks of sometimes hundreds or even more than a thousand. Every morning the crows disperse from their roosts in small flocks to feed and then return at sunset in the same way. Screech owls sometimes roost in wood duck houses.

As many as 15 bird species, including the northern cardinal, red-bellied woodpecker and dark-eyed junco, visit feeders in the southern part of the state. In the north, pine grosbeaks, pine siskins and Canada jays are among the birdfeeder birds. In northeastern Minnesota, at this time of year, male common ravens do elaborate courtship flight maneuvers, including steep dives, tumbles and rolls.

scattered events

- January 16, 1999 - The Sun shines brilliantly as temperature breaks through to 39° F. Honey bees were seen out on cleansing flights. In the Mississippi River Valley between St. Paul and the Iowa border, 750 bald eagles were counted by the Minnesota DNR.

- January 16, 2007 - Frigid air is over us. Lows of -34° at Embarrass and -22° at Faribault were recorded. The Mississippi River at Hastings is nearly frozen over and at St. Cloud is frozen over.

- January 17, 2005 - Cold morning. Negative 11 in the Twin Cities, -44° at International Falls, and -54° at Embarrass. Birdfeeders are active sites.

- January 18, 2007 - The last vessel of the shipping season left Duluth/Superior Harbor. The shipping season should start up again in late March or early April.

- January 20, 2003 - Master birder Oscar Johnson counted 176 bald eagles in the Mississippi River Valley between Red Wing and Wabasha. Most of the eagles were near the south end of Lake Pepin.

- January 20, 2005 - At Wolf Ridge Environmental Learning Center, near Finland and the North Shore, the snow depth is 48 inches, black-capped chickadees sing "fee-bee' over and over, and white-tailed deer stick to their trails and are browsing balsam fir, hazel, paper birch and speckled alder.

- January 21, 2006 - A great horned owl is seen on a nest near Faribault. They are the earliest birds to hatch young in the state. Round Lake, near Nisswa, with its 16 inches of ice cover, was the place today where 11,000 people gathered for the Brainerd Ice Fishing Contest. Lake Superior is wide open but beautiful ice formations, formed by wave spray, are seen on the shoreline rocks.

- January 21, 2007 - Ice on Mille Lacs Lake is up to 20 inches thick.

- January 23, 2000 - Wintering American robins continue to feed on crabapples and hackberry tree fruit. They will come to tray feeders offering suet mixes, raisins, bread, sliced apples and other fruit.

- January 23, 2007 - A very early spring flight of horned larks arrived in the Plato region. The open water area below Coon Rapids Dam contains 101 common goldeneyes and a few mallard ducks.

A Closer Look:

Seasonal Affective Disorder

For those people suffering from Seasonal Affective Disorder (SAD), symptoms usually begin to appear in November, which is known for its clouds and first ice on lakes, lowering angle of the sunlight, and shorter day lengths. It's the shorter amount of daylight that adversely affects as many as one in three Minnesotans during the winter months, and causes anxiety and depression. Other symptoms include a craving for carbohydrates and an urge to sleep more. Some researchers speculate that SAD may be a throwback to thousands of years ago when our ancestors sort of "hibernated" during the cold winter months, living off food they had stored up and sleeping through cold spells.

A lack of sunlight, especially during December and January, seems to affect the production of a hormone in our bodies called melatonin, leaving some people with a weak, rundown feeling. Some Minnesotans choose to winter in sunnier and warmer locations such as Arizona, Florida, and southern California. Others get help from using better lighting. Full spectrum fluorescent lights mimic the sun, giving off light in a wide range of frequencies. These lights may help

The First Northern Cardinal Sings

It is my feeling that only those of us who are close to nature during the length of a Minnesota winter can sincerely appreciate even the subtle spring signs and take joy in each happening. The wonderful whistled songs of the northern cardinal when heard in January make us take note. Our minds think of warmer days. Yes, hearing a cardinal is a sign of spring as they sing in response to the lengthening days. The females song is like the male's but softer, so always look up and see who is singing.

First northern cardinal spring song heard, "what-cheer, cheer, cheer…" in the Lake Minnetonka area—A 25-year record:

2008 January 12	1995 January 9
2007 January 26	1994 January 10
2006 January 2	1993 January 3
2005 January 15	1992 January 31
2004 January 11	1991 January 10
2003 January 18	1990 January 4
2002 January 12	1989 January 1
2001 January 5	1988 January 21
2000 January 7	1987 January 4
1999 January 16	1986 January 7
1998 January 2	1985 January 8
1997 January 31	1984 January 2
1996 January 4	

many people get out of their winter funk. But because anxiety and depression are involved, before using light or another therapy, first consult your family physician.

On the other hand, a significant segment of the state's population really enjoys winter and even thrives on our cold season climate. Ice skating, ice hockey, sledding, snowshoeing and cross-country skiing, ice fishing, walking nature trails, feeding wildlife, and other winter activities occupy people of all ages across the state.

A Closer Look: The Common Goldeneye

Coniferous forests from New York to Alaska and across Eurasia are the summer home of the cavity-nesting diving duck called the common goldeneye. Oscar Johnson, an avid birder from Brooklyn Park, called to tell me that on January 23, 2007, he had counted 101 common goldeneyes and a few mallards in an open water area below Coon Rapids Dam.

© Terry Alexander | Dreamstime.com

Goldeneyes are sometimes called "whistlers," for the sound their wings make in flight.

These mid-sized, 2-pound ducks get their name from their yellow eyes, but the males possess even more colorful features. A male has a green head, white cheek patch, and a great amount of white showing on his black and white body. Females are gray with a brown head and white collar.

The rising steam fog from waters on these winter days can make viewing difficult, but the ducks dive and feed in seeming comfort. The water temperatures are in the low 30s, warmer than the air, and the ducks' well-insulated feathers keep their wet bodies from losing much heat.

While many of the goldeneyes from Minnesota winter as far south as the Gulf, some stay here all winter especially on the Mississippi River and on Lake Superior. Come summer they return to the lakes in the northeastern and north-central regions of the state and nest in tree cavities of the boreal forest. Nesting boxes are frequently put up for goldeneyes.

Expert divers, common goldeneyes may remain under for about 20 seconds and dive to a depth of about 20 feet, but usually feed in water less than 10 feet deep. Their food consists of aquatic insects and aquatic plants, but they also eat crayfish and snails. In saltwater areas they add mussels and several types of crabs to their diet.

A Closer Look:

Shivering Chickadees

Black-capped chickadees are found throughout Minnesota and well into Canada and Alaska. These agile, seemingly cheerful, five-inch-long birds are out no matter what the weather.

Chickadees and other birds have greater resistance to cold than mammals and have many adaptations to help them deal with heat loss. Without them, the chickadee, with the core of its tiny body less than an inch from the outside air, would freeze solid almost immediately.

Sometimes chickadees shiver. Shivering allows them to make short-term adjustments to cold; it is the main way they increase their heat production while at rest. Shivering converts muscular energy into heat, but this used energy must soon be replaced through eating. To maintain their high heat and energy production, chickadees eat rich energy foods such as insects and seeds, plus suet and more seeds from our feeders.

There is still another mechanism to help chickadees reduce heat loss. Their body temperatures can drop gradually during inactive times, until they reach a regulated condition of hypothermia. In this condition they shiver just enough to maintain their colder state. A chickadee's body temperature may drop by 18 to 22 degrees, providing close to a 20 percent energy savings. Their normal body temperature is 107° F. By dropping their temperature down, the temperature variance between their bodies and the air is less and so the heat they lose will be less.

Primarily, heat loss in birds is diminished by their coat of feathers, which encircles and insulates them with confined air. Smaller birds have more feathers relative to their body weight than large birds.

Birds have tendinous lower legs and feet rather than the exposed flesh that mammals have. Their bills are made of horn, not skin, and give up little heat. They have no projecting fleshy ears or tails from which heat would be lost. Also, bird body temperatures are higher than those of mammals.

Week four (Jan 24-31)

On cold days beautiful intricate frost patterns can be seen on some windows. The patterns come in swirls and feathers, fronds and trees. During some winters, slush covers the tops of many Minnesota and Wisconsin lakes due to the weight of the snow accumulations.

The long, arching, bright golden-yellow twigs make weeping willows glow in the landscape. Try standing under a red oak tree and listening to the persistent still attached brown leaves rustling in the wind. The sound is that of a summer rainfall.

Honey bees, balled-up deep within hives, keep themselves warm with their beating wings. Coyotes begin their mating season. Red foxes are normally solitary but are now seen in pairs as the mating season approaches.

Listen for the northern cardinals singing their "what-cheer, cheer, cheer" spring songs. Downy woodpeckers are heard drumming; they hammer on resonant trees to announce territories and attract mates. Barred owls hang around some feeding stations looking for voles, mice and shrews. European starlings have started showing yellow on their bills. Starlings' bills change from black to yellow as the spring nesting season approaches.

In northern Minnesota, most bull moose have dropped their antlers by now. Once shed, the antlers are quickly chewed into oblivion by calcium-craving animals such as mice, and the porcupine and red squirrel.

Now is the time when black bear cubs are born. The young arrive in January or early February while mothers are still sleeping in their dens. At birth the young, usually two or three in number, are 6 to 8 inches long and only weigh 7 to 12 ounces, about 1/500th of the weight of their mother. It has been suggested that because the mother black bear must often nurse her cubs three or four months with no food for herself, the young have to be small.

scattered events

- January 26, 1998 - A great horned owl was observed incubating on a nest in Brooklyn Park.

- January 27, 2007 - Lake Waconia ice thickness is about 15 inches, and sunfish and northerns are biting. Wintering-over red-tailed hawks persevere in the Twin Cities area. About 20 inches of ice covers Devil Track Lake located just off the Gunflint Trail.

- January 29, 2005 - First raccoon out and about. Northern cardinals singing "what- cheer, cheer, cheer…" Today, 51 great gray owls were counted in the Sandstone and Banning State Park vicinity .

- January 31, 1995 - Midwinter heat wave with 50˚ at Marshall and 46˚ in the Twin Cities. Muskrats were out and about. Snow is nearly gone from plowed fields in Carver County where muddy spots in country roads were encountered. Some sap icicles formed on boxelder twigs. House finches sang in full song around noon in Brooklyn Park.

- January 31, 2006 - We in the Twin Cities ended up experiencing the warmest January in more than a century.

A Closer Look:
How Cold Has It Been?

The mean annual temperature across the state of Minnesota ranges from 36˚F in the north-central and northeastern counties to a bit over 46˚ F in the extreme southeast. Record temperatures have been as high as 114˚ (July 6, 1936 in Moorhead) and as low as -60˚ (February 2, 1996 at Tower), a 174-degree range that is unrivaled over most of the earth.

The record low temperature for Minneapolis/St. Paul is -41˚ set on January 21, 1888. An arctic outbreak from 5 p.m. December 31, 1911, to 1 p.m. January 8, 1912, produced 186 consecutive hours of below zero weather in the Twin Cities, second only to a spell of 226 hours in January 1864.

Here are a few noteworthy low temperature readings in Minnesota. These temperatures were taken six feet off the ground, in weather instrument shelters, and are not wind chill temperatures.

- -59° in Moorhead on February 16, 1903
- -59° at the Leech Lake Dam (Cass County) on February 9,1899
- -59° at the Pokegama Dam (Itasca County) on February 16, 1903
- -55° in International Falls on January 6, 1909. The afternoon high that day was only -29°, the daily average was -42°; no doubt one of the state's coldest days.
- -57° in Embarrass on January 20 & 21, 1996
- -53° in Moose Lake on January 15, 1972

Record low temperatures from other states include -54° at Danbury, Wisconsin, on January 24, 1922; -60° at Parshall, North Dakota, on February 15, 1936; -58° at McIntosh, South Dakota, on February 17, 1936; -47° at Elkader, Iowa, on February 3, 1996; -70° at Rogers Pass , Montana, on January 20, 1954; -66° at Riverside, Wyoming, on February 9, 1933; and -80° at Prospect Creek, Alaska, on January 23, 1971. The Russian research facility at Vostok, Antarctica, holds the record for the coldest air temperature ever recorded on Earth, -129°F on July 21, 1983.

A Closer Look:
Red Foxes

Like other wild dogs, red foxes hunt primarily at night, but they may extend this activity into daytime during the winter, when prey is harder to catch. They like to sleep in the open during the midday, curling up on the snow in some spot protected from wind, sunning themselves when they can while keeping a watchful eye or ear out for intruders. They seldom sleep deeply.

Typical length of a red fox is about 41 inches, including a 16-inch bushy tail. They weigh up to about 14 pounds. and have a pointed nose and fairly large pointed ears. Most red foxes are some shade of yellowish-red. There is usually a trace of black fur in the middle of the back, in the tail, feet and tips of the ears. The throat, underside of the body and tip of the tail are white. In winter their coat is thick and luxurious.

Red foxes are found throughout much of Minnesota. They prefer farmlands, semi-open country and forest communities. Their natural range is from the Arctic to near the Mexican border, and also across the Northern Hemisphere in Eurasia. Being primarily carnivorous, their diet includes squirrels, rabbits, muskrats, mice, voles, and birds of many species. Foxes will often cache larger kills and visit them over a period of several days. In spring, summer and fall they add a variety of insects, frogs, fruits and other items to their diet. They may be the world's greatest destroyer of mice.

Over the years that I led winter nature walks for school students in natural areas, fox tracks were always a favorite of the kids to observe. Fox tracks can be confused with the domestic dog but their overall pattern on or crossing a trail is totally different. A dog does not need to catch food so it doesn't need to be alert for game, and it can waste energy roaming through deep snow, and it basically has no enemies. The red fox is faced with the reality of winter survival, so it must spot potential food and approach it carefully enough to catch it A fox must be on alert for enemies, and in winter it must conserve energy by walking in shallow snow, staying out of the wind, and getting the Sun's warmth whenever possible. Dog tracks tend to be sloppy; they will explore, gallop and romp without much purpose. The most common fox pattern of tracks in the snow is an almost straight line of neat prints. The tracks will wander when it' s hunting, and circle when

Photo: Mike Lentz

it's about to bed down. Red foxes do not climb trees.

Red foxes are relatively solitary animals but by late January we would sometimes see two sets of fox prints, side-by-side. They are probably monogamous for one season at a time, but may mate for life. They breed in January or February, and the females usually bear 4 to 6 young after a 51-day gestation. The family occupies a burrow which the foxes dig themselves or remodel from the den of another mammal. The den usually has two or more entrances, and there may be alternative dens within the territory. The male brings food to the female and kits and leads enemies away from the den at the risk of his life. The fox kits are independent at 5 months and full-grown at 18 months. Family groups often do not persist through fall. The life-span of a red fox is probably less than 8 years but could be as long as 15 years.

A Closer Look:
Gray Foxes

The gray fox is about the same size as the red fox but not quite as heavy (weighs up to 12 pounds), prefers more secluded areas away from human activity, is able to climb trees, and frequently walks up fallen logs. It doesn't store food as does the red fox, lacks its endurance, is more nocturnal and considered less intelligent. The gray fox is only found in the New World, ranging from Latin America to the Pacific coastal states, the southern Rockies, through most of the eastern United States and north into extreme southern Ontario and Quebec.

Here in Minnesota the gray fox can be found throughout much of the state but is not common except in the southeastern counties. It prefers wooded areas or heavy brush, in contrast to the red fox that favors more open habitats. Gray foxes climb trees not only to seek refuge but also to obtain food.

Known for a "salt and pepper" look, the gray fox is beautifully marked, black and gray above with reddish-brown along its sides. A

Photo: U.S. Fish and Wildlife Service

distinct black stripe runs down the middle of the back and continues onto the tail, which has a black tip.

When abundant, insects may make up nearly half of the diet of the gray fox. Rabbits and mice are important foods and so are various fruits in season, but birds are generally not a major food item. It's probably most accurate to say that gray foxes are opportunists, feeding on whatever vertebrate or invertebrate meat is available, with some plant material also consumed.

Mating takes place in January or February, and young are born 50 to 60 days later in a clean den. The den may be in a hollow log, cave or tunnel. Probably both parents remain with the young. There is one litter per year, averaging about four kits. The family breaks up in the autumn, though parents stay together through the year. Gray foxes appear to be territorial.

A Closer Look:
January–Coldest *and* Snowiest

January 25 is statistically the coldest day of the year, with an average high of 19°F and an average low of -1°F in the Twin Cities. In recent decades January has surpassed March to become the *snowiest* month of the year in many places across the state. In the thirty-year period from 1941 to 1970, the average January snowfall for the Twin Cities was 8.2 inches a year. During the period from 1971 to 2000 it rose to an average of 13.5 inches. The snowiest January on record for the Twin Cities was in 1982 when 46.4 inches of snow fell.

A Closer Look:
Great Gray Owls

The great gray is Minnesota's largest owl. It stands about 2 feet high, and has a 5-foot wingspread. The boreal coniferous forest is its home. In this state, great gray owls are most often seen within a hundred miles of the Canadian border. However, during some winters, a few will visit the southern part of the state. Like other owls of the Far North, this species hunts during the daytime, often watching for prey from a low perch. In winter it will plunge into snow to catch rodents detected by sounds.

Because the great gray owl spends much of its time in dense conifers, it is usually overlooked. One of the most elusive of American birds, it was discovered in America by Europeans before they realized the species also occurs in Europe.

February

February is normally the most pleasant month of winter. Warmer temperatures and sunshine often appear in mid-month and continue on into March. Bird feeding stations are especially busy on snowy days. Watch for meandering finger-thick tunnels nearby made by short-tailed shrews searching for fallen seeds, just beneath the snow. It's time to prune apple and oak trees, and to plant begonia and geranium seeds indoors. If we have a warm spell, pussy willow twigs can be cut and brought indoors for a touch of spring. Warmer temperatures bring both skunks and raccoons out of their winter dens, though thousands of ice-fishing houses still dot Minnesota lakes, which are covered with ice two to three feet thick.

READING THE LANDSCAPE

Week one (February 1–7)

Red Crossbills
Pileated Woodpecker's Display
Blizzard Talk
Crows Arrive in the Arrowhead

Week two (February 8–14)

The House Finch
Pine Thoughts
Awakening in Greenhouses
Lichen Lore

Week three (February 15–21)

Boxelder Trees
Wintering Mourning Doves
The Timber Wolf
Soaring Red-tailed Hawks

Week four (February 22–29)

Circles Around Trees
Cardinals Sing Loud and Long
Eastern Chipmunks
Pine Martens

first week in february

On February 1 the normal high and low temperatures for Minneapolis / St. Paul are 25° and 6°F. The record high of 54° was set in 1931, and the record low of negative 28° was recorded in 1951. By February 1 we have gained one hour of daylight since the winter solstice.

Groundhogs, also known as woodchucks, are hibernating underground in their burrows at this time, and their internal clocks will awaken them near the end of March, not on Groundhog Day (February 2). A curled up hibernating woodchuck's body temperature may fall as low as 38°F from a normal close to 100°, they breathe once every six minutes, and their heartbeat is about 5 percent of normal.

Many people who have feeding stations derive as much pleasure from observing wild mammals such as red and gray squirrels, flying squirrels, mice, short-tailed weasels, and white-tailed deer as they do from watching the birds. Beef suet is a favorite of insect-eating birds. Chickadees, nuthatches, brown creepers, blue jays, and several woodpecker species—downy, hairy, red-bellied, and pileated—are all fond of it.

Black-capped chickadees singing "fee-bee" over and over, providing some cheery spring music on cold mornings. With a body temperature of 108° F, a chickadee must eat its weight in food each day.

Wintering bald eagles can be seen along the Mississippi River between the Twin Cities and Brownsville in the extreme southeast part of the state. And in northern Minnesota and Wisconsin, ruffed grouse commonly fly headlong into snow to spend the night or sleep out a storm. (Loose snow is a good insulator.)

scattered events

- **February 2, 1991** - South winds boost mercury to 48° F, the warmest so far this year in the Twin Cities and area. First muddy country roads. The Minnesota River at Belle Plaine and LeSueur has open areas in the ice cover. The odor of a skunk was detected in the Park Rapids area, where the temperature hit 53° today.

- **February 3, 1995** - Today in the Faribault area, naturalist Orwin Rustad notes that the spring migration of homed larks began.

- **February 4, 2003** - Red oak leaves, which have been attached since the last growing season, are now falling. A subtle spring sign.

- **February 4, 2007** - A flock of about thirty American robins comes to a heated birdbath in White Bear Lake.

- **February 5, 1994** - Ice covers about 90 percent of Lake Superior; during most winters the lake is nearly ice free.

- February 6, 2003 - The first spring bird migrants, the horned larks, have begun arriving. A few were spotted in the Faribault area today.

- February 6, 2007 - Forty-three mourning doves were observed at one feeding station in Eagan. Two male eastern bluebirds were seen in Medina, and a yellow-rumped warbler visits a suet feeder in Monticello. This morning an extremely cold -46° F was recorded at Embarrass.

A Closer Look: Red Crossbills

The conifer forests of the northern hemisphere are the habitat of red crossbills. When their population is large, or a natural food shortage occurs, they will wander great distances. Their numbers and distribution are unpredictable, especially in southern Minnesota, but when they do appear, evergreens are most appealing to them.

Red crossbills are about the size of sparrows; both sexes have black wings and tail, but the males have a distinctive brick-red plumage, while the females are olive-gray tinged with yellow. Their outstanding characteristic is the crossed mandibles of the bill. When feeding in trees, they crawl about using their bills and feet much like small parrots. The crossed bill is used to force open and hold the cone scales apart while the tongue lifts each seed out. Besides feeding from the cones of conifers, red crossbills eat insects and the seeds from birches, alders, elms, and maples.

A Closer Look:
Pileated Woodpecker's Display

The name "pileated" for the large red-crested woodpecker means crested. The species is a permanent resident throughout the forested part of Minnesota and the heavily timbered valleys and lakeshores of the prairie areas. It lives almost wholly within the canopy of the trees, easily eluding observation.

Pileated woodpeckers feed on insects infesting standing and fallen trees, supplementing this diet with wild berries and acorns. While they come occasionally to some backyard beef suet feeders, ants are their main food. (In winter they eat dormant ants.) It's the pursuit of ants that drives them to cut large furrows, four to eight inches wide and up to a foot long, deep into the trunks of living or dead standing trees. It may be difficult to spot a pileated woodpecker,

photo: Greg Gillson

but it's easy to see where they have worked in a forest.

By early February they can be heard drumming and calling in woodlands. The call is a cackle, resembling a flicker's call, but louder and richer in quality. Throughout the greater part of the year pileateds are relatively silent, but now that the nesting season is approaching, the drumming and calling are frequently heard.

A Closer Look:
Blizzard Talk

A blizzard is a severe winter storm lasting for three or more hours. It is characterized by low or falling temperatures, winds of 35 miles per hour or more, with enough falling and or blowing snow to reduce visibility to a quarter-mile or less. In Minnesota these conditions happen most often in the southwestern and western parts of the state. Annual probability for a storm like this is especially high for the Red River Valley, where there is an 85 percent chance that at least one will develop during any given winter.

When such a storm is expected, the National Weather Service issues a blizzard warning, which indicates a life-threatening risk for people caught outside. The native plants and animals should be OK. Take in your pets and make sure farm animals have shelter. Fill the feeders at your wildlife feeding station. Dress in layers if you must leave your home. Or better yet, put another log on the fire, pop some popcorn, bake cookies, and read a good book.

A Closer Look:
Crows Arrive in the Arrowhead

On February 4, 2008, friends from "Up North" called to tell me that the first migrating American crows had returned to Lutsen and to Wolf Ridge Environmental Learning Center near Finland. To them it was a harbinger of spring. Both of these locations are near Lake Superior, had deep snow, and the expectation of many more bitterly cold days before the maple sap began running and ice left the streams. But one season slides slowly into another, daylight has increased, and the crows could sense the movement of the season.

John Trott, an extraordinary naturalist from the state of Virginia, once wrote:

So, the year is turning and moving inexorably toward spring which, once started, moves like a snowball rolling downhill. It gathers momentum and mass until early May when each day brings so much newness that I am impatient and exasperated with my inability to see and hear it all. For now, I'll concentrate on the slow momentum of February.

Feeding on almost anything edible, the gregarious American crow fills the cold quiet air with a generous portion of loud "caw, caw, caw" sounds. Migrating February flocks of crows may have come from Iowa or southern Minnesota and may keep moving toward the forests of Canada. But more flocks will keep coming and some will populate the Arrowhead and other parts of northern Minnesota. Yes, American crows winter and travel in flocks, but they are solitary nesters and later in spring will choose deciduous or coniferous trees for their homes. Nests are built of sticks, bark, plant fibers, and other stuff, and are newly constructed each year. Both sexes build the nest.

Week two (Feb 8-14)

After a snowfall, tracking will be good. It's great fun to get out and see who goes where, to note the activities of neighborhood gray squirrels, cottontail rabbits, and tunneling shrews, all recorded in the snow.

House finches have begun singing and woodpeckers are drumming. Both downy and hairy woodpeckers can be heard drumming on resonant tree trunks and limbs or other "signal posts." They do this to announce territories and establish pair bonds.

Anyone who has European starlings in their locality should see some individual birds with at least partially yellow beaks. As the nesting season approaches, a starling's bill will change from black to yellow. Barred owls carry on hooted dialogues with each other. Great horned owls are on nests incubating eggs. They are Minnesota's earliest nesting bird. Pheasants look for sumac berries.

Honey bees balled up deep within their hives keep warm with their beating wings. Otters bound and slide over the snow to travel long distances with little effort. Eastern cottontail rabbits emerge shortly after sunset to feed on the twigs and bark of small trees and shrubs. Gray squirrels may use wood duck nesting boxes for sleeping, several squirrels to one box. Coyote mating season has begun.

scattered events

- **February 8, 1991** - First time we hit 50° this year. Only about one-third of the Twin Cities landscape has snow cover. First ants on the sidewalk. The fuzzy silver-white pussy willow catkins have popped out.

- **February 8, 2007** - This evening a male saw-whet owl was singing beneath Oberg Mountain at Tofte.

- **February 10, 2005** - One hundred bald eagles were counted at Colville Park in Red Wing.

- **February 12, 1991** - Wintering mourning doves began their "cooing" songs. In Kittson County the warm weather has melted all the snow on the fields, and the open fields are now very dry and subject to wind erosion.

- **February 12, 2005** - High of 53° F. Landscape about 90 percent snow-free. House finches began singing. Common redpolls are the most numerous of the birdfeeder birds. A flock of about 25 wild turkeys visits a feeding station at Rice.

- **February 14, 2007** - The "wicker" spring call of the red-bellied woodpecker is heard. Another spring sound! Our snow drought continues. Only about four to eight inches of snow covers the Arrowhead, and one to four inches over most of the rest of Minnesota. Lake Superior is wide open but the rocky shore has an elegant ice covering from wave spray.

A Closer Look:
The House Finch

Now is when we listen for the first spring music coming from the house finches. They are a recent addition to Minnesota's avifauna, and have a pleasing song, a distinctive rolling warble. The natural range of this species extends from southern British Columbia east to Wyoming and south to central Mexico. But in the late 1930s bird dealers in New York City began importing house finches to sell as "Hollywood finches." In 1940 authorities put an end to the illegal sale of these wild birds, and one dealer released, on Long Island, his now unsaleable birds, which soon became established in the wild.

By the 1960s house finches had spread throughout the Northeast, and then began expanding westward. The first Illinois record came in 1971, and in Michigan the first house finch was recorded February 13, 1972, in Berrien Springs. The first positive identification of this species in Minnesota was made on November 21, 1980, when a single male was seen at a feeder in Minnetonka. By the 1970s the wild population in the western United States was expanding eastward, and in the mid-1980s it likely reached Minnesota from the west. Since the year 2000 the colorful relative of the purple finch has continued to spread throughout much of Minnesota both as a wintering and a nesting species. They relish black oil sunflower seeds at many feeding stations.

The success of the house finch is no doubt due to its ability to use the altered landscape provided by us humans. It thrives in towns and cities, where it nests in a variety of situations such as conifer trees, ledges of buildings, old holiday wreaths near house entrances, and in baskets of living plants hung from eaves. Nesting goes on from April into August. The nest is fairly well built of twigs, roots, string, and other materials placed in any location that affords some protection from the elements.

The house finch has an interesting history in that, unlike many other introduced species, it is native to North America. Yet, as with the house sparrow (first introduced into the Twin Cities area in 1875) and the European starling (which first appeared in Minnesota in 1929), its success is based on its ability to coexist with people. House finches must have an effect on local birds which compete for the same resources, but so far there seems to be little apparent impact.

Both male and female house finches sing a flowing, cheery, variable warbling song, repeated many times. Their songs are especially appreciated by nature observers in February. They are sparrow-size, about five to six inches long. Males have brown upperparts and a bright red crown, breast and rump, but have dark brown stripes on their sides which the purple finch lacks. Female house finches lack the red, are gray-brown above and are whitish with brown stripes below.

A Closer Look:
Pine Thoughts

As kids, on road trips with our parents, my brother and I knew we were Up North when we reached Menahga, Park Rapids, and finally Itasca State Park. Mom and Dad always pointed out the tall pines, the pine scented air, and the wonderful sound of the wind through their needle-covered branches. These truly spectacular pines are the symbols of the North Woods, representing the flora in much the same way as the common loons represent the fauna. What I didn't realize until much later in life is that most of the central and northern part of the state, which is now covered with aspen, sugar maple, paper birch, and jack pine, was at one time home to similarly majestic pines—many of them more than two hundred feet tall.

The magnitude of clearing that took place throughout much of the Upper Midwest between the mid-1800s and 1930 is hard to imagine. The few remaining tall stands of both white and red pines are an accident: They were somehow missed by the lumber barons, or saved by concerned and caring citizens. In Minnesota, only 15,000 acres remain of the original old-growth pine forest. That's less than 1 percent of the formerly vast forest that took hundreds of years to grow.

Most of the old growth pine forest that does remain is found in Itasca State Park and the Boundary Waters Canoe Area Wilderness. In Itasca we can still see over 25 percent of the state's last old-growth red and white pine forests, as well as Minnesota's record white pine and red pine.

Pines existed before the age of the dinosaurs. They were among the first seed-bearing trees to have evolved. Today, in the northland, the ones we see are forms relatively unchanged from those that grew 250 million years ago. They were able to survive by adapting to changing climates and natural disasters which are part of the long geologic time scale. No doubt they will survive the attacks by humans.

Pines can survive the cold winter months because their needle-shaped leaves minimize surface area and their waxy leaf coatings cut down on evaporation and help shed snow.

Any landowner in Minnesota who has space and the right soil conditions should have success growing white and red pines. Sandy loam soil is the best for them. Both make large and handsome specimen trees. Both are native to northeastern North America as far west as Minnesota. In fact, the red pine is the state tree of Minnesota.

Red pine is sometimes called Norway pine, but it does not grow as a native in Norway or elsewhere in Europe. It is said to have received the name from the town of Norway, Maine.

A Closer Look:
Awakening in Greenhouses

On February 11, 2007, Fred Struck, from the Traverse des Sioux Garden Center in St. Peter, noted once again that plants in the greenhouse had begun to come out of dormancy and start growing. From this date on, it will be hot and humid in greenhouses on sunny days.

Fred is a horticultural science graduate of the University of Minnesota and a keen observer, and he has convinced himself (and many others) during many years in the greenhouse that the awakening in greenhouses on or close to February 11 each year can be attributed to the sun's higher position in the sky.

Even on cold days the interiors of our cars and trucks now warm up when parked in the sunlight. The rays shining through automobile windows warm up the dashboard and seats, which in turn warm up the interior air. We also see snow melting on dark surfaces when the air temperature is below 20°F. These things happen because the sun has moved higher in the sky and is concentrating its rays.

A Closer Look:
Lichen Lore

February is a good time to notice the many forms of lichens growing on tree trunks and branches, and also on rocks and bare ground if not covered by snow. Twenty-thousand species of lichens have been described and named. They grow in virtually every habitat on Earth, even on Antarctic rocks. However, they are very sensitive to air pollution and refuse to colonize areas that suffer from bad air.

More lichens are found in northern

Minnesota than in the south. They are well-suited to the northern environment because they don't require soil and can withstand extremely cold temperatures and dry conditions. They get their nutrients and water primarily from the air, not from the soil. All they need to grow is a little humidity and temperatures around 14° F. When conditions remain much colder than that, lichens simply lie dormant.

A lichen is not a single organism, but is a partnership formed between a fungus and an alga. The alga provides food through photosynthesis, while the fungus provides physical structure and the water and minerals it channels in from the environment.

One example of a lichen type is called Old Man's Beard or just beard lichen. It's very common in the spruce and tamarack bogs and nearby forests of northern Minnesota. Winter is a great time to seek out this long greenish-gray plant, which does not grow flat on rocks or tree trunks but dangles from the trees, using the live or dead branches for support without hurting them. Thus Old Man's Beard hangs on throughout the seasons, year after year.

Week three (Feb 15-21)

This is a good time to get out and prune apple trees, as the cold weather helps the wounds heal more rapidly. Cuts made in summer could invite diseases. Pruning is done to limit the number of apples a tree will produce, so the fruit will be of good size, and to open the tree up so sunlight can penetrate the interior and ripen the fruit.

All of the tree squirrels—fox, flying, red and gray—have started their mating seasons. More raccoons are moving about the landscape. In Minnesota and Wisconsin, raccoons usually den-up in early winter and remain inactive for several weeks.

By mid-February, motorists in the southern half of the state often see flocks of the small grayish-brown horned larks along roadsides and in fields. These first of the spring bird migrants each year are usually in groups of three to twenty birds that flit up as a car passes.

It's possible to count more than two hundred wintering bald eagles while on a road trip along the Mississippi River between Red Wing and Winona. Meanwhile, timber wolves in northeastern Minnesota may have begun to mate, and howl with increasing frequency.

scattered events

- **February 19, 2006** - About six hundred trumpeter swans gather in the open water area of the Mississippi River below the power plant at Monticello. Canada geese and mallard ducks are there too. A bald eagle is seen on its nest at Colville Park in Red Wing.

- **February 19, 2007** - First warm day after twenty days in a row below normal. High of 43°F. The air has the smell of spring. Lake Waconia ice is 21 inches thick.

- **February 20, 2006** - Lake Waconia ice is 17 to 20 inches thick; sunfish, crappies, northerns, and walleyes are biting.

- **February 21, 2001** - 215 bald eagles were counted by master birder Oscar Johnson as he drove between Red Wing and Wabasha. Much of the Mississippi River between Hastings and Winona is ice covered.

A Closer Look: Boxelder Trees

The leaves of the wide-ranging boxelder (*Acer negundo L.*) resemble those of an ash, so much so that it is commonly called the ash-leaf maple. The compound leaves grow in groups of three to five leaflets. It is a true maple as seen by its flowers and fruits. Boxelder is a native Minnesota tree, growing over much of the state. It occurs from southern Canada to Florida and from the east to the west coast of the United States.

Boxelders natural habitat includes stream banks, river floodplains, bottomlands, margins of swamps, and disturbed sites. It grows in a variety of soil types, often in association with eastern cottonwood, willows, and silver maple. Considered a medium-size tree, boxelder can grow to a height of 65 feet, commonly with an uneven crown and branching close to the ground. The trunk can exceed three feet in diameter and can be straight to crooked. The boxelder grows rapidly for the first 15 to 20 years, then more slowly, and can live 75 to 100 years.

Often planted in shelter belts and used as shade trees in the drier parts of western Minnesota and the Dakotas, the boxelder is very drought resistant, easy to transplant, and adapted to nearly all urban conditions. The downside is that this tree has weak wood, sheds branches readily, and attracts boxelder bugs. The partly-red boxelder bugs, which feed on the leaves, cause no serious damage but can become a nuisance to some households.

It's in February that the boxelder catches our attention for a couple of reasons. First, we notice the twigs, which are greenish or purple, shiny or with a waxy coat that easily rubs off.

Second, we notice the clusters of winged seeds on the female trees; they look like the winged pairs of helicopter seeds seen on other maples. The seeds, which ripen in autumn, are a twin samara type, hanging upside-down in a V-shape. Bunches of these seeds provide visual interest throughout winter and also attract wildlife, providing nutritious food for squirrels and a variety of hungry birds including pine grosbeaks and purple finches.

A Closer Look:
Wintering Mourning Doves

In 2008, Jim Wyer from Minnetonka first heard the hollow mournful cooing sound of the mourning dove on February 17. Such wintering over birds are usually heard cooing by the first week in March, heralding spring. It's the male mourning doves that produce the distinctive four-part song - "coah, cooo, cooo, cooo." At a distance only three coos may be audible.

Thirty years ago a wintering mourning dove was a rare sight in the Twin Cities and Lake Waconia area. Now they are quite common at feeding stations in southern Minnesota throughout the frozen season. However, most still head for the southern part of the United States in autumn. Reports from avid birders confirm that the mourning dove's winter range

is moving north, year by year. Our warmer winters and proliferating feeding stations probably account for the extended winter range.

Pairs of mourning doves are commonly seen in the summer on utility wires or picking up gravel on the ground along roadsides. These birds are a foot long, have small heads, and long, pointed tails. They are gray and brown, and their tails are bordered with large, white spots. The females are a bit smaller than the males. Mourning dove flight is swift and direct, and the whistling of the wings is distinctive.

They eat huge numbers of so-called weed seeds in fields and waste places. In fact about 98 percent of their diet consists of seeds. They also eat a few berries and insects. At feeding stations, mourning doves like millet and cracked corn, scattered on the ground, preferably near trees and shrubs with low branches that offer good protection and roosting spots.

A Closer Look:
The Timber Wolf

Although Wisconsin, Michigan, and other states now support healthy wolf populations, Minnesota's is far and away the largest outside of Alaska—about three thousand in 2008. They are the living symbol of the wilderness.

Photos: David Brislance

The typical wolf pack is a family group usually made up of four to ten individuals. The pack has a dominant adult pair with their sub-adult and juvenile offspring, although the pack may include other subordinate adults. In order to live together in a pack, young wolves must learn to respect authority, and older individuals must show restraint. Food needs to be shared and the young of the dominant pair must be protected and cared for by the entire pack. Only the dominant pair breeds, which prevents the production of a high density of wolves. The social organization of wolves tends to prevent over-utilization of its prey resource, but also insures that areas of suitable habitat will be occupied.

Wolves mate in February; after a 63-day gestation period, four to seven pups are born in April or May. Pups are generally reared in an underground den with both parents involved in care and feeding. The young stay with their parents until 2 or 3 years of age.

The wolf is the common ancestor of all our modern dog breeds. Most people will never see a live wolf in the wild but we can see remnants of their structure and behavior in domestic dogs.

An adult male timber wolf is about 64 inches long, including its 16-inch tail; shoulder height is about 27 inches and weight up to 150 pounds. (A female can weigh up to 80 pounds.) These animals are usually gray, sprinkled with black. In Minnesota, they feed primarily on deer, especially in winter. In summer they supplement their diet with other prey and some wild fruits.

Wolves once occurred throughout most of North America and were also widespread in Europe. Now they are gone from most of the contiguous United States and occur in the sparsely settled parts of Alaska, Canada, in northern Minnesota, Wisconsin and Michigan, and a few western states. But their population is increasing, and they were recently removed from the Endangered Species List.

When it comes to wolves in the wild, there is a lot of misunderstanding and fear among people. Although timber wolves have lived in a balanced predator-prey relationship with deer for thousands of years, many people who live in wolf country are convinced that wolves must be eliminated to save the deer. In fact, a good supply of browsing and grazing plant material, combined with adequate cover for the deer, is the key to both a thriving deer population and healthy wolf population.

There are no confirmed instances of wolves killing or injuring people in Minnesota.

A Closer Look:
Soaring Red-tailed Hawks

During the third week in February and on into early March, red-tailed hawks arrive and begin their nest-building duties. Some return to the same nesting site each year. Only a few remain in Minnesota during the winter; most others migrate to southern states.

The red-tailed hawk is a summer resident throughout the state, except in the coniferous forests of the northeast and north-central regions. It is one of the most numerous breeding raptors in the state.

Soaring in wide circles with little movement of its wings, the adult red-tailed hawk can be recognized by the bright reddish-chestnut color on the upper surface of the tail that is fully extended like an open fan. The reddish tail can be seen when the bird dips and turns to bring its upper half into view. This reddish colored tail is not acquired until the bird is a little over a year old. Until then it is immature and does not mate, and it is nearly two years old when it does.

The red-tailed hawk is a large bird. It nests in woodlands but feeds in open country. The large nest is made of sticks and smaller twigs. Two eggs are usually laid and have an incubation period of about 28 days. Since the red-tail's food consists mainly of rodents, it does very little damage to domestic poultry or wild birds.

Week four (Feb 22-29)

The long, bright, arching golden-yellow twigs of weeping willows glow on the landscape. Red-osier dogwood twigs appear to have become a brighter red. Between now and the last of March is a good time to prune grape vines.

Usually the first few eastern chipmunks have

emerged from their underground burrows and are out and about. Eastern cottontail rabbits come to feeding stations during the night.

Wild tom turkeys gobble and fan their tails on warm winter days. American crows make rattle calls, a spring sound. Ring-necked pheasants have started to crow; this loud double squawk is the sound of a courting male. A small amount of yellow is appearing on some American goldfinches—another spring sign, as they have been in their somber brownish plumage since late fall. Expect to observe a feeding frenzy at wildlife feeders just before a snowstorm hits. Gray squirrels, juncos, tree sparrows, cardinals, chickadees, and other species come in numbers and eat in earnest.

With about two hours extra sunlight since January 1, we notice a big increase in bird vocalizations. Tiny springtails, also called snow fleas, jump about on the snow when the air temperature is above 27°F. Red foxes are seen in pairs. White-tailed deer have begun shedding winter fur.

Black bear cubs, now about a month old and weighing less than three pounds, nestle close to their mothers. Migrating American crows are returning to northern Minnesota.

scattered events

- **February 24, 2006** - At Wolf Ridge Environmental Learning Center, near Finland, 28 inches of ice covers Wolf Lake, and 30 inches of snow covers the ground, making for very good snowshoeing, cross-country skiing, and animal tracking. Hundreds of pine siskins come to the feeders. Lake Superior is wide open and the water showing beautiful tinges of blue.

- **February 25, 2001** - On this snowy day, birds are very active and numerous at feeding stations. About 20 inches of snow covers the Twin Cities landscape, and 60 inches on the Gunflint Trail area.

- **February 26, 1998** - First migratory American robins, red-winged blackbirds, and common grackles return. Rhubarb is beginning to poke up above ground, and many crocuses are blooming in protected outdoor spots.

- **February 27, 1991** - White-tailed deer are commonly seen near the edges of Hwy. 61, along the North Shore of Lake Superior. Driving from Duluth to Little Marais, we notice that ice covers about 80 percent of the Lake Superior surface visible to us. First migratory bald eagle spotted at Finland today, where pine grosbeaks are numerous at feeders.

- **February 27, 2000** - First male red-winged blackbirds return. First wood duck. Migratory Canada geese arrive. Red-tailed hawk seen on a nest. Maple syrup producers are tapping trees.

- **February 27, 2007** - A bald eagle is on a nest in Lake Elmo. Only 22.6 inches of snow for the season so far at Minneapolis/St. Paul International Airport. About 8 inches of snow covers the Twin Cities.

- **February 29, 1988** - On this "Leap Day" the first woodchucks were seen out of hibernation, in Carver Park Reserve, near Victoria. Also, tapped sugar maples ran well, and a great horned owl is on a nest.

A Closer Look:
Circles Around Trees

Yes, there will be much more snow and cold weather, but by the end of February we notice circles of bare ground around tree trunks. This sure sign of the changing of the seasons is very welcome. In a little more than a month we may find some green grass or other growing plants in these spots

The increased amount of daylight makes for lighter days. Sunlight is mostly reflected off snow, but not off dark tree bark, which absorbs heat from the lengthening light and slowly radiates it back to the surrounding snow. The melted snow may extend out from trees several inches to a foot or so. Because evergreens with branches way down near ground level have shaded trunks, snow melt around them is not likely, but in the maple-basswood forest or around other deciduous trees the snow melt tells us that winter is losing its grip.

A Closer Look:
Cardinals Sing Loud and Long

The northern cardinal is a permanent resident in southern Minnesota. A few are heard singing the rich whistled "what-cheer, cheer, cheer" song even in January but by the end of February this sound is commonly heard. There are many variations of the song. Both sexes sing, and sometimes together. These are territorial songs. So the very early start of the nesting season is marked by renewed singing, and at feeding stations we will notice mate-feeding now in late winter. The male often feeds the female, a courtship gesture. This is also the time when a cardinal starts to respond to its reflections in a window, displaying and attempting to drive-away a bird it thinks is an intruder. I have seen both sexes do this.

Nesting generally takes place between the later half of April and into August. In Minnesota, most northern cardinals raise two or possibly three broods. Nests are built by the female while the male is close by in full song. The female incubates the 3 to 4 eggs for about 13 days, but the male feeds her on the nest. They work together feeding the nestlings protein-rich insects. Young cardinals leave the nest about 11 days after hatching. The nests are usually only 4 to 5 feet off the ground but could be as high as 10 feet, and are built in young evergreens, tangles of vines, or thick deciduous shrubs.

A Closer Look:
Eastern Chipmunks

Photo: David Brislance

Being woodland squirrels, eastern chipmunks do climb trees but each individual spends most of its time in a relatively complex underground burrow that typically has food storage chambers and two or more entrances. This makes them essentially woodland ground squirrels. Like

---

First Active Chipmunk - Carver County

Because I have worked in nature centers and schools for many years, I have had countless students and teachers helping in the search for the first eastern chipmunk each year. The results seen in this sidebar are a real team effort.

2008 • February 21	1998 • February 19	1988 • March 1
2007 • February 21	1997 • February 26	1987 • February 26
2006 • February 27	1996 • no record	1986 • February 24
2005 • February 4	1995 • January 29	1985 • February 26
2004 • February 24	1994 • February 21	1984 • March 23
2003 • February 20	1993 • March 3	1983 • February 23
2002 • February 19	1992 • March 4	1982 • February 23
2001 • February 26	1991 • February 7	1981 • February 19
2000 • February 22	1990 • March 3	1980 • March 12
1999 • February 15	1989 • March 12	1979 • February 22

many other ground squirrels, chipmunks hibernate. Their body temperature decreases and they fall into a relatively deep sleep from October through March. Yet unlike the thirteen-lined ground squirrels and woodchucks, chipmunks do not put on much pre-hibernation fat, but awaken frequently during the winter and feed in their underground pantries. Stored food consists of acorns and other seeds and nuts.

Eastern chipmunks are relatively light hibernators, and sometimes even emerge during warm spells in the winter. But we can expect to see the first one out for sure by late-February or early March, as this is the beginning of their mating season. The first litter could be born in April, and there may be a second in late August.

Found in the eastern half of the United States, except in the southern coastal plains, eastern chipmunks occur in woodlands throughout Minnesota except in the southwestern corner. Like other woodland squirrels they have a varied diet, but the bulk of their food consists of various buds, seeds, and fruits in season. Chipmunks also eat mushrooms and some animal food.

A Closer Look:
Pine Martens

The "martin" is a bird in the swallow family that we won't see until April, but a "marten" is a mammal in the weasel family. We need to be careful with the spelling. Pine martens are relatively unknown in Minnesota. They became vary rare by the late 1800s because of their value as pelts and the ease with which they could be trapped. When European explorers first came to the state, the marten was a common animal in most of the forested areas in the northern half. Now they seem to be making a comeback in the northeastern part of Minnesota; I have only seen pine martens twice, once coming to a feeding station at Wilderness Canoe Base, located near the end of the Gunflint Trail, and another time also in the Arrowhead region. Both sightings were in the winter.

Pine martens do best in boreal forests. They reside in a belt stretching from eastern Canada through most of Alaska, occurring in the contiguous United States only in northern New England, northeastern Minnesota, and the northern Rockies. They are active throughout the year and are thought of as a large, arboreal weasel about the size of a mink. Being as comfortable in trees as a squirrel and being tireless hunters

photo: David Brislance

in treetops, night or day, they are one of the few predators of squirrels, particularly the red squirrel. About the only protection a squirrel has is to get into a hole too small for a marten to enter, as the marten can outrun it in the treetops.

Martens are about two feet long, including an eight-inch bushy tail, and slender. They can weigh two to three pounds, and have thick, soft fur that is dark brown, except for a a lighter patch on the throat. They are solitary creatures, largely but not entirely nocturnal, and will hunt on the ground as well as in trees. Hollow trees are favorite denning sites. The diet of the pine marten is varied and includes mice, squirrels, birds, insects, fruits and nuts, though mice probably make up the bulk of its food.

March

THE ROOT OF THE WORD "March" comes from *mar*, meaning a region of interaction, where, or when, things meet. Here in Minnesota, March is the center of the season when cold meets warm. Warm weather may actually start in late February, while cold can easily still occur in early May, but in March we have a mixture of warm and cold. March could be the peak of the snow season, but it's also our first month of real spring, the awakening season. By the end of the month, storms are more likely to bring rain than snow.

READING THE LANDSCAPE

Week one (March 1–7)

Is It Winter or Is It Spring?
Migrating Canada Geese
Tapping the Maples
Looking for the First Robin

Week two (March 8–15)

Red-wings Return to Marshes
First Wood Ducks Appear
Honey Bees' Cleansing Flights
Begin Recording Your Own Observations

Week three (March 16–23)

First Bluebirds
Blue Herons are Here
Woodchucks Come Out in the Sun
Gopher Wake-Up Time

Week four (March 24–31)

Ruffed Grouse Drumming
Woodcocks in Concert
Where the Green Grass Grows
Cricket Frogs Calling

first week in march

Ah, the sounds of spring! Northern cardinals whistle loud and clear and for long periods. They do this to declare territories. Male mourning doves which have wintered over begin their cooing songs. Canada geese are flying and honking, with pairs claiming nesting territories. Ring-necked pheasants can be heard "crowing," the loud double squawk is the sound of a courting male.

For March 1, in the Minneapolis and Saint Paul area, the normal high temperature is 34° and the low is 17° F, with the record high of 59° set in 1990.

We begin looking for the first migrating American robins and red-winged blackbirds to return, but cold temperatures and strong winds from the north can hold them in Iowa for another week. House finches and juncos are the most numerous of the birdfeeder birds at many stations.

It's the mating season for red foxes. As skunks move about the landscape searching for companionship and trying to fill their stomaches with food, they sometimes relax their caution and pay little head to traffic. We may see the flrst garter snakes out sunning. Tiny springtails, also called snowfleas, jump about on the snow when the air temperature is above 27°.

Between now and the last of March is a good time to prune grape vines, and continue pruning apple trees. Oak trees can be pruned at this time but not maples. However, now is the time to tap maple trees. Maple sap flow is triggered by thawing days reaching into the 40s.

In southern Minnesota, temporary ponds may begin to dot the landscape as snow melts and frost remains in the ground. Also, wild turkeys have started their spring courtship with the tom turkeys gobbling and flaring their tails.

American crows and bald eagles return to northen Minnesota, where deep snow usually covers much of the landscape, offering the best cross-country skiing and snowshoeing of the entire winter.

© Robert Hambley | Dreamstime.com

scattered events

- **March 1, 1998** - Eastern bluebirds claim nestbox at River Bend Nature Center in Faribault. The fuzzy silver pussy willow catkins are out in Fairmont.

- **March 1, 2001** - At Leech Lake the snow is 2 feet deep, the ice is about 30 inches thick, and yellow perch and tulabees are biting. Close to 45 inches of snow on the ground at Finland, 30 inches at Roseau, 28 inches at Duluth and 19 inches in Chanhassen.

- **March 4, 2000** - A farmer from the Truman, MN, area seeded oats.

- **March 5, 1983** - First great blue herons return to the rookery near Cold Spring.

- **March 6, 1995** – First migrating flocks of Canada geese returned to the Twin Cities area. Canada geese move northward at the edge of the 32°F isotherm; their travels often come to standstills by snowfalls and blizzards.

- **March 7, 1999** - More than a hundred white-tailed deer and a few bald eagles seen while driving Highway 61 along the North Shore of Lake Superior. Returning migrating horned larks observed in northwestern Minnesota.

■ **March 7, 2000** - High of 80°F at Winona, 73° in Twin Cities, and 67° degrees at International Falls. At the Minnesota Landscape Arboretum, located just west of Chanhassen, the vernal witch hazel shrubs are in full bloom, the ice cover left Green Heron Pond, and honey bees visited crocus and common snowdrop flowers. Nearby, in Victoria, the first painted turtle of the year was seen sunning on a log in Kelzer Pond, which lost its ice cover yesterday.

A Closer Look:
Is It Winter or Is It Spring?

This certainly is a transition time. Climatologists and meteorologists here in the Upper Midwest consider winter to be the months of December, January and February. Following this scheme winter, the season of frozen beauty and survival, gives way to spring, the season of hope and renewal, on March 1. Astronomers, on the other hand, would have us wait until March 20, the vernal equinox, for spring to begin. The Latin word *vernal* means "belonging to spring" and the Latin word *equinox* means "equal night," so our astronomical spring in the Northern Hemisphere begins on the vernal equinox. At that time the sun reaches the celestial equator, an imaginary line through the sky above the earth's equator. At this moment each place on earth receives 12 hours of sunshine and 12 hours of night. But because the earth's axis is tilted 23½ degrees from an upright position with respect to the sun, this moment of equipoise is a fleeting one. From then until June 21, nights in the Northern Hemisphere continue to grow shorter while the days become longer.

If the earth was not tilted on its axis, climates would still vary from place to place, but there would be no spring, summer, fall or winter. Because the earth is tilted, at times the North Pole is leaning toward the sun and at other times it leans away from it. When the North Pole leans toward the sun, the rays of the sun strike the Northern Hemisphere in a more direct and concentrated manner per unit, bringing summer, the season of sunlight and possibilities, to the northern half of the earth.

A Closer Look:
Migrating Canada Geese

Few of nature's very early spring events are more thrilling to behold than a V-formation of Canada geese, heading north, flying at speeds of up to 45 miles per hour, with males and females honking as they

© Denise Campione/ Dreamstime.com

aggressive during the spring breeding season.

The Canada goose has become the most numerous and widespread goose species in North America. This large goose is rarely confused with any other bird. Look for its black head and neck and white chinstrap, and otherwise gray-brown body except for a white rump. Males and females look alike but there are several races which vary greatly in size. The population of giant Canada geese has been growing at a phenomenal rate in the last 35 years. This growth is very evident in the Twin Cities area, one of the homes of the "giants." Male giants weigh about 14 to 16 pounds and females 10 to 12 pounds. Smaller races of Canada geese may weigh a little over 5 pounds.

Nesting sites are usually chosen in March and eggs are laid in late March or sometime in April. Egg laying is triggered by open water. The female chooses the nest's location, generally close to where she was hatched herself. The nest is most often by water, and preferably on a small island, a muskrat house, or a beaver lodge. She alone will incubate the eggs—usually five or six—although clutch sizes can vary from one to ten eggs. Normally, 28 days after the last egg is laid the young hatch and are ready to leave the nest. During the nesting period the female will lose 25 to 30 percent of her body weight due to the fasting that incubation imposes.

Many times, the only indication of a

communicate to each other. These geese are returning from states south of Minnesota, and it should be noted that some local flocks are made up of non-migrators. To know that migrants have arrived birders look for a build-up in the total population. In 2006, migrating Canada geese were observed over Waconia and the Twin Cities on February 28, and by March 2 we were seeing and hearing them in pairs standing on the ice of marshes and other wetlands, declaring nesting territories.

Canada geese were eliminated from Minnesota in the 1930s and early 1940s, but were reintroduced and by the 1970s had adapted to our changed environment. Although the elaborate courtship rituals, the raising of young, and their flights enchant us, the fact that they have adapted to city landscapes so well has created a major problem in many parks, golf courses, and other outdoor spaces where the geese foul lawns, overgraze grasses, and become nest is the outstretched head of the male standing guard. Hidden in the grasses, the female maintains a low profile with her neck down while the male makes sure that late-arriving geese do not enter the territory and that foxes, raccoons, and other potential predators of the eggs are driven off. Females will also help defend against predators. Males do not incubate but they are so essential that if killed during the incubation period the female will give up the nest. Soon after hatching, both parents lead their brood of four-ounce, downy, yellow-and-brown goslings across a waterway to a safe hillside on which to graze on the tender new green grass blades. The Canada goose's diet consists mainly of grasses, seeds, and small aquatic plants and animals.

We expect to see the first newly-hatched goslings by the end of April or in early May.

A pair of Canada geese stays with their young for about nine months. They are very attentive parents. The goslings learn survival techniques early. Only hours after hatching they venture out on the water where they are soon able to swim up to fifteen feet under water. If danger threatens on land, they flatten themselves to resemble rocks or other objects. The fortunate goslings survive to become adults, and some pairs may have as long as twenty years together.

"© Anikasalsera | Dreamstime.com

A Closer Look:
Tapping the Maples

It's sapping and sugaring time in New Hampshire, Vermont, and here in Minnesota. There still may be snow in the forests from Quebec and New England to Ontario, Wisconsin and Minnesota, but cold nights and warm days mean that the sap is running.

Settlers from Europe learned the art of tapping maples and making syrup and sugar from the local Indians. Earlier generations looked forward to spring days when the sap would begin to flow, and they and their neighbors could gather for sugaring. Before the 1860s maple products were the principle sweetening material used in the United States, and today Americans continue to enjoy their unique flavor. But during the past two or three generations, the art of tapping maple trees and preparing syrup and sugar has been largely forgotten except by a few enthusiasts who follow this as a trade or hobby.

During the summer months sugar is manufactured in the leaves of the maple tree. The process is a complicated one involving the chemical action of water supplied by the soil, carbon dioxide from the air and chlorophyll from the leaf plastids. Within the plastids these raw materials undergo a chemical change with sunlight providing the energy. The result is glucose, a simple sugar that is later stored in the trunk and roots of the tree as starch. By the time the sap drips from the tapholes, the compound has again been transformed, this time into sucrose. Sap contains from 1 to 6 percent of this sugar, with water making up the remainder of the volume. The presence of small quantities of organic acids and other compounds give the sap its maple flavor.

Maple trees will produce sap any time from late fall, after leaf drop, until well into spring.

photo: NJDEP, Division of Parks & Forestry

Sap flow is triggered by thawing days following freezing nights. In southern Minnesota, the best sap flows tend to come between the last week in February and the first few days of April, at which point leaf buds swell and sap becomes bitter. The sap will flow from a wound in the sapwood, whether the wound is from a hole bored in the tree or from a broken twig. By mid- to late February some of us start looking for icicles forming on the ends of maple twigs that have been browsed by deer or broken in a storm. We call these "sapcicles" and they are a tasty treat. Ideal weather for tapping involves nights with temperatures near 20°F, together with sunshine and daytime temperatures reaching the 40 to 50 degree range. Late afternoon is a good time to collect the day's flow. Sugar maples, black maples, and boxelders, also known as ash-leaved maples, are best for tapping. The red maple and silver maple can also be tapped but their sap is less sweet. A forest of many maple trees together is called a sugarbush.

Maples are tapped using a carpenter's brace with a ⅜-inch bit. Trunks smaller than ten inches in diameter should not be tapped. A tree at least 14 inches in diameter gets two taps, and one 24 inches or more in diameter three taps. More that three taps may undermine the health of even the biggest tree.

Maples tapped in different spots each year rarely suffer from their loss of sap. Holes two inches deep are bored into the tree trunk about three feet above ground. A small metal or wooden tube called a spile is inserted into the hole and tapped lightly with a hammer so it fits snugly. The spile supports the container and carries sap into it. The old wooden buckets and metal pails have now largely been replaced by plastic bags and tubing, which are easier to use and store, and which inhibit the growth of microorganisms when sunlight filters through the plastic. A plastic pipeline can be used to collect sap from trees on a hillside, enabling the sap to be carried directly to a storage tank by gravity.

The average amount of sap collected from each taphole is 15 gallons. Occasionally, a single taphole will produce 40 to 80 gallons of sap in a season. A taphole is usable from the time the sap begins to flow until the buds of the tree begin to swell and the syrup takes on a bud-like flavor. The spile is then removed. In a healthy tree, the taphole will be completely covered over with new wood in a single growing season.

Maple syrup is made by condensing the sap until it contains a high percentage of sugar. The best way to do this is to boil the maple sap in a shallow pan. A large surface area will allow for maximum evaporation. To determine when the finished product is close at hand, a candy thermometer is necessary.

Maple syrup has arrived when it has reached a temperature of 7° F above the boiling point of water. The syrup is then strained and bottled. The quality of the finished product depends on the flavor, the color and the density. Usually 30 to 40 gallons of sap are necessary to produce a gallon of syrup; the amount depends on the percent of sugar in the sap.

A Closer Look:
Looking for the First Robin

Spring doesn't truly arrive in the northern states until the robins fly back from the south and we see them hopping across our lawns and calling and singing from neighborhood trees. For many people the sight of that first American robin, no matter what the weather or the exact timing, means that spring is here and all, or mostly all, is right with the world. It's hard to know if American robins spotted in southern Minnesota in early March are migrants or wintering-over birds. A small percentage in Minnesota don't migrate but spend the winter in spots protected from cold winds, searching for leftover wild fruit, insects and other animal matter. Don't be surprised to see them relishing the fruit from backyard crabapple trees. Some of these non-migrators do not survive the winter.Migrating American robins are very flighty and noisy, and usually return in small to medium-size flocks. These birds are all males. The first female robins return about a month later.

Photo: Jim Gilbert

A male American robin has a black head with white eye-ring and a dark rusty-red breast; a female looks similar to a male but has a lighter gray head and pale reddish breast. Other than this, the only behavioral clues to distinguish the sexes are that the males are the only ones to sing and the females do all of the incubation.

Soon after the first robins arrive there is a breakdown of the male social flocks of the winter. The males become less tolerant of other males and show this intolerance by scolding calls, chasing, and fighting. Along with these interactions, each male American robin will begin to restrict the majority of his movements to a particular area about the size of a football field. This area may broadly overlap the areas of other males—hence the aggressive behavior.

After the females arrive and join with their mates, these territories shrink to about one-quarter of their original size. This territory is a place where mating, nesting, and most of the feeding takes place.

The American robin females and males generally return to the same areas for breeding every year, but banding studies have shown that they do not always breed with the same mates. They are one of our earliest birds to nest, and their first nests are often built in evergreen trees for protection because the deciduous trees haven't leafed out yet.

The female American robin does the most of the nest-building but the male may help bring materials to the nest site. The nest takes two to six days to build, and may be used for more than one brood. Nests are always a sturdy cup of small twigs, mud, and grasses, with an inside diameter of 4 inches, placed on a horizontal limb or building ledge anywhere from 5 to 30 feet off the ground. Three to six blue eggs hatch in about 13 days, and in another 13 days or so the young leave the nest. Two to three broods are expected during the nesting season. By early to mid-summer, after the breeding season, robins flock together and go to large communal roosts at night.

While watching robins hop about on lawns, meadows, and golf courses searching for earthworms, we will see individuals stop with their heads cocked. Robins seem to listen for worms but in fact they hunt by sight. They also eat insects, berries, and other fruit.

First American Robin arrives in the Waconia area

Observations by Jim Gilbert

1971 • March 13	1981 • March 8	1991 • March 11	2001 • March 21
1972 • March 14	1982 • March 14	1992 • February 28	2002 • March 17
1973 • March 5	1983 • March 3	1993 • March 26	2003 • March 16
1974 • March 5	1984 • March 15	1994 • March 12	2004 • February 29
1975 • March 21	1985 • March 10	1995 • March 12	2005 • March 18
1976 • March 18	1986 • March 12	1996 • March 13	2006 • March 7
1977 • March 8	1987 • March 4	1997 • March 7	2007 • March 12
1978 • March 19	1988 • March 8	1998 • February 26	2008 • March 11
1979 • March 19	1989 • March 9	1999 • March 8	
1980 • March 16	1990 • March 9	2000 • March 1	

Average First Sighting

1970s **March 12**   1980s **March 11**   1990s **March 9**   2000s **March 11**

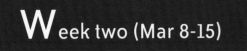

Week two (Mar 8-15)

The sunlight is powerful now and we notice melting in streets and on rooftops even when the air temperature is well below freezing. The normal high temperature on March 8 for Minneapolis/St. Paul is 36°F, and the low is 21°F.

Watch for the first migrating American robins to return. Many flocks of male red-winged blackbirds arrive and some are seen and heard on their wetland territories. It's time to get the wood duck and eastern bluebird nesting boxes up. House finches are investigating nesting sites; they often nest in old holiday wreaths and hanging plant baskets. Cedar waxwings are nomadic and can appear at any time to relish fruit from crabapple trees, highbush cranberry shrubs or other woody plants.

Gray squirrels collect and eat old apples that have been clinging to trees all winter. Short-tailed weasels are turning from their white winter coats to brown summer ones. Woodchucks that went into hibernation in October can once again be seen above ground about this time in March. Pussy willow twigs could be ready to cut and bring indoors for a touch of spring. Red-osier dogwood twigs look bright red—the veins of spring. Weeping willow twigs have an amber glow.

scattered events

■ **March 9, 1999** - Biggest snowfall since the 1991 Halloween snowstorm. Up to 17 inches fell on the Twin Cities, 14 inches at Hastings, 11 inches in St. Peter, and 10 inches at New Ulm. Northern cardinals whistled, woodpeckers drummed, and both house finches and black-capped chickadees sang their spring songs.

■ **March 9, 2000** - The ice covers left Lake Calhoun in Minneapolis, Lake Minnewashta near Excelsior, and Lake Jennie located south of Dassel.

■ **March 11, 1878** - After the warmest winter on record, the ice was out of Lake Minnetonka on this date (still the earliest on record).

■ **March 11, 2003** - More than 90 percent of Lake Superior's surface is frozen over.

■ **March 13, 1996** - The first western meadowlarks returned to the Mountain Lake area.

A Closer Look:

Red-wings Return to Marshes

The widespread and familiar red-winged blackbirds winter in southern states, sometimes gathering in large flocks along with common grackles and brown-headed cowbirds. But at the first hint of spring, mature males head north to stake out their territories. Marshy areas with old tan-brown cattail plants are where we look for the glossy blackbirds, flashing bright red epaulets and singing their cheery songs. These harbingers of spring with their "o-ka-leeee" or "tonk-a-leeee" songs, are observed by mid-March, with females spotted about a month later. The female looks very different from the male; she is brown with well-defined striping on her lower body. Red-wings prefer to nest in marshes and swamps, but will nest near most any body of water. They like to feed in open fields and plowed lands. Although they have been condemned as grain eaters by farmers, only about one-eighth of their diet is made up of this food. Insects and weed seeds make up most of their diet.

A Closer Look:
The First Wood Ducks Appear

Russ and Sandy Rippberger, who live on the edge of Bass Creek in Brooklyn Park, have forty wood duck nesting boxes on or close to their half-acre yard. During spring into summer of 2005, thirty-seven of the forty were occupied. Russ notes that over the years March 12 is the average date for the first wood ducks to arrive at their place. In 2005 the first woodies

Photo: Dave Menke

returned March 23; this was late but Bass Creek was still about 80 percent ice covered. On March 14, 2006 at 6:20 p.m. the first ones arrived in the Rippberger's yard. Eight wood ducks came walking in single file down the center of ice-covered Bass Creek and into their yard to feed on whole kernel corn scattered on the ground. There were six males and two females. Russ said "spring has begun."

Early March is a good time to put up one or more wood duck nesting boxes in a yard or area, even if the spot chosen is a block or two from a stream, pond or lake. Since migrating wood ducks are still arriving the third week of April, it may still be OK to get a nesting box up that late. The ideal height is 12 to 15 feet up on a tree or pole, with the entrance facing out into an open area. Compass direction doesn't matter. Nesting boxes on poles over water should be about 6 feet above surface. Being cavity nesters, wood ducks often use old woodpecker holes. Watching a duck fly into a hole in a tree or perched high on a branch, or seeing the day-old young jump from a height of up to 50 feet to the ground or water to follow their mother can be enlightening experiences.

Wood ducks winter from Missouri south to the Gulf states and into Mexico. Around 1900 due to overhunting and habitat destruction this splendid species was almost wiped out. Protective laws ended the slaughter in time, and now the wood duck is doing well due to nest box programs and habitat conservation.

The gentile wood duck is regarded as one of the most beautiful birds. It's always a thrill to see a pair floating contentedly in a spring pond. The male has a green head and crest patterned with white and black, red eyes, a rusty chest and whitish belly; the female is a brown dabbling duck with a broad white eye-ring. Their food consists of nuts and other seeds, fruit, plus aquatic plants and animals, including small fish.

Photo: USDA

Eggs of wood ducks are found in a nest of wood chips and down in a cavity. Only the female incubates the 10 to 15 eggs. Incubation period is about 27 to 30 days. Sometimes eggs will be layed in a neighboring female's nest, resulting in some clutches having an excess of 20 eggs. This is called egg dumping.

A Closer Look:
Honey Bees' Cleansing Flights

At this time area honey bees are still living off their honey reserves, but are waiting for their chance to get out and collect some early pollen and nectar. It probably will be another two weeks or so of waiting, but during warm days in March the honey bees will leave their hives on short cleansing flights. Many times in very early spring we have found some dead and chilled bees stranded in the snow as far as 300 feet from the hives.

Dead bees in the snow may worry new beekeepers who wonder why the bees are in the snow and how they got there. This occurs when winter or early spring sunshine raises the temperature on the inside and the front of the hive sufficiently to cause bees to fly out a short way to void themselves, the excrement causing dark spots on the snow. Bees that fly even a few feet from the hive sometimes become chilled because they are cold-blooded and in moments their bodies cool down so their wings are unable to get them back to the hive. They drop to the snow, casualties of the cold, but a common occurrence in the bee cycle.

We have seen them out of hives on sunny days with temperatures in the 20s and 30s even though the bees must realize it is too cold for them. They often choose to fly rather than foul up the combs and hive when they have been forced to remain inside for a long time. Ideally, they should have a warm flight day every four to six weeks. Beekeepers hope for a few warm days in December, a mid-January thaw and a few more warm days in February and again in March. Confinement for over six weeks becomes serious, and disease becomes a problem if feces are discharged within the hive.

🐝 MOST NEW PHENOLOGISTS get their start in spring. What follows are several spring signs that you may enjoy observing in your own area. Be sure to add more. If you keep accurate records, you and others will enjoy referring to them in the months and years ahead.

Spring Signs (In each case, record the date)

_____ First migratory American robin returns

_____ First time it smells like spring to you

_____ Grasses turning green in ditches and on south-facing slopes

_____ First day when at least 90% of the (name) lake is free of ice

_____ First lawn mowing

_____ Common dandelion—first flower seen near wall of building

_____ First rhubarb pulled for sauce

_____ House wren first arrives

_____ First baby robin seen out of nest

_____ Common purple lilac first flower open on a cluster

_____ First apple blossoms (type of tree, if known) _____

_____ First garden strawberry picked

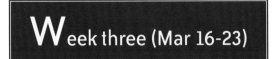

Week three (Mar 16-23)

The normal maximum and minimum temperatures for March 16th in Minneapolis/St. Paul are 40° and 24° F. Spring really moves in; much of the snow turns to water and now temporary ponds dot the landscape because of frost in the ground. This can be the week of many firsts, as the first killdeers, great blue herons, song sparrows and brown-headed cowbirds return. And the first garter snakes may come out of their underground dens for some early spring sunning.

Migratory American robins, eastern bluebirds, wood ducks and common grackles arrive in numbers. With much honking and fanfare, Canada goose pairs claim their wetland nesting territories. Pairs of American crows check out possible nesting sites and carry nesting materials in their bills.

We expect to see many eastern chipmunks above ground by this time in March. Sugarbush operators look for some of the best maple sap runs of the year. March 17 is the average date for the shipping season to begin on the Mississippi River at St. Paul. Yet this period could also provide some of the best dogsledding and cross-country skiing in northern Minnesota. Deer are numerous along the North Shore of Lake Superior, coming out of the deep snow to feed along bare roadside ditches and enjoy the warmer air down by the lakeshore.

scattered events

- **March 16, 2003** - Only patches of snow left. First migratory American robins, male red-winged blackbirds, common grackles and wood ducks returned. Parkview Golf Course in Eagan opened for first time this year; about 200 golfers came out to play.

- **March 18, 2000** - The official ice-out for Lake Minnetonka today was the second earliest on record.

- **March 18, 2001** - Jack rabbits in St. Peter area are turning from white to brown. Three to four feet of snow covers much of the BWCA, where snowshoeing is great, and black-capped chickadees sing their "fee-bee" spring songs.

- **March 19, 2000** - Fishing boats are seen on Minneapolis area lakes, while 200 miles north at Leech Lake the ice is 20 inches thick and people continue driving cars and pickups to their favorite fishing spots.

- **March 21, 2001** - The landscape is covered with 14 inches of snow. First migratory American robins and red-winged blackbirds arrive.

■ **March 21, 2005** - First crocuses blooming in outside gardens. Male red-winged blackbirds are singing from their wetland territories. The Minnesota River at LeSueur and Belle Plaine is wide open; just some ice on edges.

■ **March 22, 1998** - American crow seen flying with nesting material in its beak. A clutch of five screech owl eggs is seen in a wood duck nestbox. Northern flickers are back and calling. House finches heard in full-song.

A Closer Look:
First Bluebirds

A few eastern bluebirds attempt to winter over in Minnesota but nearly all of them spend the cold months in states south of us, returning in greatest numbers between mid-March and mid-April. Their habitat includes farmlands, orchards, roadsides and open woodlands. They nest in natural tree cavities, old woodpecker holes, wooden fence posts and the nest boxes we put out for them. Insects make up the main part of their diet, but they also eat fruits and seeds during the months when insects are scarce.

A female eastern bluebird is a dull version of the male. He has a sky-blue head, back and tail, a rusty-red throat and breast, and white belly. This 7-inch bird is a favorite of many people, but 50 to 70 years ago was nearly eliminated in Minnesota due to the increasing use of insecticides, the dwindling number of wooden fenceposts, and a competition for nest sites from two introduced species—the house sparrow and the European starling.

Numerous individuals and organizations have helped bluebirds make a remarkable comeback in the last forty years by putting up thousands of nesting boxes, and the bluebird has responded well to such management efforts. The best hope for their survival in our human-changed landscape seems to be bluebird trails. Such a trail consists of five or more nesting boxes set out by late March along a rural roadside, or along a trail or fence line in an area of mixed woodland and grassland or grazing pasture.

© Steve Byland | Dreamstime.com

A Closer Look:
Blue Herons are Here

In 2005 the first great blue heron was spotted in the Waconia area on March 22, and in 2006 we saw the first one on March 17. They winter in a range extending from our southern states down to Central America. They always return to their breeding range and, specifically, to their nesting rookeries early in the season. There is a heron rookery on Coney Island in Lake Waconia. The great blue heron, or "blue crane" as it is often called, is the largest and best known of American herons. Like most of the heron species, it is very sociable, preferring to nest in congested communities that vary in size from a few pairs to hundreds of birds.

Herons are stately, graceful birds, flying with slow, steady wing beats, with necks drawn in and legs stretched out behind. They stand more than three feet tall, with much of their height made up of long legs and a long neck. From tip to tip, their wings measure six feet. In addition to its height, the heron has a very distinctive appearance, with its blue-gray color, largely white neck and head, black eyebrows extended into several long plums off the back of the head, and six-inch yellow bill. The feathers at the base of the neck drop down to form a kind of necklace. Males and females look alike and seldom weigh more than seven pounds.

Photo: Gren Gillson

The great blue heron often is seen standing motionless in shallow water, patiently waiting for prey. When an unwary fish or frog comes within striking distance, its sharp beak shoots forward and down with lightning speed, seizing the fish or other animal crosswise between mandibles. Seldom does the heron miss its mark.

The bird's hunting routine, which might be done by day or night, also involves stalking on dry land for snakes, mice, shrews, grasshoppers, and other insects. When necessary, the heron also will alight on water and swim for its food.

Great blue herons usually nest in colonies.

The nest is a platform of sticks high up in a tree. Both male and female build the nest and incubate the 3 to 5 eggs. Incubation lasts 28 days. The downy young leave the nest about 8 weeks after hatching. There is only one brood per year.

© Photawa | Dreamstime.com

A Closer Look:

Woodchucks Come Out in the Sun

Woodchucks hibernate for nearly half of every year, and during those intervals the heartbeat slows from 80 beats per minute to only 4 or 5, and body temperature drops over 60 degrees to about 38° F. This pudgy creature, also known as a groundhog, does not appear above ground on its official day, February 2. That idea is a delightful hoax. Its internal clock awakens it usually in early to mid-March. (In 2006 I observed a woodchuck above ground for the first time on March 21.)

The woodchuck is the largest member of the squirrel family. It can reach a weight of 10 pounds as an adult and measures close to 2 feet long. It feeds primarily on green vegetation and other plant materials, though it also eats insects, mice, and even birds from time to time—consuming as much as a pound of food a day.

Woodchucks are found throughout Minnesota, especially at the edges of forests and in hilly areas where they dig an extensive burrow system. To the dismay of gardeners and farmers, clover, alfalfa, peas, beans, corn, melons and apples are some of the groundhog's favorite foods. However, woodchucks also benefit the wildlife community (and the farmer) by constructing burrows that serve as homes for animals that are important in controlling insect pests and small rodent populations. The tunnels also permit rain water to enter the ground easily.

Mating takes place in early spring immediately after hibernation. Two to eight young are born 31 to 32 days later. They young ones can crawl at 3 weeks and will be out playing in the sun at 5 weeks.

A Closer Look: Gopher Wake-Up Time

The Minnesota gopher, a symbol of the University of Minnesota, is also known as the 13-lined ground squirrel. Found in pastures and other short grassy areas, it is common throughout the state except in the northeast. Most of these creatures have been underground since October, but now some have begun emerging from winter hibernation.

A gopher runs to 11 inches in length and can weigh from 5 to 9 ounces. It is buff-colored with a compact set of light and dark stripes and rows of spots running down its sides and back. Seeds and insects are its main food. While many burrowing animals leave piles of soil about their burrows, gophers scatter the soil widely, so that entrances to their burrows appear on the surface only as small holes.

Facts about gopher hibernation are interesting. A gopher plugs the burrow opening before beginning its long sleep, then curls into a ball, nose touching its belly and tail over its head. The heartbeat drops to just 5 beats per minute from a normal active rate of between 200 and 300 beats per minute, and its oxygen consumption drops more than 90 percent. At the same time, the body temperature sinks from about 105° to 37° F. Severe cold, with freezing temperatures penetrating deep into the soil, can awaken gophers from their dormancy several times during the winter. This causes their body temperature to rise and prevents them from freezing to death, but unusually warm temperatures might also awaken them.

Week four (Mar 24-31)

It's good to hear the red-wings trilling and Canada geese honking. Eastern bluebirds claim nesting boxes. Tundra swans migrate in large Vs through southeastern Minnesota, including the Twin Cities, and many flocks stop to rest on open water. Listen for eastern phoebes and song sparrows, and watch for the first turkey vultures.

This is the time for some excellent maple sap runs. Rhubarb and chives begin poking up in gardens. American elm and silver maple trees are in bloom, and honey bees and other insects gather the pollen. More eastern chipmunks, 13-lined ground squirrels and woodchucks are out and about after spending the winter in underground burrows. The ice cover begins to leave southern Minnesota and Wisconsin lakes, while the snow lies deep in northern forests.

The normal high and low temperatures for March 31 in the Twin Cities are 49° and 29°F, but the record high is 82° set in 1986.

scattered events

▪ **March 27, 1999** - First Canada geese incubating eggs. First spring rain. Ice-out date for Mountain Lake in Cottonwood County.

■ **March 29, 1998** - American robins singing and hunting on lawns. Ice-out date for Stone Lake near Victoria. Tornadoes hit south-central Minnesota and cause huge amount of damage in Comfrey, St. Peter, and nearby rural areas.

■ **March 29, 2003** - The Port of Duluth officially opened at noon today when the Canadian ship Frontenac came in with a load of salt.

■ **March 30, 1999** - Ice-out date for Lake Waconia, Lake Calhoun and Lake Harriet in Minneapolis, and Forest Lake in Washington County. Both wood frogs and chorus frogs first calling. Maple syrup producers pull taps. Grasses now green on south-facing slopes. In Rice County, an American woodcock nest has four eggs, and both pasqueflower and sharp-lobed hepatica have begun blooming. First migrating American robin spotted in Bemidji.

■ **March 30, 2005** - Western meadowlarks, Canada geese and flocks of sandhill cranes have returned to northwestern Minnesota.

■ **March 31, 1997** - Best maple sap flow of the year. Large flocks of common grackles are moving through. Skunk cabbage now blooming along Nine Mile Creek.

Photo: David Brislance

A Closer Look:
Ruffed Grouse Drumming

A brown, chicken-like bird with a fan-shaped, black-banded tail and black "ruffs" on the sides of the neck, the ruffed grouse is a permanent resident throughout the deep woods of Minnesota from the southeast to the northern half of the state, excepting the northwestern tier of counties. With the coming of winter, these birds grow comb-like rows of bristles on the sides of their toes, converting their feet into snowshoes. When there is enough snow they may dive into a snowbank to keep warm at night.

In spring, a male ruffed grouse stands on a log, stump or boulder, raises the tuft of feathers on his head, fans his tail feathers, and drums with his wings to stake claim to his territory and to attract females. The drumming sound comes from cupped wings moving in the air, not by pounding on its chest or the log. With each wingbeat, the resulting compression of the air produces a low thump that can be heard half a mile away. Beginning with a steady thumping rhythm, it speeds faster and faster and then abruptly stops. And then it begins again. The drumming can continue for hours throughout the day, and it could go on for half the night as well. An individual male ruffed grouse will return to the same log or stump day after day for drumming.

The drumming of the ruffed grouse is, to the uninitiated, one of the most mysterious and puzzling sounds of the forest. It may be mistaken for distant thunder or the rumbling of a gasoline engine. It's the "love-song" of the male grouse and, at the same time, a challenge or warning to would-be rivals. Heard most frequently in spring, the main drumming period lasts from late February or early March until June. Drumming is not uncommon in the fall and even may be heard in the winter.

At this time of year, ruffed grouse can still be seen up in aspens and other trees, feeding on buds. Other food includes catkins, seeds, wild fruits and insects.

The male is promiscuous and no pair bond is formed. In late April or early May, the female makes a small depression in the soil and lines it with leaves. It may be located at the base of a tree, under dense brush, or near a log, stump, or rock. She lays 9 to 12 eggs, one daily, until the clutch is complete, and then incubates the eggs for more than three weeks. The chicks leave the nest as soon as they dry off after hatching, fly in one week, and stay with their mother about three months.

A Closer Look:
Woodcocks in Concert

By this time in March, the ground has usually been thawing sufficiently to unlock the food supplies of earthworms and insects for the newly-arrived American woodcocks, which can be heard "peenting" like giant insects.

American woodcocks are stocky birds, about 11 inches long, with 3-inch bills, short necks and a dead-leaf pattern on their upper bodies. They begin their calling and display flights soon after they arrive from the southern states.

The emergence of spring is widely announced by the noisy courtship displays and vocalizations of many bird species. Canada geese are flying and honking; woodpeckers

Photo: U.S. Fish and Wildlife Service

drum and house finches sing. Ring-necked pheasants can be heard crowing; the loud double squawk is the sound of a courting male, heard often in corn-growing areas. To this chorus the male American woodcock adds his special music at a quiet time of day. He begins his performance soon after sunset and it ceases when the glow in the western sky disappears, only to begin again in the morning twilight or on moonlit nights when it continues throughout the night.

Woodcocks nest in wooded or brushy uplands not far from wetlands, and they perform their courtship displays in open pastures or fields. The bottomlands of the Minnesota and Mississippi Rivers provide good observation spots. The loud nasal "peenting" sound is uttered every few seconds as the woodcock struts about. Suddenly he rises and flies off at an angle, circling higher and higher until he reaches a height of perhaps

200 to 300 feet. The flight is accompanied by twittering musical notes. As the bird flutters back to the ground, a series of chipping whistles completes his elaborate performance. He soon begins his "peenting" again, and the whole act is repeated. So the cock courts the hen by the twittering calls, high spiral flights, the plunges to earth, and the strutting along with "peenting" calls on the ground.

These woodcock concerts could begin in mid-March and might continue into June, but April is the liveliest month, since the female nests in May. For any humans fortunate enough to witness this rite of spring, the memory lasts a lifetime.

Nests are on the gound. Eggs, three to four in number, hatch after about 21 days of incubation. The downy young woodcocks leave the nest soon after hatching, are watched over by the female only, and become independent at about 2 weeks.

Woodcocks feed by plunging their long bills deep into the soil. Each bird can eat its weight in earthworms within 24 hours; they also eat insects and seeds.

A Closer Look:

Where the Green Grass Grows

By the last week in March, grass is often turning green along roadsides and on south-facing slopes in the Waconia and Twin Cities area, though the variation from year to year is pronounced. Late dates for this spring happening are April 16 (in 1972 and 1979) and April 18 in 1975. Early dates include March 6, 1987, and March 9, 2000.

However, the last week of March is about average. To winter weary eyes, big patches of green look good and can lift one's spirits. For many years I have been recording the day when green grasses, probaby of several species, are first noticed on south slopes and along highways. These green carpets remind us that the Earth on which we live is partly green and that the green comes from plants that are essential to the life and welfare of humankind. People and animals could not exist on this planet without the green coloring found in plants and without the activities of the leaves containing this pigment.

Green plants possess the ability to manufacture food from raw materials derived from the soil and the air. They make this food to sustain themselves—though many other living creatures also benefit from the process—by means of photosynthesis, producing sugar (food) from carbon dioxide and water in the presence of chlorophyll, the stuff that makes them green. Sunlight is the energy source and oxygen is the by-product.

All living things require energy for growth and to maintain life, though not all life forms can draw it from the sun and soil the way plants can. Many organisms depend on sources of energy that only green plants can generate, and this is why photosynthesis has been called the most important chemical process known.

A Closer Look:
Cricket Frogs Calling

By the end of March, the swamp cricket frogs, also called western chorus frogs, can usually be heard calling from grassy ponds and roadside ditches. The great volume of the mating trills produced by these tiny frogs, which have bodies a little over an inch long, suggests that it is coming from much larger frogs. The sound is like that of a metallic clicker.

It's the males that call, and I have watched them at night with the aid of hip boots and a flashlight. Only their tiny heads with extended bubble-like throat sacs stick up above the water. With many males calling in a small pond, their combined chorus is continuous and quite deafening, but in the daytime the slightest disturbance causes them to remain quiet. A person walking near a pond of singing frogs causes the chorus to stop short.

April

April is the windiest month of the year here in Minnesota. Mild days with occasional rain or snow and a greening landscape also characterize the month. It's ice-out time for most Minnesota lakes. Leopard frogs leave their lake-bottom hibernating spots and are seen up on land. Expect to see painted turtles sunning on logs or other objects just above water. Canada goose egg-laying, triggered by open water, has usually begun by this time. The female chooses the nest's location, generally close to where she herself was hatched.

Reading the Landscape

Week one (April 1–7)

Don't Miss the Spring Signs
Listen for the Swans
Spring Walks
Crocuses and Pasqueflowers

Week two (April 8–15)

The Ice-out Process
Lake Minnetonka Ice-out History
Dandelions and Purple Martins
Bird Sounds

Week three (April 16–23)

Those Terrific Trees
A Taste of Rhubarb
Wild Ginger and
    other Wildflowers
Earth Day, 2007

Week four (April 24–30)

Loons are Back
Arbor Day
Urban Trees
Daffodils and Tulips

first week in april

Pairs of eastern bluebirds, tree swallows, and wood ducks check out nesting boxes, while black-capped chickadees excavate nesting cavities in rotting tree trunks. House finches have also begun nestbuilding. Look for tundra swans to migrate through and for belted kingfishers and common loons to arrive.

Common dandelion flowers are seen next to buildings, and crocuses bloom in gardens. Lawns begin greening. Golf courses should be opening. The maple syrup season may be ending in southern Minnesota, but expect good sap runs in the central and northern regions. Migrating American robins, red-winged black-birds, brown-headed cowbirds, and Canada geese begin to arrive in the northern third of Minnesota and Wisconsin.

On April 1, the normal high temperature for the Twin Cities is 49° and the low is 30°F. The record high for this date is 75°, set in 1963.

scattered events

- **April 1, 2002** - Snowy day. Six inches fell on parts of the Twin Cities area. Juncos are the most numerous visitors to the birdfeeder.

- **April 2, 2001** - Excellent maple sap flows. Last snowfall; less than an inch fell, but we still have 8 inches on the ground. First tree swallows returned.

- **April 4, 1998** - Wood ducks are laying eggs. Screech owl eggs hatched. Waterfowl numerous on southern Minnesota lakes. Common loons first arrive in Aitkin area.

- **April 4, 1999** - Bald eagle on nest in Carlos Avery Wildlife Area. First purple martins at Hawick in Kandiyohi County.

- **April 6, 1998** - Female American robin seen gathering nesting material. First fox and vesper sparrows, hermit thrush, and ruby-crowned kinglets. We enjoyed the green-smell of first mowed lawn grasses.

- **April 6, 1999** - In forests at St. Peter, thousands of sharp-lobed hepaticas bloom, and wild ginger begins flowering. In northern Minnesota, black bears are coming out of their dens, maple syrup production continues, and snowshoe hares are changing from white to brown.

A Closer Look:
Don't Miss the Spring Signs

No winter lasts forever, and April proves it. Each of us has something special that catches our attention and tells us personally that spring is on its way or has arrived. It may be the lengthening of daylight, the taste of freshly evaporated maple syrup, crocus flowers, open windows, seeing temporary ponds, or the first field work on a farm. But whatever it is that gets us thinking "spring," it lifts our spirits and nudges us onward in this period of newness.

After spring arrives for us, we then have appointments to keep that will help make our spring season complete. Listed below are just a few spring thoughts from people who have shared their nature observations with me for many years.

The first arriving of the migrant horned lark, and hearing its "tinkling" call above the winter winds—that's spring.

(happens in February in southern Minnesota)

– Orwin Rustad, naturalist
Faribault, MN

With noticeably longer days I wake earlier, eager to observe spring's unfolding: the first spring songs of year-round birds, the earthly scent of soil just thawed, the greening of plants and trees, the first insects, the waves of returning bird migrants, the ice going out on lakes, and then the frogs and toads announcing in chorus that spring has arrived.

– Julie Brophy, environmental educator
Victoria, MN

Spring is the time for the western chorus frogs to take center stage as their persistent trilling resonates over a secluded woodland pond.

– Matt Schuth, wildlife manager
Minnesota Landscape Arboretum

Every event in spring—returning bird, opening bud, frog call—is filled with the hope of better things to come. Opportunities to observe multitudes of changes with our own senses abound. Those of us who are students of spring feel as if the days just fly by and that we are always somehow behind in making our own personal nature discoveries which help us keep pace with the world around us.

Try to get outside as often as you can. Feel the warm rays of the sun on your face and arms, listen to the American robins singing, smell the wet soil, look for new green blades of grass next to sunny walls. Make the most of every spring day; each is one of nature's many fine gifts. Take pleasure in the beauty and wonder of the Earth and its creatures, and take time to learn about and enjoy nature.

It seems that only those of us who have been close to nature during the length of a Minnesota winter can truly appreciate the subtle signs of spring and rejoice in each happening fully. But if you have been away enjoying the plants of the Arizona desert, orange groves in Florida, or harbor seals and shorebirds on the beaches at San Diego or La Jolla, it won't take you long to get back in the Minnesota groove and once again take pleasure in our many spring signs.

Photo: Mike Dunn

A Closer Look:
Listen for the Swans

My listening point for more than thirty years has been our yard on the northwest side of Lake Waconia. Sandra and I were walking in the neighborhood with our dog Gilbey on the evening of April 1, 2006, when we heard the muffled musical whistles of five magnificent flocks of tundra swans passing overhead, traveling west. It was still light enough at 7:15

to see the first flock of about ninety birds in a big V-formation. We can count on observing these white, long-necked swans at some time each year between the end of March and into the first half of April.

The tundras migrate by day and night, flying in long Vs from their winter range on the Atlantic coast, where they are most abundant between Maryland and North Carolina. They breed on the seacoast within the Arctic Circle.

Trumpeter swans are the largest North American waterfowl and hundreds of them winter on the Mississippi River at Monticello. Tundra swans, also known as whistling swans, are the second largest. The tundras are snow white with black feet and bills, and the adult's black bill often shows a yellow spot at the base, up near the eye. They weigh 10 to 19 pounds and have a seven-foot wingspan.

When traveling long distances, tundra swans fly in V–shaped wedges for the same reason that geese do. The resistance of the air is less if each bird flies in the widening wake of its predecessor. The leader has the hardest work to do as he or she "breaks the trail" but is relieved at intervals and drops back into the flock to rest.

A Closer Look: Spring Walks

Walk and be happy, walk and be healthy.

-Charles Dickens

Many of us in the United States are not physically fit, and neither are we as aware of our natural surroundings as we would like to be. We hear statistics such as: the average American spends no more than 5 percent of their time outdoors, and more than 64 percent of Americans are overweight or obese. It's true that taking a brisk walk over your lunch break can help ward off heart disease, the number-one killer among women. It's also true that for nearly all of us, a brisk walk for thirty minutes each day improves the efficiency of our hearts and lungs and burns substantial extra calories. It also promotes psychological well-being and, not incidently, helps us to get to know our neighborhoods better.

After the long, dark, and often inhospitable winter, April is the perfect time to start walking. Walking requires no special equipment or skill. It's the easiest exercise there is and one of the best, and it can be done in the great outdoors. Enjoyment of the outdoors is independent of age, income, occupation, culture, and locale—it doesn't matter if you live in a city, on a farm, or deep in the woods. Walking outdoors is healthy, reenergizing, and enlightening. It clarifies what is important to us all—healthy bodies and a healthy environment.

Of course, walking on an interpretive trail at a nature center or state park will help you gain new insights and awareness of the natural habitats around you, but it's amazing what you can learn on your own about plants, animals, and the natural processes taking place all around us if you use your senses and really pay attention.

My wife Sandy and I try to walk two miles each day, year-round, in our Lake Waconia neighborhood, and after each walk I quickly write a few lines in my nature notebook about what I have observed. I'm always alert for the first sighting of a returning bird species, the first chirp of a frog species, and the final disappearance of ice from a pond or lake. The first week of April is a fantastic time to make and record these and many other nature observations. If you keep your observations from year to year, like I do, then you'll be able to anticipate upcoming events and compare present happenings in your own neighborhood with those of previous years.

Listed below are a few entries in my notebook for early April walks along North Shore Road of Lake Waconia.

April 1, 2004 - Clear sky all day with a high temperature of 57°F. Dandelions are blooming next to buildings, and crocus flowers are open in gardens. We were fortunate to hear the muffled musical whistles and see tundra swans in a flock of nearly a hundred, headed west over (still) ice-covered Lake Waconia. Male red-winged blackbirds sang and showed off their red as they perched on cattails in marshy spots. House finches vocal.

April 3, 2005 - Warmed up from the 30's to a high of 68°. Small ponds nearly ice-free. South-facing slopes now showing bright green blades of grass. Silver maples in bloom. Many American robins hunting on lawns; saw one female robin, my first this year. Common purple lilac shrubs have buds that are showing some green and opening.

April 4, 2007 - Only 17° this morning and new ice sheets can be seen on small ponds that had been ice-free since March 25. Flocks of American robins are on sunny south-facing grassy slopes out of the strong northwest winds. We watched a flock of a thousand-plus ring-billed gulls, some swirling in the winds and many floating on the deep blue Lake Waconia water surface.

April 5, 2006 - Warmest day in nearly five months. High of 63°. Lake Waconia ice cover is very dark and there is a ring of open water around the shore. Heard and saw a belted kingfisher near the open water. Western chorus frogs very vocal in ponds. Red-winged blackbirds trilling and song sparrows singing. Saw my first female American robin of the year; she was on our lawn near a male. Neighbors just starting light raking and yard cleaning.

April 7, 2006 - 5 pm, clear and 45°, strong NE winds. The ice cover left Lake Waconia today. It's great to see the deep blue water and whitecaps. The lake smells SO good! First wind-surfer is out enjoying the sport. Western chorus frogs sing in neighborhood ponds.

A Closer Look:
Crocuses and Pasqueflowers

Meteorologist Bill Endersen called me early in the afternoon on March 19, 2007, to say that the first crocus flower—a golden-yellow one—had just opened on the south side of his Minneapolis house, out about five inches from the foundation. Snow still covered one-third of the landscape but in this tiny microclimate the spring blooming season had begun.

Crocuses bloom in gardens and the native pasqueflower blooms on prairies, both usually starting by very early in April. To most gardeners, the crocus flower means spring has arrived, but there are also crocus species that bloom in the autumn here. All are wildflowers native to southern Europe and Asia.

Crocuses are among the best known of the early spring-flowering bulbs. The bulbs (corms) are planted in autumn, not closer than two or three inches apart and about two inches deep. The best effects are usually obtained by spacing them casually to get a naturalistic look. Plant in lawn areas as well as on the edges of gardens, between shrubs and beneath small trees. They will give you spring flowering beauty for many years. The plants grow about six inches tall, have linear leaves, and flowers about an inch or so in diameter. Garden crocus blossoms come in yellow, golden-yellow, orange-yellow, white, various shades of blue or purple, and some are bicolor. The flowers are closed at night and on overcast days.

The showy pasqueflower (*Anemone patens*) of native prairie areas, so called because it blooms around the Easter (Paschal) season, is also called crocus by some people. The plants are usually found on sunny slopes. Flowers are about two inches across and have five to seven pale-purple to white petal-like sepals. Within the flower is a ring of golden stamens and a central tuft of grayish pistils that become plumed fruits. The flowers appear before the leaves. The entire plant, including the flowers, is covered with soft silvery hairs that no doubt trap warm air next to the plant in the cool spring air.

Less than 2 percent of Minnesota's precious native prairie ecosystem remains, but in the last thirty years or so there has been great interest among individuals and groups in restoring former prairie areas. Planting more land to diverse prairie would restore valuable wildlife habitat if managed (and possibly harvested) properly. Harvesting the priaries? A University of Minnesota study has shown that mixed prairie plants can provide more usable energy per acre for ethanol or biodiesel production than either corn or soybeans. Prairie plants don't require herbicides, pesticides or energy intensive cultivation. They prevent erosion and remove carbon dioxide from the air, storing it as carbon in their roots. So not only are prairies beautiful and full of plant and animal diversity but they just might be able to reduce our nation's use of oil.

Photo: Anders Bjorling

pasqueflower

Imagine the small pasqueflower helping us to reduce our dependency on fossil fuels. Hopefully readers of this entry can get out on a native Minnesota prairie and see the pasqueflower, the early flowering spring perennial, which happens to be the floral emblem of South Dakota and Manitoba.

Week two (April 8 -15)

Pasqueflowers bloom on prairies and bloodroots in forests. Crocuses and snowdrops flower in gardens. Forsythia shrubs and red maple trees bloom and crabapple trees have tiny leaves.

Wood frogs, which make barking calls, and western chorus frogs, which sound like metallic clickers, are very vocal.

American robins are now building nests. Many Canada geese have begun incubating their eggs. Wood ducks and house finches begin laying eggs. The first chipping sparrows arrive. A few of the other migrating birds seen include yellow-rumped warblers, purple martins and northern flickers.

Listen at dusk in open natural areas for the nasal "peenting" sound of a male American woodcock trying to attract a female. He will continue the "peent" sound for several minutes, then spring into the air and spiral upward maybe 300 feet before dropping to earth again in a set of swoops, chirping all the way. The courtship flight occurs over and over until darkness sets in, and then is resumed at dawn.

Ice covers leave central Minnesota lakes. Farmers in the southern part of the state begin soil preparation for planting.

For Minneapolis and St. Paul, the normal high temperature on April 8 is 53° and the low is 33°F. The record high is 83° degrees set in 1931, and the record low is 9° set in 1997.

scattered events

- **April 8, 2000** - Many daffodils blooming. First great egrets, sandhill cranes and ruby-crowned kinglets.

- **April 10, 2005** - Merrill magnolia trees and Northern Sun forsythia shrubs are blooming nicely. First leaves out on common purple lilac shrubs.

- **April 14, 2003** - High of 89°F in the Twin Cities (warmest it has ever been this early in the year). First mosquito bite. Dutchman's-breeches first blooming.

- **April 15, 2002** - Record high of 91°F in the Twin Cities; the earliest 90° or above ever recorded here. In Faribault it's 93°. Ice-out date for Lake Waconia, to which the first American white pelicans and belted kingfisher have returned.

A Closer Look:

The Ice-out Process

People living near ponds and lakes have the good fortune to be able to directly observe the ice-out phenomenon. Although some people believe that ice sinks when it goes out, that is not the case; the ice is lighter than water.

The process starts with ice retreating from the shore, creating a belt of open water around the lake with a temperature of about 45°. A wide band of ice beyond the open water then becomes soft and rotten while the rest of the ice cover turns dark. At this point, turtles and leopard frogs begin to break their winter hibernation in the water near shore and emerge from the bottom sediments, although they are

Photo: Bruce Wahlstrom

still sluggish in the cold water.

The main ice sheet weakens and begins to fracture in large sections when winds become strong enough to move it. This is followed by rapid melting of ice crystals on the edges of the floating sections as they come in contact with the warmer water. Eventually wind will sweep the last ice sheets from the lake. As the sheets are pushed ashore, the remaining ice is generally in chunks up to seven inches thick and honeycomb-shaped.

Some loose ice along a shore doesn't constitute the condition of ice still being in, because a boat can easily be pushed through it. I consider ice-out to have occurred when at least 90 percent of the lake is free of ice.

Ice-out is an exciting time and people are anxious to get on the lake. Soon fishing boats and sailboats will appear and docks will go in, as we are off and running into summer.

Listed in the sidebar is a ten-year record of Lake Waconia (Carver County) and Wolf Lake (Lake County) ice-out dates. Wolf Lake is located at the Wolf Ridge Environmental Learning Center near Finland, Minnesota. The variations from year to year and between a southern and a northern Minnesota lake are interesting.

❈ ICE-OUT DATES ❈

Lake Waconia	Wolf Lake
1997 April 18	May 2
1998 April 3	April 19
1999 March 30	April 29
2000 March 15	April 4
2001 April 20	May 2
2002 April 15	April 30
2003 April 10	May 2
2004 April 4	April 24
2005 April 8	April 18
2006 April 7	April 17

A Closer Look:

Lake Minnetonka Ice-out History

The tenth largest of Minnesota's lakes, Lake Minnetonka is the largest in the metropolitan area. Its watershed is 123 square miles of which about 22 square miles make up the lake itself, and it has approximately 110 miles of shoreline. The average depth is 30 feet and greatest depth 104 feet.

Minnetonka is more of a meeting of waters than it is a single lake. In addition to the Upper Lake and Lower Lake there are about 23 named bays and areas. It's actually a complex of 16 interconnecting lakes formed mostly by ice blocks falling off the front edge of a retreating glacier 11,000 years ago. Because of the many bays and areas it is difficult to determine ice-out times for the lake as a whole.

Scientist and writer Dick Gray, who founded the Freshwater Society in 1968, has collected Lake Minnetonka ice-out dates going back as far as 1855. That's more than a century and a half of records. But Dick is missing a few years here and there, and actually has ice-outs for 127 years. According to Dick, the ice is designated as "out" when it is possible to travel by small boat from any one shore to another shore through any passage on the lake. I simplify this and say ice-out is the first day when at least 90 percent of a lake is free of ice. For the past 30 years both of our methods of determining ice-out have ended up with the same dates.

The ice-out date for Lake Minnetonka, or any other lake, is a significant time because it represents the beginning of a whole new season, the season of open water, waves shimmering in the sunlight, and all that comes with it. With April 13 as the average ice-out date, it's interesting to look at the recent past—the years between 1981 to 2005. During that period the ice cover left the lake later than normal in eight years and earlier than normal in fifteen years. On two occasions it left on the average date.

In 2007 the official ice-out date for Lake Minnetonka was on April 3—earlier than average by 10 days. In 2008, ice-out was April 23—ten days later than average.

[**For a detailed record of ice-out history on Lake Minnetonka, see Appendix I, page 300.**]

A Closer Look:

Dandelions and Purple Martins

This is not an essay about how to attract purple martins to our yards or how to get rid of dandelions, but rather some notes on two living species that share the Earth with us. One only has to examine each one thoughtfully to stand in awe of their adaptability, determination and beauty.

In 2007 I spotted my first bright-yellow dandelion flowers of the year on the sunny afternoon of March 26. That day the temperature hit 81° at the International Airport in the Twin Cities, which was 35° above normal and a new record high.

It was 80° that afternoon in St. Peter. I was out searching for spring signs to show my environmental studies classes when I found five wide-open, 1½-inch dandelion flowers. One was touching the south side of the St. Peter Fire Department building, and four others were as close as they could get to the south side of Christ Chapel on the Gustavus Adolphus College campus.

Coming as it does in early spring, the golden flowers and lush green leaves of the common dandelion catch our attention and help us celebrate the start of the growing season. While they are targets of lawn herbicides, dandelions are also much admired, and they have been widely used for food and medicine over the centuries.

Most authorities believe that the common dandelion came to the United States from Europe but originated in Asia Minor. It eventually spread across our continent and across much of the world, and is now found in both the Northern and Southern Hemispheres. As a weed, this plant is a bother to those who cherish a uniform green lawn, though the water contamination that results from treating lawns with chemicals to eradicate the dandelion ought to be an even greater concern. Why not just appreciate some lawn diversity?

Back in the Middle Ages the plant's deeply toothed leaves gave someone the idea that they resembled lion's teeth in profile. The plant was called "dents-de-lion" (French for "teeth of the lion") and from this the name "dandelion" has come. The young leaves have long been used fresh in salads, though as they mature they become bitter. Yet even older leaves are edible. They can be boiled twice, changing the water after the first boiling, and served like spinach. Dandelion leaves are rich in vitamin A, thiamine, riboflavin and calcium. In fact, ounce for ounce, the leaves have more potassium than bananas, a popular source of that mineral.

The blooming flower heads are often used

in the preparation of an excellent wine. And the roots, gathered in early spring or fall, can be used as a substitute for coffee after being baked in an oven until brown and brittle, ground, and then perked like commercial coffee. The dandelion root has also been an ingredient in medicines to treat constipation, insomnia, and other problems.

Given these many beneficial attributes, it should come as no surprise that animals also consider the dandelion to be a tasty treat. Birds and mice eat the seeds. Rabbits, pigs and goats devour the entire plant. Dozens of insect species visit the flowers for nectar and pollen.

On sunny days dandelion flowers open in the morning and close in the afternoon. They remain closed on overcast days.

We look for these sunny yellow flower heads from early spring well into November, with the greatest masses appearing along with the blossoming of crab apple trees.

The flower of this non-native perennial is actually a composite of many tiny flowers clustered together. It is made up of numerous bright yellow straps, plus stamens and pistils, but the pollen is sterile and so there is no true pollination or fertilization. Fortunately for its survival, the seeds of dandelions contain little buds of the parent plant and do not require fertilization. Thus dandelions are asexual. Wind scatters the seeds, which are attached to the "parachutes" that make up the fluffy white seed heads.

Soon after we see the first dandelion flowers we can expect the first purple martins to return, usually during the first week of April but always by the second week. In 2006 in the Twin Cities area the first purple martin was spotted April 9. Purple martins spend their winters around the farmlands and cities near Sao Paulo, in southern Brazil, and the peak of their migration back to Minnesota is between late April and early May.

Martins are such agile fliers that they often drink and bathe while flying by skimming water or flying through rain. My dad and others

around me enjoyed the sight of the graceful martins gliding in the air, and since boyhood I have felt that the bubbling chirps and trills of purple martins coming from high overhead have made spring and summer days extra special. The happy sounds are so attractive that many people put up and maintain multi-unit apartment houses, or gourd houses in clusters, for the birds to nest in. Native Americans developed a friendship with martins long before European settlers arrived; they hung hollow gourds near their lodges to attract the birds.

The purple martin is the largest member of the swallow family. They are 7 to 8 inches long, have a wingspan of 15 inches, and weigh about 2 ounces. They have pointed wings and notched tails. Their bills, which they use for scooping insects from the air in flight, are short and wide. Males have glossy purplish-black plumage over their entire bodies, while females are duller with grayish underparts. Purple martins are cavity nesters, and they prefer to nest in colonies. They often nest within a hundred feet of human dwellings and it's a fact that the most successful colonies are located within this distance.

Martins come to Minnesota to feed on insects and to nest. The earliest arrivals get the best nesting sites, but those who jump the gun and arrive too early may face disaster. A late-season cold snap or spring snowstorm can kill migrants, mainly because they can't find the flying insects they need to survive.

The martin's reputation as a great mosquito controller is not borne out by the facts, as they prefer large insects such as dragonflies, butterflies, moths, and both deer and horse flies. No doubt martins eat some mosquitoes, but they do not feed much after sunset, when mosquitoes are most active.

Martins raise only one brood of young per year. Nest building is a cooperative effort by the pair. A clutch of four to six white eggs is laid which the female incubates for 15 to 18 days. Both the male and female feed the young that remain in the nest for 28 to 35 days after hatching, until their flight feathers are fully developed. By late July and into August, martins congregate in big flocks as they stage for migration.

Our family once spent several summers on the shore of Leech Lake, and when the martins departed in August it seemed very quiet and vacant without them. We were cheered by the fact that the martins return to the same nest sites each year, while the young strike out to form new colonies. We could expect apartments full of martins the next summer.

Most purple martins probably live only a year or two at most, but there are a number of banding records of martins living eight years and beyond. The oldest documented one was alive at 13 years.

A Closer Look:
Bird Sounds

The air is filled with spring bird music in April. We hear the loud rattling sounds of belted kingfishers, the winnowing of the common snipe in flight, woodpeckers drumming, the chattering of tree swallows, mourning doves cooing, and Canada geese honking. Added to this is the "cheer-up" song of the American robin and the remarkable melodic accomplishments of the song sparrow. The song sparrow song is three or four repeated notes followed by a rich and varied chuck-chuck warble; put into the English language it might come out as "Marge-Marge-Marge, put-on-your-TEA-kettle-ettle-ettle." There are hundreds of variations of this basic song sparrow theme.

So, why do birds sing, call, or make mechanical sounds? It's their means of communicating with other birds and the world around them. The chief function of song in most species is to proclaim territory. It warns males of the same species to stay away and attracts females, and subsequently helps maintain and strengthen the bond between the mated pair. There are social songs such as a canary-like one used by American goldfinches in flock formation. At times a bird sings because it is bubbling over with the pure joy of living. Call notes are used in a variety of situations. There are calls of alarm, anger, scolding, and location. As an example, the cheeps of warblers help these nocturnal migrants stay together in flight.

Even though birds do not call and sing for our benefit, we can still enjoy their efforts, and it keeps us in tune with the changes that are coming our way, especially in spring. Described below are three well-known Minnesota birds that we often hear and see in April.

Killdeer

The killdeer is probably most often identified by sound. This bird repeats its name as a call—"killdeer, killdeer, killdeer." In southern Minnesota we usually first hear this call by the second week in March.

Photo: Greg Gillson

The killdeer is also easily recognized by its distinct color pattern—brown on the upper body and pure white on the lower, with two black bands across the breast. It is the size of an American robin, with long legs that are used extensively for running. When running, the bird holds its body rigid, and its legs are a blur of motion. Killdeers are famous for their predator-distracting "broken-wing display" in which they run along the ground dragging their wing, appearing to be injured, and thus lure a potential predator away from a nest or chicks.

Although the killdeer is a shorebird, it commonly nests far from water on athletic fields, agricultural lands, golf courses, gravel rooftops, or any area that has short sparse vegetation. They are common throughout the state except in deep forest areas.

Brown Thrasher

We first hear them and then see them. One arrived in our yard April 19, 2006, a typical time to first observe the brown thrasher returning from its winter home in the southern United States.

A secretive bird, the brown thrasher is most commonly glimpsed as a cinnamon-shape escaping into the brushy woodlands or garden shrubs it chooses for its home. A member of the mockingbird family, the brown thrasher is known for its rich, musical phrases, which are usually sung in pairs. With such a beautiful song, the notes are well worth repeating. To explain the tempo of the song, one listener wrote it down as a type of telephone conversation: "Hello, hello; yes, yes; Who is this? Who is this? I should say, I should say; How's that? How's that?" The male brown thrasher usually sings from a lofty perch with his body trembling, head upraised and bill wide open.

Common Grackle

Millions of our Minnesota common grackles winter in Arkansas, Louisiana and Mississippi; and the first ones return to the St. Peter and Twin Cities area by the first or second week of March. The grackle is the foot-long blackbird with bright yellow eyes. They appear black at a distance but are highly iridescent. The head iridescence may be green, blue, or purple, depending on how the light hits. They have a long, keel-shaped tail and fairly long black bills. Female grackles look similar to males, only duller and bit smaller.

The range of the common grackle extends east of the Rocky Mountains from southern Canada to the Gulf States. They are a summer resident throughout nearly all of Minnesota and often nest in evergreens. Their food includes insects, frogs, mice, seeds, and wild fruits. Large flocks may damage grain crops. At feeders they especially like cracked corn.

The word "grackle" is derived from the Latin word "graculus" meaning "to cough," and the bird does have a loud raspy call. Common grackles don't really have a song. We may hear clucks and high-pitched rising screeches like a rusty gate hinge, which in no way can compete with the refined notes of American robins and northern cardinals. Yet female grackles have always found the rasping notes of the male common grackles attractive.

Week 3 (April 16 - 23)

These spring mornings are the best time of year to hear the symphony of bird music. Listen for tree swallows chattering, mourning doves cooing, ring-necked pheasants crowing, both northern cardinals and black-capped chickadees whistling, common grackles squawking, red-winged blackbirds trilling, Canada geese honking, American robins singing, woodpeckers drumming, and more.

Lawns are greening-up and the first mowers are heard. Magnolia and apricot trees bloom with showy flowers. Gardeners plant potatoes and onions, and seed-in leaf lettuce, radishes, peas and spinach. Common dandelions, tulips and daffodils bloom next to south-facing walls.

Weeping willows have an elegant yellow-green glow with their tiny new leaves. Woodland wildflowers such as bloodroot, sharp-lobed hepatica, white trout-lily and Dutchman's-breeches have showy flowers.

Brown thrashers, barn swallows and yellow-headed blackbirds first return, and more yellow-rumped warblers and chipping sparrows arrive. Eastern bluebirds, wood ducks and mallards are nesting, and we may even spot the first mallard ducklings.

Southern Minnesota and Wisconsin farmers are busy doing field work, including soil preparation and early planting. Ice could still be going out of central Minnesota lakes. As ice covers leave, common loons are returning to northern Minnesota and Wisconsin lakes and are filling the spring air with their enchanting calls and yodel-like songs.

scattered events

- **For Earth Day, April 22**, the normal high temperature in Minneapolis/St. Paul is 60° and the low 39°. The record high is 90° set in 1980 and the record low is 23° set in 1874. On April 22, 1963, the Twin Cities received 5.4 inches of snow.

- **April 17, 1997** - Ruby-crowned kinglets moving through. Grass fires in Hastings area. Flooding bad from Fargo to Grand Forks area.

- **April 17, 2005** - First rhubarb pulled for sauce. First yellow-headed blackbirds arrive. Last day this spring for skiing at Lutsen Mountains.

- **April 19, 1998** - Dandelions blooming on sunny slopes. Eastern cottonwood trees began leafing out. Carver County farmers planting field corn.

- **April 21, 2002** - 6.2 inches of snow fell on crocus, scilla and early daffodil flowers.

- **April 22, 1999** - Black-capped chickadees are nest building. Sod is being cut for new lawns. Ice-out date for Leech Lake in Cass County.

- **April 22, 2005** - First house wren. First shade in forests from emerging leaves.

A Closer Look:
Those Terrific Trees

All of us are familiar with trees. These large, amazing plants grow all around us—in our yards, on school grounds, at work places, and in parks and forests. Minnesota is home to 43 native tree species and several hundred introduced species and varieties. By definition a tree is a woody plant which usually reaches a mature height of at least 10 to 15 feet, and has one main trunk which develops many branches and a crown of leaves.

Trees, powered by the sun's energy, are remarkable natural resources. Without trees the world would be bleak and life as we know it impossible. They provide innate beauty and are especially admired in their natural forest settings. Trees can reduce the heat of summer and block the cold of winter. They absorb sound, decrease noise pollution and serve as screens for privacy.

From early times humans used wood for such purposes as home building, rafts, canoes, fuel and weapons. Too often, however, so-called advanced civilizations have recklessly destroyed trees. The great forests of the cedars of Lebanon, for example, were virtually eliminated in lumbering operations during early historic times for such purposes as the construction of King Solomon's temple and palace.

Carbonized and fossilized wood, known as coal, remains as a fuel for energy we need. Trees provide us twenty-first century people with paper, cardboard, and building materials. Leaves of palms and other trees continue to be used for thatching roofs and for clothing. Edible fruits and nuts produced by trees such as apple, cherry, pear, and black walnut in temperate climates, and citrus fruits in warmer climates, are important to us. So are dates, coconuts, olives, chocolate and coffee, all tree products from warm regions. Medicines, including quinine, plus dyes, spices, turpentine and cork come from trees.

Trees are of immense importance in helping to purify the atmosphere by absorbing carbon dioxide and other pollutants, and releasing oxygen. Trees help control soil erosion, prevent flooding, and protect and conserve water supplies. They also play a vital role in creating habitats for wild animals, from tiny insects to large birds and mammals, by providing them with food, water, shelter, and places to raise their young.

A Closer Look:
A Taste of Rhubarb

It's fun to taste spring. By mid-April I'm anxious for the first rhubarb. In 2006 our neighbors Joe and RaeAnn Tewinkel pulled their first rhubarb and made sauce on April 17, the same date as in 2005. They shared with us a jar of rhubarb sauce, a delicious spring treat

with an agreeable acid flavor.

A harbinger of spring, rhubarb is grown for its large thick leaf stalks which are popular for tangy pies and sauce. I personally like to pull, not cut off, a stalk out of the crown and eat it fresh while working in our garden. (The leaves are poisonous and should not be eaten.)

Native to southern Siberia and the Volga region, rhubarb is a cool climate perennial that has been cultivated for centuries. It was introduced to Europe about 1600, and by 1800 many different varieties were listed by horticulturists in America. It is most productive in the northern third of the United States; one of the few vegetables that can be grown in Alaska but can't be successfully grown in the

First Rhubarb Pulled for Sauce (Carver County) - A 16 year record	
1992 - April 17	2000 - April 8
1993 - April 24	2001 – April 11
1994 - April 20	2002 - April 25
1995 - May 11	2003 - April 21
1996 - April 28	2004 - April 19
1997 - May 1	2005 - April 17
1998 - April 10	2006 - April 17
1999 - April 14	2007 - April 23

southern Gulf states, as it requires a cold period of dormancy.

Propagation is by division of the root. Each division planted should contain a bud and a piece of root. Plant rhubarb in spring or fall, but don't harvest until the second year. Rhubarb likes heavy soil with lots of organic matter such as rotted manure and decayed leaves mixed in before planting and added year after year. About six plants set four feet apart in a row will provide enough rhubarb for average family use.

Rhubarb is ready at least a month before the first ripe garden strawberries and can be harvested for about two months. After that, allow the plant to build up a large crown for the following year. Also, it is best to remove the flower stalks and not let them produce seeds, as seed production saps the energy of the plant.

A Closer Look:
Wild Ginger and Other Wildflowers

By mid-April, or soon after, in the southern half of Minnesota, and into May up north, the woodland wildflowers such as bloodroot, white trout-lily, wild ginger, Dutchman's-breeches, spring beauty, downy yellow violet, and cut-leaved toothwort have sent up leaves

---

SIMPLE RHUBARB SAUCE RECIPE

4 cups of rhubarb stalks,
        cut in 1 to 2 inch lengths
1 cup of sugar
1/2 cup water
add a bit of cinnamon if you want

Bring to a boil and then cook for 10 minutes at a lower temperature. Cool and enjoy.

❀

RHUBARB REFRIGERATOR JAM

5 cups of rhubarb stalks cut in about
        1 inch lengths or shorter
3 cups of sugar
3 oz. package of strawberry
        or raspberry gelatin
1 cup of water
Bring rhubarb and water to a boil. Add sugar and boil until mushy. Remove from heat and add the small box of gelatin. Stir until completely dissolved. Store in refrigerator.

---

and begin blooming. At least two dozen other woodland wildflowers spread their green leaves and then produce flowers followed by mature seeds, taking advantage of the spring sunshine before the deciduous forests become shady. There is a mystique to the forests now making any person interested in the early growing season want to walk wooded paths often, almost daily if possible, so as to catch the progression of wildflower bloom. Some species like the sharp-lobed hepatica bloom soon after the snow melts and others bloom several weeks later.

The perennial plant called wild ginger is one of those early spring wildflowers found in deciduous forests throughout Minnesota, Wisconsin, and across temperate eastern North America. It has a pair of fuzzy heart-shaped leaves at the end of a rather thick, elongated rootstalk. Because the single flower is at ground level between the stalks of the paired leaves, springtime hikers may pass a hundred of them in the woods and never see their flowers. But there is a purpose for the dark red flower with three triangular lobes to be touching the soil. The flower stays low because the ground is the source of the insects that visit and pollinate it.

As an early bloomer, wild ginger attracts the early emerging types of spring flies and other insects that come out of the ground looking for the thawing carcasses of animals that died over the winter. The insects are probably drawn to the flower by the dull red color, similar to carrion, and to the pollen, much of which they eat but some of which they transfer to other wild ginger blossoms. The cup-like shape of the flower also provides insects with shelter from the cold winds of April and early May.

Later, when the plant produces seeds, wild ginger uses ants to disperse them. Like the seeds of many other spring woodland wildflowers, wild ginger seeds have oily "elaiosomes," appendages that ants find tasty. The ants carry the seeds to their underground chambers, eat the elaiosomes, and then discard the seeds which will have a safe place to sprout.

Wild ginger is not related to the common flavoring herb of the tropics, although the root-stalk has a mild ginger flavor and has been used in folk medicine for centuries. The powdered root was also widely used as a flavoring substitute for real ginger in the late 1700s and throughout the nineteenth century.

A Closer Look:
Earth Day, 2007

The first Earth Day, April 22, 1970, was a day set aside to think about creating life-styles to reduce the waste and destruction of our environment. One of the main messages many of us heard that day was that human life can continue on Earth only if people cooperate with nature. During the last 37 years strides have been made in cleaning up many of our rivers and lakes, recycling, protecting natural ecosystems, hazardous materials awareness,

Photo: NASA

Week four (April 24-30)

and the list goes on. But, we have a long way to go if we are to live in a sustainable way in harmony with nature.

There are long lists of things to do and things not to do when it comes to being a good steward of our Earth, but one of the best may be to take pleasure in the true beauty of the Earth's ecosystems and its creatures, and to take time to learn about some of the plants and animals that share the Earth with us. It's just about impossible to destroy something you understand and love.

Throughout the year, and especially on April 22, with the wonders of spring all around us, we should make it a point to get out and observe. Every forest, every marsh and prairie remnant, is full of spring signs—evidence that our Earth is designed as a place for life, no matter what foolish acts people may commit.

We begin the emerald-green time, with many tones of green and the lush-green look to the landscape. Basswoods, sugar maples, bur oaks and other trees start to leaf-out, and a bright green tinge is seen in deciduous forest canopies along with the first shade from emerging foliage. Backyard and wild plum trees are in bloom and covered with white flowers. At least a dozen species of woodland wildflowers such as spring beauty and large-flowered bellwort cover forest floors. Sod is being cut and put down for new lawns. In gardens, tulips, daffodils, hyacinths, the PJM Rhododendron, dwarf irises and Arctic phlox all have showy flowers.

American toads and common tree frogs can be heard calling. Green herons first return, and migrating white-throated sparrows are numerous at feeding stations.

It's early, but in the past few years we have observed crabapple and apple trees, as well as lilac shrubs, starting to provide fantastic floral displays and fragrances in late April.

Southern, central, and western Minnesota farmers plant corn, soybeans, spring wheat, oats, sugarbeets, and green peas. Ice-out time continues for northern Minnesota lakes.

scattered events

- **April 24, 1997** - Carver County farmers busy doing field work. Ice-out date for Kabekona Lake in Hubbard County. Cross-country skiers still able to ski on ice and snow cover of Caribou Lake near Lutsen.

- **April 24, 1998** - First shade in deciduous forests. Truck farmers in Belle Plaine area are planting sweet corn, potatoes, cabbage, broccoli and radishes.

- **April 26, 2006** - First house wren. Rafts of American coots are back. Eastern bluebirds incubate eggs. Juneberry shrubs blooming nicely and crabapple trees starting. Masses of yellow common dandelion flowers brighten the altered landscape.

- **April 28, 1998** - Crabapple trees starting to bloom. Between LeSueur and St. Peter, there are beautiful green tones in the Minnesota River valley from all the newly leafed-out deciduous trees.

- **April 29, 1994** - This morning my neighbors in Waconia were out shoveling five inches of wet snow from their driveways. Trees were decorated with snow for Arbor Day. American robins were feeding on sumac fruit clusters. Both song- and white-throated sparrows, along with mourning doves, northern cardinals and other birds were scratching for seeds at our feeding station. We heard on WCCO Radio that Cold Spring had a foot of new snow.

- **April 30, 2004** - Common purple lilac shrubs begin flowering. At Nerstrand Big Woods State Park, twenty-two species of wildflowers are now blooming, including the Minnesota dwarf trout-lily and marsh marigold.

- **April 30, 2005** - Many crabapple trees now blooming and very showy. Also, backyard plum and pear trees are in bloom. House wrens very vocal.

Photo: David Brislance

A Closer Look:
Loons are Back

Common loons appear in spring at the same time that ice is leaving the lakes—often returning to a lake when it's still half-covered. They are beautiful black and white birds about 2 feet long, and weighing 8 to 9 pounds. Males and females have identical plumage. Their wild echoing calls are a symbol of the Minnesota wilderness. In fact the calling no doubt does more to create the indescribable feeling of being apart from civilization and being close to nature than any other phenomenon in the wilderness country. The common loon was designated as the Minnesota state bird in 1961.

Much has been learned about the life of the common loon but just a few notes may help readers to better appreciate the presence of these birds in Minnesota.

Loons have the least wing surface in proportion to body weight of any flying bird. Unlike other large birds such as Canada geese and great blue herons, a loon's wing beats are very rapid, about 250 beats per minute. Their speed is surprisingly fast, up to 100 mph. But it's the take offs which are arduous, starting with a long run and gaining altitude slowly. While common loons sometimes need up to a quarter mile of aquatic runway, they can often break water contact after a run of about 80 yards. On many small lakes they must fly in a curve around part of the lake before ascending high enough to clear the trees.

Cold, clear water, an ample food supply, and a feeling of solitude are the qualities the loon seeks in a lake. Clear lakes are preferred because loons hunt by eyesight. Fish, which are the principal food, are pursued beneath the surface of the water with great speed and power. Loons also eat frogs, leeches, and other aquatic creatures. The average dive time while feeding is 40 seconds, but loons can stay under for up to five minutes or so, and can certainly dive to depths in excess of 100 feet. Only the feet are used for propulsion, although the wings facilitate underwater turning maneuvers.

The loon's webbed feet are located back on the body, which aids in diving, but there is a drawback to this design: when a loon comes up on shore to nest it must propel itself forward on its belly. The parents take turns incubating the two olive-brown eggs for 29 days. Newly hatched young begin to swim and dive in just a day or two, and during their first few weeks the young often travel on the backs of their parents.

The name "loon" means lummox or awkward and refers to the bird's on-shore movements and perhaps its inability to fly from the ground.

Scientists believe the common loon is long-lived, estimating the life span at 15 to 30 years. One banded individual was still alive 18 years later. We expect to find common loons on Minnesota lakes from the central part of the state to the north and northeast. By a survey conducted in 1989, non-game wildlife biologists calculated the statewide population of these majestic birds to be about 12,000. Almost one-third of the estimated loon population was on lakes 10 to 49 acres in size. Of course they are well-known summer residents on Mille Lacs Lake, Leech Lake, and other large Minnesota lakes. As of 2007, loons continued to be plentiful in Minnesota but are always susceptible to changes in lake water quality. Acid rain, leaky septic systems, erosion, over-development of shore-lines and intensive lake recreation are all problems that effect the loon.

The breeding range of the common loon includes most all of Alaska, much of Canada, and the northern parts of the states next to the Canadian border from Washington to Maine. They also breed in such countries as Greenland, Iceland, and Norway. However, Minnesota has the distinction of providing summer homes for more than half of the common loon population in the lower forty-eight states.

Loons begin their autumn migration in September and by the first part of November nearly all are gone, with only a few lonely stragglers to be seen in their simpler winter plummage. Without the loon's haunting cry the woodland lakes become empty solitudes. The two things that northerners love about loons—their beautiful plumage and the haunting calls—are not enjoyed by southerners. Along the Atlantic and Gulf coastal waters, where loons winter, they are usually silent, and their plummage lacks the brilliant contrasts of their summer dress. Like many other birds utilizing the marine environment, loons are capable of coping with salt water by secreting excess salt through a nasal gland.

A Closer Look:
Arbor Day

A civilization flourishes when people plant trees under whose shade they will never sit.

– A Greek proverb

The Latin word "arbor" means tree. Arbor Day—the last Friday in April—is a special day set aside for people to learn about trees and to plant trees in their communities. It is celebrated in all fifty states and in many Canadian provinces.

Arbor Day started in Nebraska—a state not known for its trees. Among pioneers moving into Nebraska Territory in 1854 was J. Sterling Morton from Detroit. Morton and his wife liked plants, and the home they established in Nebraska was quickly planted with trees, shrubs and garden flowers.

Morton was a journalist and soon became editor of Nebraska's first newspaper. Given that forum, he spread agricultural information and his enthusiasm for trees to a wide audience. His fellow pioneers on the plains missed their trees, and they also recognized the need for trees for fuel and building materials, and to serve as windbreaks to keep the soil from blowing away.

Morton not only urged individuals to plant trees in his articles and editorials, but also encouraged civic organizations and groups of every kind to join in. He eventually became secretary of the Nebraska Territory, which gave him another forum to stress the values of trees. On January 4, 1872, at a meeting of the Nebraska Board of Agriculture, Morton proposed a tree-planting holiday to be called "Arbor Day." The date was set for April 10, and prizes were offered to counties and individuals for planting properly the largest number of trees on that day. More than one million trees were planted in Nebraska on the very first Arbor Day.

A century and more later, the last Friday in April is officially recognized as National Arbor Day. Numerous communities hold special tree-planting and educational events. In addition, the whole month of May is recognized as Arbor Month in the state of Minnesota.

The year 2007 marked the 135th anniversary of the first Arbor Day, and we continue to mark it by reflecting on the importance of conservation, promoting the value of trees in our lives, and renewing our commitment to tree planting and care.

Each time we plant a tree we give to the world a new source of beauty, shade, oxygen, and habitat for creatures of many sizes. We plant trees to celebrate our hope for the future.

A Closer Look:
Urban Trees

In recent years, as the effects of global warming have become clearer and more pronounced, trees have taken on a new level of environmental importance. Above and beyond their many practical virtues, trees are vital to life on Earth. They sustain our soil, moderate our climate, provide dwelling places for wildlife, conserve our water, clean our air, cool our streets and homes, and smooth the edges of our lives. Of perhaps even greater importance, they take in and use, for their growth and development, carbon dioxide, the main global warming gas.

Dr. Gary Johnson, professor of urban and community forestry, University of Minnesota Department of Forest Resources, says that "the urban forest softens our environment," making it more livable for us humans. When thinking about trees in our urban environment, Gary considers small towns also to be urban, and he has come up with his top ten trees for planting in urban forests of southern and central Minnesota. They are: bur oak, white pine, sugar maple, northern white cedar, Ohio buckeye, larch (the native tamarack or European or Japanese larch), Japanese tree lilac, crabapples (many excellent varieties), Norway spruce, white fir.

Photo: Jim Gilbert

A Closer Look:

Daffodils and Tulips

Narcissus is the generic or scientific name for the well-known spring-blooming plants called daffodils and jonquils. All three names are used indiscriminately for the perennial plant that comes up each year from a bulb and has a star of petals surrounding a trumpet-like structure. Daffodil is the name most often used in Minnesota. The flowers come in yellow, white, yellow and white, or yellow and orange.

Daffodils are native to Europe and Asia. Most grow to a height of about two feet, and all have blade-like leaves. Plant in mid-August or as early as bulbs are available from garden centers. Place bulbs about six to nine inches apart and six inches deep. They like moist soil that has good drainage and will grow in sunny locations or partial shade. The bulbs can be planted between shrubs, under small trees, in gardens, and also in lawn areas. Do not cut the lawn until the daffodil leaves have died down or the bulbs will be weakened and future flowering impaired. There is no need to lift daffodil bulbs after bloom time until they become crowded. Just enjoy the blossoms each spring.

The tulip has been the most popular spring-flowering bulb for centuries. Bulbs are planted in late October or early November; placed six to eight inches below ground level in a sunny garden location with well-drained soil. There are thousands of varieties, some of which can thrive and bloom in the same spot for 10 to 20 years, though most remain productive and healthy for just a few years.

Most tulip plants have solitary, single, bell-shaped flowers which are red, pink, white or yellow. Bluish-green leaves are clustered around the base of the plants.

The Dutch have been in the tulip bulb business for more than 400 years, but tulips did not originate there, nor from Turkey where the Dutch got theirs. The flowers are native to the Mediterranean region and Asia. (Tulip is the Turkish word for turban.)

May

In May, warm temperatures and showers work to continue the greening-up process. It's the month of many woodland wildflowers and delightful weather, neither too hot nor too cold. Rose-breasted grosbeaks, Baltimore orioles, and indigo buntings arrive at feeding stations. Lilac shrubs, crabapple and apple trees bloom. White tailed deer fawns are born. Corn, soybeans, spring wheat, potatoes, and other crops are planted.

READING THE LANDSCAPE

Week one (May 1–7)

The Baltimore Oriole
Fantastic Fragrance of Lilacs
American Toads Trilling
Attracting Hummingbirds

Week two (May 8–15)

Season Creep
Planting for Birds
Busy Bees
Barn Swallows Nest Building

Week three (May 16–23)

Northern Lights Azaleas
White-tailed Deer Fawns
Naming Plants and Animals
The Monarch Butterfly Returns

Week four (May 24–31)

Snags
Butterfly Gardening
Young Common Grackles Fledge
Cattails—Very Important Plants

first week in may

Rose-breasted grosbeaks, ruby-throated hummingbirds and chimney swifts return. Also look for the first Baltimore orioles. They winter in Costa Rica and other parts of Central America, and arrive in numbers the first two weeks of May. These orioles have a strong homing instinct and often return year after year to nest in the same yard and even the same tree. Expect to see the first tiny Canada goose goslings swimming with their parents and grazing on fresh green grasses. Ring-necked pheasants, blue jays, and northern cardinals are among the birds incubating eggs. Red-winged blackbirds build their nests.

It's time to enjoy the superb fragrances and visual beauty of crabapple, apple, and lilac flowers, and to hunt for the Minnesota State mushroom, the common morel. Tulips and daffodils bloom nicely. Asparagus is up tall enough to harvest, and gardeners continue pulling rhubarb. Cattle graze on lush green pastures. Forests are carpeted with blooming wildflowers such as the cut-leaved toothwort, wild blue phlox, and various violets. Wild grape and staghorn sumac start to leaf out.

Leopard frogs, American toads, and chorus frogs add their captivating vocalizations to the spring air. Young gray squirrels leave their nests. Red fox kits are out of their dens.

In southern Minnesota, the first jack-in-the-pulpits are up and open, and as deciduous trees continue leafing out, we are noticing shade in urban and natural forests. In northern Minnesota, quaking aspens start to leaf out and spring peepers call, as the last lakes lose their ice sheets.

On May 1 the normal high temperature in the Twin Cities is 65° and the low is 42° F. The record high is 91° set in 1959, and the low is 24° set in 1909.

scattered events

■ **May 1, 2005** - On this windy day with some snow showers, American robins eggs continue hatching, and colonies of wild plum trees have showy white flowers. From Owatonna to Mankato and the Twin Cities, there are beautiful tones of green in urban and native deciduous forests. The trees have leafed out but many still have tiny leaves.

■ **May 1, 2007** - I walked Hidden Falls Trail in Nerstrand Big Woods State Park, located northeast of Faribault, with my Gustavus Adolphus College Environmental Studies class. The students and I found and identified 23 species of blooming wildflowers in this maple/basswood forest, including wood anemone, early meadow-rue, wood betony and the Minnesota dwarf trout-lily. Nerstrand is well-known for spring wildflowers.

■ **May 4, 1995** - Green tinge first noticed in Twin Cities area urban forest; willows, boxelders and other trees have started leafing out. Up to a foot of snow covers the forest floor off the Sawbill Trail out of Tofte. Ice cover left Gunflint Lake in Cook County.

■ **May 5, 2001** - New migrants observed include bobolink, scarlet tanager, black-and-white warbler, and eastern kingbird. Ice-out date for Devil Track Lake in Cook County, near Grand Marais.

■ **May 6, 2000** - Common purple lilac shrubs and apple trees at bloom peak and very fragrant. In wetlands, new green cattail leaves are up one to two feet.

■ May 7, 2007 - Overall bloom peak for the University of Minnesota Landscape Arboretum crabapple collection. Also blooming nicely in the Arboretum are the eastern redbud trees, lilac shrubs, tulips, and many woodland wildflowers such as the large-flowered trillium. All of these offer a fleeting spring show.

A Closer Look:

The Baltimore Oriole

May first is a good time to put out the orange halves or grape jelly to welcome back the orioles. Mix the jelly half-and-half with water using an eggbeater, then pour it into glass jars set out in feeders. The Baltimore oriole, which winters in Central America, is an insect eater but also feeds on wild fruits and may probe flowers for nectar.

The bright orange and sharply contrasting black plumage of the male Baltimore oriole makes it very conspicuous as it searches for food. These colors must have caught the attention of early European settlers in Maryland because the bird was named in honor of George Calvert, Lord Baltimore, an early colonizer there, who had chosen orange and black as his family colors.

Orioles also attract attention with their loud, clear voices. The presence of this small bird's cheerful series of whistles and chattering is a sure sign that the month of May is here.

A Closer Look:
Fantastic Fragrance of Lilacs

It's time for the common purple lilac to be flowering. Our area is perfumed with a scent that Edward Bunyard, a British horticulturist, called "the very heart and soul of memory." Other writers have also stated that the common purple lilac essence is one of the most memory-stirring of all fragrances. Longfellow firmly declared, "I shall not go to town while the lilacs bloom," nor did he. The bloom period is about 10 to 14 days.

To most people lilacs mean fragrance, and it

is true that the flowers of the most popular kinds are what some could describe as deliciously perfumed. The common purple lilac, a native of Central Europe, has been a favorite in gardens for centuries, no doubt because of its sweet floral essence. It often maintains itself in a wild state for long periods around abandoned farms and other settlements, and was one of the earliest plants to reach North America from Europe.

Exactly when the common purple lilac was brought to America is in doubt, but we have records dating back to 1652 when it was the modest ornament of many a cottage yard. As European settlers moved westward, the lilac was the first flowering shrub that bloomed by the side of log houses in the frontier settlements, having been brought from New England along with the household goods. At the time of fullest bloom, lilacs were brought to country churches where the fragrance mingled with the sounds of prayer and song.

The common purple lilac is a large multi-stemmed shrub that can grow up to twenty feet tall. The pale to deep lilac-colored, sweet-scented blooms come after the bright-green foliage emerges in spring. Individual flowers, each about ⅓ inch long, are grouped together in panicles 6 to 10 inches long. Lilacs grow best in full sun. They should have at least 6 hours of direct light per day to bloom prolifically. To start new plantings, dig up the suckers around the base of the mother plant and transplant these in early spring before any new growth emerges.

In 2007 the common purple lilac shrubs were at bloom peak on May 8, and in 2006 it was May 9. Residents and travelers to the North Shore of Lake Superior can enjoy lilac blossoms there the first week of June.

A Closer Look:
American Toads Trilling

In 2007 we heard the first American toads calling on April 22, and in 2006 it was on April 13. In autumn these toads burrow into the soft soil to depths below the frost line to hibernate. They emerge from hibernation in middle-to-late April or the first part of May, and then move to grassy ponds for breeding, where the males can be heard trilling to attract females. This captivating sound is made when the throat is puffed out and almost globular, but the actual sound is made by the air drawn in at the nostrils and passed back and forth from lungs to the mouth over the vocal chords, the puffed-out throat acting as a resonator.

The high-pitched trills may continue uninterrupted for twenty seconds or more. The females arrive at the ponds a few days after the males and lay long strands of eggs, which are then fertilized by the males. The strands of eggs attached to submerged vegetation are like tiny strings of beads.

Toad eggs hatch in two to 12 days, depending upon the water temperature. The tadpoles transform into small toads in 40 to 60 days, depending on food available and water temperature. Toads mature in two to three years and reach a length of about four inches. The tadpoles feed mostly on vegetation but the adult toads live entirely on small animals, including insects that are injurious to grasses and other plants. This makes American toads useful creatures to have in fields and gardens.

Toads are colored from gray to brown. The topside of an American toad is covered with warts, which do not transfer to us humans. But the warts do discharge a poisonous substance that creates a bad taste in the mouth of its predators, often causing the toad to be released. These toads can also fill themselves with air which prevents snakes from swallowing them.

A Closer Look:
Attracting Hummingbirds

Weighing less than a penny, with a length of only three inches from tip of the bill to tip of the tail, the ruby-throated hummingbird is the smallest of our Minnesota birds. Its plumage is a metallic green above and white below. Only the adult males have the iridescent ruby-red throat, which looks black in many lighting situations.

Most of the 300-plus hummingbird species live in the American tropics. Of the more than 20 hummingbird species in North America, only the ruby-throat is regularly found in the eastern half. Its breeding range extends into the lower parts of southern and central Canada and includes all of the eastern states south to Florida and Texas. The ruby-throat is a strong flier for its small size, traveling considerable distances over land and water, even crossing the Gulf of Mexico to reach its wintering grounds. Most winter from southern Mexico to Costa Rica and Panama, although a few remain stateside along the Gulf.

Photo: David Brislance

The ruby-throated hummingbird is a regular spring and fall migrant throughout Minnesota except in the southwest where it is uncommon in both seasons. This tiny jewel is a common summer resident in the northern part of the state with numbers decreasing southward in the state until it becomes rare or absent in the south-central and southwest.

Usually we expect to see the first hummers about May 1 in southern Minnesota and by May 15 in the north. In the Waconia/Lake Minnetonka area we begin looking for the first ruby-throat the last week of April. A good share are gone from the north by September 15 and the south by September 30, with a few late birds remaining into October.

People who see these remarkable birds regularly in spring and summer are usually homeowners who landscape their yards with a variety of red and orange tubular flowers, and who have placed sugar-and-water feeders in their yards. Food coloring or honey is not recommended in these solutions.

At feeders, and sometimes in gardens, these little birds can be very feisty and territorial. In less populated areas, especially in northern Minnesota and Wisconsin, ruby-throated hummingbirds are at home around woodland edges, not far from beds of blooming wildflowers. In August they are especially attracted to edges of wetlands with blooming jewelweeds.

It should be noted that in many cases the plants that hummingbirds depend on for food are, in turn, dependent upon hummingbirds for their pollination. These native plants evolved at the same time as hummingbirds. Also important is the fact that hummingbirds cannot survive on nectar or on sugar-water solutions alone. They time their migrations to coincide with the blooming season of favorite flowers and with the appearance of small insects. Hummingbirds visit flowers not only for nectar, but also for insects, an essential source of protein. They also capture spiders in their webs and insects on the wing.

Listed below are a few useful plants for home landscaping which have flowers that can produce a lot of nectar and so will increase your chances to observe ruby-throated hummingbirds on a regular basis.

Bee-balm	*Nasturtium*
Columbine	*Lilies and daylilies*
Coralbells	*Petunias*
Delphinium	*Snapdragons*
Fuchsias	*Trumpet honeysuckle*
Hollyhocks	*Virginia bluebells*
Lantana	*Zinnias (especially red*
Lilacs	*daisy-like ones)*

Week two (May 8-15)

House wrens and Baltimore orioles have become very vocal. American robins and eastern bluebirds feed young nestlings, while barn swallows gather mud for their nests. The first gray catbirds and indigo buntings arrive, and waves of migrating warblers are passing through the treetops. Many pairs of Canada geese can be seen with young goslings. Expect the first young wood ducks to jump from their nesting boxes or tree cavities. The new growth on most spruce trees is bright green. It's the peak of the lilac bloom in southern Minnesota. Ohio buckeye, eastern redbud, and many crabapple tree varieties have colorful flowers. Showy blooming woodland wildflowers at this time include large-flowered trillium and columbine.

Typical lake surface temperatures are in the 50- to 60-degree range for the Minnesota fishing season opener. Ovenbirds, Baltimore orioles, rose-breasted grosbeaks, and ruby-throated hummingbirds begin returning to northern Minnesota and Wisconsin.

Statewide, farmers continue to plant field corn, sweet corn, soybeans, sugar beets, potatoes and spring wheat.

scattered events

- **May 9, 1995** - Ice floes seen on Lake Superior out in front of Lift Bridge in Duluth. At the Laurentian Environmental Center near Britt, MN, evening grosbeaks and pine siskins are numerous at feeders, leaves are not out yet on deciduous forest trees, but the common snipe is heard "winnowing" and winter wrens sing.

- **May 12, 2007** - Apple and crabapple blossoms, and tartarian honeysuckle and lilac flowers continue to give us great fragrances and visual beauty. Junebugs have been hitting screens of lighted rooms at night since May 7. Tim Kornder, from Brewery Creek Farm in Belle Plaine, transplanted cantaloupe and watermelon plants into outside gardens. In the Lutsen area, along the North Shore of Lake Superior, paper birches and quaking aspens have small leaves, marsh marigolds and wood anemones are among the blooming wildflowers, and at 9 p.m. American woodcocks were heard "peenting" and spring peepers calling.

- **May 13, 1999** - Morel mushrooms are up in some places. (They should not be eaten raw, but when sautéed in butter and served on toast, the texture and flavor of the morel are hard to beat. In fact, use them in any dish which emphasizes the mushroom.) Wild columbine is in bloom. American robin parents are feeding their nestlings. Many Canada geese pairs are seen with young goslings.

- **May 14, 1999** - Tartarian honeysuckle begins blooming. Full shade now in deciduous forests. June bugs hitting screens and outdoor lights this evening. House finches eat dandelion seeds from seedheads. White-tailed deer fawns are being born.

- **May 14, 2001** - Overall peak of bloom for the Minnesota Landscape Arboretum crabapple collection. Beautiful! House wrens laying eggs. First common nighthawks and monarch butterflies return. First 90° day (high of 94°F in Twin Cities).

A Closer Look:
Season Creep

Properly recorded and correctly interpreted, there is nothing perhaps to equal the records of the dates of periodic events in the lives of plants and animals as indices of the bioclimatic character of a place or local area, because such events are in direct response, not to one or a few, but to all the complex elements and factors of the environment, which no artificial instrument, or set of instruments, yet available, will record.

– A. D. Hopkins, 1918

Phenology is the science that studies the timing of natural events from year to year and from place to place, and their relationship to weather and climate. Most events of the annual cycle recur in regular order near, and sometimes even on, the same date as previous years. By studying this timetable we can learn much about the environment around us.

Since 1971 I have been observing the crabapple collection at the University of Minnesota Landscape Arboretum. What follows in this essay are two entries from my field notebook, three short features I wrote for WCCO Radio Nature Notes, an article I wrote on "spring creep" in May of 2006, and the result of my 37 years of studying the crabapple collection bloom peak dates.

April 26, 1987 – The University of Minnesota Landscape Arboretum crabapple collection trees are at overall bloom peak today and are beautiful. Very early this year! Peak of bloom about three weeks ahead of normal. I really like the fragrance of the five-petaled flowers. 'Flame' with its white flowers and 'Sparkler' covered with rose-red blossoms are just two of the dozens and dozens of varieties with excellent bloom. Some other phenological events taking place today that we can correlate with the great crabapple show include:

- We are in the midst of the biggest dandelion bloom of the year

- ginkgo trees have tiny leaves

- poison ivy shrubs and butternut trees have begun leafing out

- leopard frogs and American toads are very vocal

- large numbers of daffodil and tulip flowers can be seen in gardens

May 14, 1991 – The Arboretum crabapple collection is at overall bloom peak. Superb! Fantastic again this year. Some trees white, some pink, some rose-red and others are dark rose-red.

From **May 16, 1984** WCCO Radio notes:

"Crabapple trees have begun blooming in southern Minnesota. Often people ask how to tell an apple tree from a crabapple tree. The difference is somewhat questionable but many horticulturists consider apple trees with fruit two inches in diameter or less to be crabapples. These trees have multiple uses, both ornamental and economic. Those in the Twin Cities probably were planted primarily for their beautiful five-petaled flowers that range in color from pure white to dark purplish-red, with many variations in between. Most have small red fruit that clings to the small trees throughout the cold months and provides food for cedar waxwings and other wildlife."

From **May 21, 1984** WCCO Radio notes: "At the University of Minnesota Landscape Arboretum the crabapple collection is at its best now. Some of the trees are covered with dark red flowers, some pink and some white. The colors and rich fragrances are outstanding. More than 400 individual crabapple trees representing 150

different species, cultivars and selections are found in the arboretum. Each spring a good-sized apple tree can produce from 50,000 to 100,000 blossoms, most of them grouped in clusters of five or six. In an average year, no more than two to five percent of the blossoms develop into apples.

From **May 18, 2004** WCCO Radio notes: "At this time of year the various apple blossoms open to fill our yards, gardens and orchards, and neighborhoods with one of the best spring scents. It is soft, permeates like an invisible

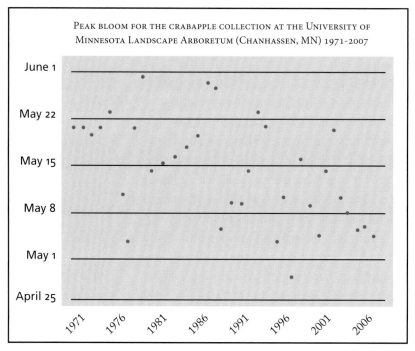

PEAK BLOOM FOR THE CRABAPPLE COLLECTION AT THE UNIVERSITY OF MINNESOTA LANDSCAPE ARBORETUM (CHANHASSEN, MN) 1971-2007

For a complete record of peak bloom see Appendix, page 300

fog, and is with us day and night. The violet-like fragrance lasts only about a week, for apple blossoms of every kind are fragile and go quickly with the first rainfall or warm wind."

From a **May 11, 2006**, *Waconia Patriot* article I wrote on May 8, 2006:

"This last month we enjoyed watching the progression of blooms and the fantastic beauty of about two dozen native woodland wildflowers, including the bloodroot, Dutchman's breeches and large-flowered trillium; all blooming more than two weeks earlier than they did in 1970, the year of our first Earth Day. There is an unnatural aspect of these too-early events. Now all over the Twin Cities and Waconia area, we are seeing the beautiful crabapple trees covered with flowers; 35 years ago these same trees were at their peak of bloom two weeks later.

The term for this is "season creep" and this is one example of the impact of climate change on seasonal cycles and how global warming is already affecting the world around us. (see chart). Although the date of peak bloom continues to vary widely, we may note on the chart that during the first five years (1971–1975) that I kept records, May 21 was the average bloom peak, while during the most recent five year period (2003–2007) the average bloom peak was almost two weeks earlier, on May 8.

A Closer Look:
Planting For Birds

Whole books are available on what to plant to attract birds to our yards and neighborhoods. The most important thing to remember is to keep natural areas natural, so the native birds continue to have nesting, roosting, resting and feeding areas. It's fun to garden for birds. What follows is just a small list of plants that are suited for Minnesota backyards and will produce food that draws many birds.

TREES

Crabapple: Choose varieties that have small fruit that clings on through the winter. Cedar waxwings and wintering-over American robins relish the fruit.

Birch: Seeds are eaten by dark-eyed juncos, black-capped chickadees, pine siskins, and many others. Grouse eat the catkins, buds and seeds.

Red mulberry: This and other mulberry trees are outstanding for attracting birds. At least two dozen bird species including the American robin, gray catbird and brown thrasher eat the ripe fruit.

Mountain ashes: The fact that the reddish or orange fruits persist on the trees through winter makes them especially valuable to wildlife.

SHRUBS

Elderberries

Red-osier dogwood

Choke cherry

Sumacs -offer spectacular fall color, along with
colorful seedheads

Viburnums

VINES

Virginia creeper: Also called woodbine, its leaves turn brilliant scarlet in the fall. About 20 species of our native birds, including eastern bluebird and red-bellied woodpecker, eat the bluish-black, grape-like berries.

Wild grape: Fruit eaten by almost 100 species of birds, including northern cardinal and wood duck.

GARDEN FLOWERS
(LET THEM GO TO SEED)

Columbines

New England aster

Sunflowers

Coneflowers

A Closer Look:
Busy Bees

The use of bees for human benefit is not new. The people of ancient Egypt knew about honey bees and put them to good use.

The colonists introduced honey bees into New England at least as early as 1640, to provide them with honey and wax. Honey is a natural food composed of simple sugars, minerals, and water (17 percent). Beeswax is prized for its use in candles, polishes, and cosmetics. Honey bees are now found all over the United States, thanks to beekeepers and the bees' habit of swarming. The fact that often an old queen departs from the hive with a major portion of the worker bees to seek a home elsewhere insures survival of the species. Minnesota ranks in the top five honey producing states, producing 12 to 16 million pounds annually.

To me the sight of honey bees on early blooming snowdrops, crocuses, and willows in late March and early April is truly a sign of spring. Now we are seeing them on apple blossoms and the flowers of many other plants, including several wildflower species.

Don't miss out on the close-up beauty of flowering plants or the intriguing display of worker honey bees because you're afraid of getting stung. The bees are so busy with their work that they won't notice you. Bees don't sting unless frightened or hurt. But when they do sting, of course, it hurts!

Though other species of bees can sting as often as they want, a honey bee worker can sting only once, because its stinger is covered with tiny barbs like fishhooks. When the bee flies away after stinging, the stinger and poison sac are torn out of its body and the bee dies. If you do get stung, therefore, use a fingernail to quickly scrape away the stinger, which will otherwise continue to pump venom into the wound.

In the colony of honey bees, there are three different forms of bees: queen (female), worker (female) and drone (male), which are determined by genetic make-up and the type of food they are fed. Each hive contains approximately 45 to 60 thousand workers, 200 drones and one queen. The job of the drones is to mate with new queens, an event in which all of the drones swarm around the queen while a few mate with her, most often fertilizing enough of her eggs to last her entire lifetime.

The queen's role is to lay eggs, up to 2,000 per day in the summer. During its short life a worker bee does practically nothing but work. The average worker born in the summer lives not over three months, and perhaps during the height of the main bloom not over six weeks. Those born in late summer could live through the winter and into the next growing season. The workers long list of duties include building wax cells for brooding and honey storage, digesting and evaporating nectar to make honey, regulating hive temperature, feeding the young, defending the hive, cleaning out cells, removing dead bees, feeding and caring for the queen, collecting water, and foraging for and collecting pollen and nectar. They also collect sticky liquids from the buds of plants and make them into a kind of glue which is used for hive repair work.

Worker honey bees usually find flowers within two miles of the hive by sight and smell, and by communication with other bees. They cannot see "red" as humans see it, but are sensitive to ultraviolet light which allows them to see color in flowers we may only see as white. A returning forager will "dance" to communicate to other workers the direction, distance away, and quality of food sources in the field.

So it's the worker honey bees that we observe collecting nectar and pollen from flowers. Nectar is the thin, sugary solution produced by special glands on flowers, called nectaries. Workers suck up the nectar with their long tongues and store it in their honey stomachs. The honey stomach is not the true stomach of the bee and has nothing to do with digestion. It is simply a receptacle for storing the nectar, which is mixed with some secretions from the glands of the bee that brings about chemical changes. The main one is the changing of the cane-type sugar into a more easily digested grape sugar and fruit sugar of the honey.

After the honey is emptied from the honey stomach into the comb cells, it remains exposed to the air for some time before the cell is capped, and thus ripens. It takes about 40,000 bee loads of nectar to make a single pound of honey. Many bees may have to fly as much as 55,000 miles and visit about two million flowers just to make one pound of honey. It takes 12 bees to produce one teaspoon of honey in their collective lifetimes.

As the honey bee flies from flower to flower, her hairy body picks up a lot of pollen. Occasionally she uses bristles on her legs to brush the pollen down into pollen baskets on her rear legs. During the flight back to the hive these baskets are a very handy place to store the pollen.

The honey bee plays an important role in assuring pollination of many of our useful plants. Pollination is simply the transfer of pollen from the anther or male part of a flower to the stigma or female part. The honey bee transfers pollen from one flower to another while making her rounds. If the transfer takes place on the same blossom or on another blossom on the same plant, we call it self-pollination. If the pollen is carried from an anther of one plant to the stigma of another plant of the same type, we call it cross-pollination. Some plants are self-sterile. This means they must be cross-pollinated or they will not bear fruit or seeds.

About one-third of our human diet involves crops which require insect pollination. For this reason, the pollination services of honey bees is worth much more than honey and wax combined. Common crops requiring bee or other insect pollination include almond, apple, apricot, blueberry, many species of clover, cucumber, grape, pumpkin, raspberry, strawberry, sunflower, and watermelon.

A Closer Look:
Barn Swallows Nest Building

For barn swallows, a series of twittering notes serve as a song. Here in southern Minnesota each year we can usually enjoy their musical chattering and watch them glide with the ease and grace of Olympic figure skaters starting about mid-April, when the first ones return from South America. Insects tossed up by a farm or lawn tractors provide easy pickings for these swift, strong, and tireless flyers. Barn swallows are present each year to feed on Minnesota's flying insects; a majority of them leave in September. Like other swallows, they migrate by day, often feeding on insects as they travel.

The barn swallow nests all across Eurasia as well as much of North America, and is our most familiar swallow. It is the only swallow with a deeply-forked "swallow" tail. It is sparrow-sized, dark blue-black above, with a rusty throat and buff or pale rusty underparts.

Photo: Linnette Hulbert

The barn swallow is a mid-spring to early fall resident throughout the state of Minnesota, least numerous in heavily wooded areas and most common in farm—formerly prairie—areas. Originally they nested on the rocky faces of cliffs, in caves, and also perhaps attached their nests to tree trunks. But this species has long since abandoned natural nest sites in favor of docks, bridges, and barns. Outbuildings with wide-open doors and windows, through which the swallows can come and go at their pleasure, and the eaves of other buildings, are also good spots for the half-cup-shaped nest, built of mud pellets reinforced with grass and lined with feathers and fine grasses.

Nests are usually fastened against an upright surface. We see the first nests being constructed in May. Both sexes take part in building the nest, incubating the eggs, and caring for the young. Two broods can be raised each spring/summer.

Red-eyed vireos arrive and begin singing in the forests. The warbler migration is at its peak, and on a good day, an expert might spot twenty species or more. Female Baltimore orioles are weaving their nests. New broods of Canada goose goslings and mallard and wood duck ducklings are numerous. White-breasted nuthatches, downy woodpeckers, eastern bluebirds, northern cardinals, barred owls, American robins, and blue jays are among the bird parents busy feeding young nestlings.

We continue to enjoy the visual beauty and fragrances of the blooming crabapple trees and lilac and azalea shrubs, and the taste of freshly gathered and cooked morel mushrooms. There is heavy shade in southern Minnesota and Wisconsin deciduous forests, while in the northern parts of the states such trees as quaking aspens and sugar maples have tiny leaves.

In northern Minnesota, moose calves are now being born, opening balsam poplar buds perfume the air, veerys and wood thrushes return, and flocks of cliff swallows arrive at their favorite nesting sites—the undersides of bridges near water. Along the North Shore of Lake Superior, the paper birches and native mountain ash trees have small leaves, spring-beauty and nodding trillium wildflowers bloom nicely, and winter wrens and white-throated sparrows fill the air with their songs. Also, the native serviceberry (Juneberry) trees are loaded with white flowers—the "crabapple trees" of the North Shore. Very Showy!

scattered events

- **May 16, 1998** - First common nighthawks. Bridal wreath spirea shrubs at bloom peak, and they look like white fountains. Baltimore orioles, house finches, red-bellied woodpeckers and gray catbirds come to a grape jelly feeder in New Ulm.

- **May 16, 2005** - Morel mushroom hunting is good. Common purple lilac flowers still showy. First common nighthawks return.

- **May 17, 1998** - Black locust trees first blooming (June 5, 1997). Lightning bugs seen tonight in Hastings. Luna moths on the wing near Park Rapids. Statewide, 98 percent of field corn has been planted, with potatoes at 83 percent and sweet corn at 58 percent.

- **May 21, 1997** - At 4:30 a.m. CDT, American robins begin singing. Crabapple trees blooming nicely and very showy. Green ash trees have small leaves. First Baltimore orioles and ruby-throated hummingbirds of the year in Grygla area. Also, first hummingbird at Lutsen.

- **May 21, 1998** - The surface temperature of Lake Waconia reached 70° F, the cut-off for safe swimming. Wild grape is well leafed out and in full bloom with clusters of fragrant small greenish flowers.

A Closer Look: Northern Lights Azaleas

During the spring of 1979 the Northern Lights azaleas were available through Minnesota nurseries for the first time. Since then these azalea hybrids have changed the spring landscape in Minnesota and the whole Upper Midwest. For many decades gardeners and landscape observers have enjoyed the progression of spring bloom of daffodils and tulips, crabapple and apple trees, lilacs and tall bearded irises. And now we have the Northern Lights azaleas which flower at their best after the crabapple bloom but when the old favorite, the bridal wreath spirea, is in full bloom with each shrub looking like a white fountain. This happened on May 16 in 2007.

Northern Lights azaleas were developed by the late Albert G. Johnson, taxonomist and plant breeder at the University of Minnesota Landscape Arboretum. These hybrids were produced from crosses between Mollis Hybrids and the Rose Shell azaleas. Plants from the initial crosses, made in 1957, have continued to

produce outstanding bloom every year since in the Arboretum.

Azaleas are in the genus Rhododendron, which contains approximately one thousand known species. In the moist mountain areas of the Himalayas and adjoining Asian regions nearly nine-hundred species are native. There are no native rhododendrons in Minnesota. The species with leather-like evergreen leaves are usually called rhododendrons and those with deciduous leaves are normally called azaleas. Most rhododendrons have ten stamens, and azaleas only have five.

Plants of the Northern Lights hybrid azaleas are the only winter hardy azaleas that can be counted on to produce full bloom every year in the Upper Midwest. Flower buds can withstand winter temperatures of -30° to -45°F without injury. Plants are compact in growth habit and mature at six to seven feet in height and spread.

They grow best in full sun or partial shade and need an acid soil, though they also thrive in soil of neutral pH if acid peat is used for filling around the roots and if plants are fertilized with an acid fertilizer once or twice annually.

Flowers of the Northern Lights hybrid azaleas are funnel-shaped, usually 1.5 to 2 inches across, and are in clusters. Most have a spicy fragrance. Cultivars developed and released by the University of Minnesota Landscape Arboretum include 'Pink Lights' with a light pink flower color and 'White Lights' having virtually white flowers; both introduced in 1984. Other Northern Lights cultivars have yellow, orange, or purple flowers. All produce a spectacular display of blossoms in May.

A Closer Look:
White-tailed Deer Fawns

The rutting (or mating) season for white-tailed deer centers on the month of November. By the end of that month, most does have been bred. In southern Minnesota, about 20 percent of fawn does are bred in late November and into early December.

After a gestation period of 196 to 213 days, most fawns are born in late May and into early June. As the time of birth arrives the doe lies down. Her body strains and movements aid in her labor. In a normal birth, the forefeet of the fawn appear first, followed quickly by the head. The entire birthing time requires from 10 to 60 minutes. A doe giving birth the first time will usually have one fawn. From then on twins will be most common. Triplets are fairly common. At birth the weight of a fawn is about 7 pounds.

Mothers vigorously lick their newborn young with their rough tongues. This washing process may imprint the doe with the particular odor of her own young, enabling her to distinguish them from other fawns. A fawn, except for the nursing time, is inactive for the first three or four days of its life. During this same time period the fawn is further protected by being odorless, or nearly so. Its spotted coat is great camouflage and allows the fawn to blend into most natural backgrounds. In addition, during the first few days of a fawn's life, the doe stays away as much as possible to prevent her own body scent from giving away the fawn's location. She does return to nurse her young up to 10 times in a 24-hour period. After the fawn nurses, the doe makes it lie down, and she goes off to eat a variety of plant material—mostly leaves and twigs. The young are spotted, but molt to the solid brown-gray winter coat in September. Fawns usually remain with their mothers through their first winter, and sometimes a doe in winter may be accompanied by both first-year and second-year young.

A Closer Look:
Naming Plants and Animals

The famous Swedish botanist Carl Linnaeus (1707–1778) from Uppsala, who never left Europe in his lifetime, described and named 7,700 plants and many animals, including 133 species of American birds such as northern cardinal (*Cardinalis cardinalis L.*) and Canada goose (*Branta canadensis L.*). From specimens sent to him he named quite a few of the well-known living things in the United States that are part of our Minnesota landscape. Some examples:

Danaus plexippus L., monarch butterfly
Actias luna L., luna moth
Esox lucius L., northern pike
Canis lupus L., gray (timber) wolf
Caltha palustris L., marsh marigold
Rudbeckia hirta L., black-eyed susan
Morus rubra L., red mulberry tree
Pinus strobus L., eastern white pine
Acer negundo L., boxelder, ash-leaf maple
Acer rubrum L., red maple
Acer saccharinum L., silver maple

Linnaeus came up with the binomial system of naming living things. Each species of plant or animal is given a name consisting of two words, usually in Latin or Latinized, the combination of the two being exclusive to that species. Before

Carl Linnaeus

applied only to a single species within a genus. The "L." at the end stands for Linnaeus, who originally named the organism.

A Closer Look:
The Monarch Butterfly Returns

The word "monarch" means king or ruler and probably no other accepted common name could better describe this regal insect of bright orange and black, with white spots. Monarch butterflies have a four-inch wingspan and glide about the countryside and city landscapes in a most dignified way.

Now it's time to welcome the monarchs back. Each year they spend the winter in Mexico, where they congregate in selected trees on mountainsides in an area west of Mexico City. They leave Minnesota from late August into October, and the first ones arrive in the wintering site about November first, a most amazing flight for an insect. In late February, as spring approaches, the monarchs start migrating northward, following the development of milkweeds on which they lay their eggs. However, the butterflies that leave Mexico are not the same ones that will fly to the northern limits of milkweeds in Canada. I have seen some very faded and frayed individuals nectaring on lilac blossoms in the University of Minnesota Landscape

Linnaeus there was not an accepted method for naming plants and animals. He made a huge contribution to natural science, because only when an organism has a specific name of its own in a universal language can people communicate their findings to each other.

In writing a scientific name, the genus is always listed first and begins with a capital letter. This name is shared by all closely related species in a group. The species word listed next begins with a lower case letter and can be

Arboretum, which leads me to think that those few individuals made it to the Mexican wintering site and came back this far north in the spring. Spring migrating monarchs enter Texas from Mexico during March and April. Females lay their eggs on milkweeds and their progeny appear in April or May. So by mid- to late May, when common milkweeds are up about six inches, a scant few of the fall migrants and many of their offspring that hatched in Texas find their way into Minnesota from the southlands.

The monarch is the only butterfly to truly migrate to and from overwintering spots. It is also the most readily identifiable butterfly in our country. If the United States had a national butterfly, this would undoubtedly be it. In Minnesota, the monarch as been the official state butterfly since 2000.

Monarch butterflies are found throughout most of North America, and occasionally errant migrants have reached England and the South Pacific. The northern limit of the summer range is around St. John's, Newfoundland, and stretches across Quebec to near Churchill, Manitoba, and southwesterly through Saskatchewan to Vancouver Island in British Columbia. Monarch females lay their eggs on various milkweeds or closely related dogbane plants; the larvae dine on these leaves. All adults feed on nectar of various wild and cultivated plants.

During my thirty-eight years of monitoring the return of this insect, the earliest arrival date has been May 5, and the latest June 11.

Week four (May 24-31)

White-tailed deer fawns are now being born. Baby woodchucks can be seen out and about. Eastern tiger swallowtail butterflies are on the wing. The first monarch butterflies arrive from Mexico. Common tree frogs and American toads are very vocal.

Gardeners harvest leaf lettuce, radishes and green onions, and the first ripe strawberries. Now is the time to plant watermelon, squash, pumpkin, and muskmelon seeds directly into the garden.

FIRST MONARCH BUTTERFLY RETURNING TO THE

UNIVERSITY OF MINNESOTA

LANDSCAPE ARBORETUM IN CARVER COUNTY—

A 38-YEAR RECORD

1971 - May 30	1981 - May 14
1972 - May 20	1982 - June 11
1973 - June 1	1983 - June 10
1974 - May 21	1984 - May 31
1975 - May 20	1985 - May 17
1976 - June 3	1986 - May 28
1977 - May 14	1987 - June 1
1978 - May 25	1988 - May 25
1979 - May 29	1989 - May 20
1980 - May 28	1990 - May 28

1991 - May 11	2000 - May 5
1992 - May 14	2001 - May 12
1993 - May 13	2002 - May 28
1994 - May 29	2003 - May 27
1995 - May 30	2004 - June 3
1996 - May 22	2005 - May 24
1997 - June 1	2006 - May 22
1998 - May 20	2007 - May 15
1999 - May 10	2008 - May 28

EARLIEST ARRIVAL DATE: MAY 5, 2000.

LATEST ARRIVAL DATE: JUNE 11, 1982.

AVERAGE RETURN DATE: MAY 24.

Yews, firs, and spruces are evergreens that now look especially attractive with their new bright green growth. Lawns, trees and shrubs, and whole forests are lush green. The tan-brown silver maple seeds are falling. Red pine pollen is carried through the air. New cattail leaves have grown up two to five feet so marshes have also begun looking green again.

Scarlet tanagers and indigo buntings relish sunflower seeds at some feeding stations. More common nighthawks return. House wrens, purple martins, yellow warblers, American robins, ovenbirds, and many more bird species fill the air with their special music. Juvenile common grackles leave their nests and parents feed them on lawn areas.

Woodland wildflowers blooming nicely include wild geranium, Virginia waterleaf, and large yellow lady's-slipper. European mountain ash, choke cherry, and Ohio buckeye trees all have showy flowers. Racemes of fragrant, white pea-like flowers droop from black locust trees.

In northern Minnesota and Wisconsin, common loons incubate their eggs. Black flies become bothersome and wild blueberry shrubs have their first white flowers in the BWCA. In southern Minnesota, eastern cottonwood trees begin shedding seeds on cotton carriers, and alfalfa hay cutting starts.

On May 31 the normal high temperature in the Twin Cities is 75° and the low is 53°F; with a record high of 106° set in 1934.

scattered events

- **May 26, 1998** - Russian olive trees in bloom; the small four-pointed, star-shaped yellow flowers have a spicy fragrance. Snapping turtles are up on dry land, laying eggs. Young moose calves can be seen in the BWCA.

- **May 26, 2003** - At Walker, the surface temperature of Leech Lake is 65°, purple martins and yellow warblers are vocal, and tiger swallowtail butterflies nectar on common purple lilacs.

- **May 28, 1995** - Baltimore orioles like grape juice and jelly at feeding stations. Cedar waxwings feed on late apple blossoms. Statewide, the planting of field corn is at 87 percent, soybeans at 63 percent, and sweet corn at 44 percent.

- **May 31, 1998** - Gardeners are picking buckets of strawberries. Rugosa roses are blooming nicely. Chipping sparrows call over and over. Statewide, an estimated 55 percent of the first crop of alfalfa has been cut; 4 percent is average for this date.

A Closer Look:
Snags

In the wild, numerous species nest in cavities of standing dead trees, which are sometimes called snags. Many people are not aware of the value of dead, dying and hollow trees, as well as logs on the ground, for birds and other wildlife, and the loss of suitable nesting sites is a major factor in the decline of some bird species.

Dead trees provide homes to hundreds of species of birds, mammals, amphibians, insects, fungi and other plants. Consider leaving dead and dying trees in your yard standing unless they pose a safety or property hazard. Also, be sure to use old logs and stumps in your gardens and landscaping for the benefit of wildlife.

A Closer Look:
Butterfly Gardening

Butterflies are interesting and colorful. Worldwide there are about 20,000 species of butterflies. Close to 700 inhabit North America, north of Mexico; in Minnesota we have 172 types. These insects are part of the summer scene, and when we see them fluttering about in the warm sunshine, we may take them to be an expression of all things

Host plants for caterpillars: milkweeds, parsley, dill, nasturtium

Nectar plants for butterflies:		
Astilbe	Joe-Pye weed	New England aster
Blanketflower (Gaillardia)	Lantana	Petunia
Butterfly-bush (hardy to zone 5)	Liatris	Phlox
Butterfly-weed	Lilacs	Purple coneflower
Coreopsis	Lupine	Rudbeckia
mints, thymes and sages	Marigold	Sunflowers
Goldenrods	Mexican sunflower (Tithonia)	Verbena
Hollyhocks (single flower)	Monarda	Zinnia
	Nasturtium	

tranquil and ethereal. That such charming creatures exist at all is cause for wonder. It's part of the miracle of life that includes us humans too. The adults with their straw-like mouths can't bite, but dozens of species visit our yards searching for nectar.

Butterflies are thought to possess the broadest known visual spectrum of any animal on earth, and they must appear even more colorful to one another than they do to us! Some species have ultraviolet wing patches which are invisible to humans but obvious to potential mates. Being sensitive to ultraviolet light also helps them find nectar flowers. Their senses of smell and taste are also acute and are vital to feeding and mating. You may have watched butterflies walk on their food; this is because they have taste organs in the soles of their feet.

To allure more butterflies to your yard, use the chart above to choose plants for a small butterfly garden. Do not use pesticides, locate the garden in a sunny area, plant a selection of flowering plants that will provide nectar over a long part of the growing season, and include a few host plants. For example, black swallowtail butterflies eat parsley and dill, while monarch butterfly caterpillars eat milkweeds. Remember that not all butterflies feed on nectar, the sweet liquid formed by flowers to attract pollinators, and there are dozens and dozens of host plants on which they lay eggs. If the correct host plant is not available, the caterpillar will starve to death rather than eat another kind of plant. That's a good thing to think about when putting a caterpillar in a jar to observe it. Fortunately each butterfly lays eggs on or near the correct host plant for her species.

The end of May is a great time for planting.

Young Common Grackles Fledge

At the end of May we notice many young grackles on our lawns, fresh out of their nests. These young can fly well soon after leaving the nest and are fed by their parents for only a few days. After that, they join in with other juveniles to form flocks that feed and roost together, and in turn join bigger roosts of adults and juveniles. Common grackles produce only one brood each year so now is the time to watch for fledglings taking their first flights.

On March 12, 2007, I observed my first common grackles of the year. It was 9 a.m., sunny, 37°F, and we still had seven inches of snow on the Lake Waconia area landscape. First I heard their high-pitched screeches sounding like rusty hinges on a garden gate, and then I spotted several blue jay-sized black-colored birds flying by. Yes, the grackles were back!

Its early spring arrival, habit of feeding on lawns, and frequent appearances at feeders combine to make the common grackle one of our best-known birds. They may appear uniformly black from a distance, but are highly iridescent at close range, with colors varying from purple and blue to green and bronze. The bright yellow eyes are easy to spot with binoculars or when the birds are close. Males

© Steve Byland | Dreamstime.com

have slightly longer tails then females, and more iridescence on their heads and necks.

Grackles are members of the blackbird family. They are classified as songbirds not because of the beauty of their songs but because they have all the vocal equipment a songbird needs. Birds do not have vocal cords. All of their sounds come from a resonating voice box down at the bottom of the windpipe, just where the bronchial tubes branch off to the lungs. By varying the pressure of air from the lungs as it passes through the voice box, a bird changes both the loudness and the pitch of its notes. A common grackle's voice includes gurgling and creaking "kssh-ka-leeeea" and a rough "chack."

In the spring we often see a male grackle striding elegantly across a lawn area and pausing by a group of three or four females. He will lift his head, ruffle his feathers, open his beak … and sing like a creaking rusty gate. No matter how unmelodious it may sound to us, the female grackles like it. It's the spring mating song of the grackle.

Another major component of pair formation is a flight involving a single female and up to five males, which follow her while keeping their tails strongly keeled.

Common grackles are found throughout Minnesota but they are uncommon in the heavily-wooded parts of the northern regions. They arrive early in the spring and depart late in the fall. They are very social and known for their communal roosts in swamps and marshes. Flight to and from roosts in the evenings and mornings may involve from a few dozen to thousands of birds, and the sounds we hear from the wetlands themselves, where the grackles mix with red-winged blackbirds for the night, can be deafening.

After pairing occurs, the females begin to select nest sites. Their mates defend only a small area of the nesting tree, frequently a good-sized spruce or pine. Nests are often found in loose colonies. The female constructs the nest in about 11 days. The nest is a bulky structure of grasses and other plants, sometimes reinforced with mud, lined with fine grasses and occasionally with feathers. The 4 to 5 eggs are pale greenish-white or pale yellow-brown, with dark brown or purple spots and scrawls. The incubation period is about 13 days. Only the female incubates and broods, but both sexes feed their young, which leave the nest 10 to 17 days after hatching.

Grackles rank high in intelligence. Like American crows they are omnivorous. They can be seen, for example, in shallow water along lakeshores and streams (with tails elevated to keep them dry) catching minnows. (I have even seen grackles fishing at minnow tanks in marinas.) They also invade the nests of other birds, breaking eggs and eating young. More often they feed on cutworms, beetles, crickets, and various insects which could harm farm crops. In addition, they feed on the seeds of many noxious weeds.

On a constant lookout for food, grackles sometimes attack corn fields and may ruin ripening apples and pears by pecking them and eating only a little from each fruit. At our feeding station I scatter cracked corn on the ground under a couple of feeders. The grackles, red-wings, mourning doves, and northern cardinals relish the cracked corn, and it keeps the grackles out of the feeders.

A Closer Look:
Cattails–Very Important Plants

By the end of May, the long, sword-like leaves of cattails are up several feet, so marshy areas look quite green. Stands of cattails can also be found along shores of lakes, in river backwaters, and in roadside ditches. They grow from moist soil into water up to about 3 feet deep. Cattails rule many wetlands through their gigantic capacity for growth. A single seed can result in a network of rhizomes and a hundred shoots in one growing season.

Cattails are of great value to aquatic communities. They provide nesting habitat for many marsh birds including red-winged blackbirds, yellow-headed blackbirds, marsh wrens, least bitterns, and American coots. Shoots and rhizomes are consumed by muskrats and geese. Submerged stalks provide spawning habitat for sunfish and shelter for young fish. Many insects and other invertebrates live in and on cattail leaves, stalks, rhizomes, and roots. These small animals, in turn, provide food for birds, fish and frogs.

Muskrats and cattails go together like American goldfinches and thistles. Muskrats harvest numerous cattail leaves and plaster them together, creating a lodge with an underwater entrance. Cattail shoots and rhizomes are the core of the muskrat diet. In the absence of muskrats, cattails take over shallow ponds and other wetlands. The openings created by muskrats provide space for waterfowl, and their lodges can serve as nesting platforms for Canada geese.

Almost everyone is familiar with the cattail plant. Young people on my interpretive hikes refer to them as hotdogs on sticks. Ancient people collected the cigar-like seed heads on stems and soaked them in animal fat to become torches to light up the night. Cattails continue to have many uses in cultures throughout the world. The leaves are dried and woven into mats and baskets. The pulp has been used in paper-making. The down from the spikes can be stripped off and used as stuffing in quilts, pillows, and life preservers, and in wall insulation. Native Americans used the fluff to line diapers.

The common cattail is similar to the narrow-leaved cattail but has the wider sword-like leaves and no gap between the staminate (male) and pistillate (female) flowers on the spike. Breezes cause the pollen of both cattail species, during June, to rain down on the cylinder of female flowers directly below, or over female flowers on neighboring cattail plants. Male flowers fade after the pollen is shed, leaving a bare stalk above the pistillate flowers that then develop into a brown, cylindrical seed mass that bursts into a fluff of fine hairs that allow seeds to be carried by the winds of autumn, winter and into spring. The best time for collecting the brown cattails on sticks is in early July; they can then be dried for fall home decorations that won't burst open.

People past and present have found cattails to be a good source of food. In spring the young shoots, about 4 to 16 inches long, can be easily pulled from the rootstalks, pealed to the tender white core and eaten raw or cooked like asparagus. In June, when the flower spikes provide heavy coats of bright yellow pollen, a surprising amount of the yellow dust can be collected by shaking the flowers in a bag. After being sifted, the pollen produces an excellent nutritious flour when mixed half-and-half with wheat flour; and can be made into delicious pancakes, cookies

© Elena Elisseeva | Dreamstime.com

and muffins. In fall, winter, or early spring, the core of the rhizomes can be eaten raw, roasted, or dried and ground into flour. The rhizomes are said to contain as much protein as rice and more carbohydrate than potato.

Sadly, many people don't value the importance and versatility of the cattail, and even encourage their destruction by dredging, or by draining and filling in marshes. These people should consider that cattails are natural sewage treatment plants, more efficient than any process we humans have invented. They help us live sustainable lives.

Kathy Heidel, former Senior Interpretive Naturalist from Lowry Nature Center, located near Victoria, MN, drew my attention to a most interesting true story a few years ago. Kathy said: "A Wisconsin dairy farmer's milkhouse wash water and runoff from the cowyard ran through a cattail mat in an adjacent roadside ditch. The water entering the ditch was high in fecal matter, nitrogen, and phosphates. Water leaving the cattails 300 feet farther along the ditch was tested and found to be pollution-free and fit to enter a nearby trout stream." Wow! Nature's water purifier, the cattail, has roots that contain an antibiotic substance that attacks and kills fecal bacteria in human and animal waste. Cattails can absorb industrial pollutants such as phenols, cyanide, zinc, and hydrogen sulphide. Through their roots the plants absorb these contaminants, trapping the toxins in plant tissues or breaking them down into harmless elements.

June

Historically, June can be the month of rains. Temperatures above 95°F may occur on any June day over most of Minnesota, and yet frost is always possible in low areas and in the north. Many of us think of June as rose month because both cultivated and wild roses bloom with elegance. But the month also blossoms with new animal life—emerging butterflies and bees, more mammals taking their first steps, fish and bird eggs hatching. Also, farmers finish up harvesting the first crop of alfalfa, and gardeners pick ripe strawberries.

READING THE LANDSCAPE

Week one (June 1–7)

Summer Begins
The Western Meadowlark Sings
Brake for Turtles
Listening to Loons

Week two (June 8–15)

Joys of Bird Watching
Rose Notes
Nesting Warblers
Wild Lupines

Week three (June 16–23)

Chimney Swifts Overhead
Arboretum Reflections
Summer Solstice
Bee Watching

Week four (June 24–30)

Dragonflies, the Superb Flyers
What is a Bird?
Basswoods Blooming
Birds on Hot Days

first week in june

For June 1 the average high temperature in the Twin Cities is 75°F and the average low is 54°. The record high is 96°, set in 1852, and the record low is 37°, set in 1946. Expect lake surface temperatures to warm up to 70° soon—the lowest temperature for safe swimming.

White water lilies start blooming on the quiet waters of lakes, ponds and rivers. Blue flag, a native Minnesota iris, is flowering in wetlands, and tall bearded irises continue to be showy in gardens. Double peonies have large scented flowers. Rugosa roses and golden mockorange shrubs also have very fragrant flowers. Eastern cottonwood trees shed myriad seeds on cotton carriers. Russian olive trees are full of small yellow flowers with a spicy smell. The Minnesota state flower, the showy pink and white lady's slipper, is blooming at the Minnesota Landscape Arboretum. (Many botanists and naturalists feel that the bloom of this plant marks the onset of the state's summer flora.) Honey bees forage on white Dutch clover blossoms on lawns. As the flowers of prairie smoke plants mature on native prairies, the styles elongate to form brushes of soft, slender plumes—the "prairie smoke."

Both red-eyed vireos and warbling vireos are very vocal. Cedar waxwings begin nest building. Mourning doves are egg-sitting on loose platforms of twigs, down low or up in trees. They raise two or three broods during the nesting season, which for them lasts into September. Newly hatched wood duck ducklings jump from their nest boxes. Canada geese and trumpeter swans begin to shed flight feathers.

Juvenile eastern chipmunks and gray squirrels dart about exploring their new environment. Throughout the state, the tiny lights of fireflies can be seen. In central and northern Minnesota, baby common loons hatch and ride on the backs of their parents who catch fish and floating insects for them.

scattered events

- **June 1, 1996** - First day mosquitoes have become bothersome. Wild columbine is at bloom peak. The surface temperature of Lake Waconia is 65°, the temperature at which largemouth bass spawn.

- **June 2, 1998** - Young red-tailed hawks are about ready to fly. Lupines bloom at Lutsen. Tulips, crabapple trees, and lilac shrubs flower in Grand Marais, where the Lake Superior fishing catch includes herring and whitefish.

- **June 3, 2003** - We enjoy the superb fragrance of the clusters of diminutive, greenish wild grape flowers. There is great bird music in the air. A few of the songsters include: song sparrows, warbling vireos, house wrens and common yellowthroats.

- **June 4, 2007** - In the Lutsen/Grand Marais area, black-throated green warblers and white-throated sparrows sing frequently, bunchberry and starflower bloom nicely, Canada tiger swallowtail butterflies are on the wing, and common purple lilacs and crabapple trees have vivid flowers.

- **June 7, 1998** - The big double garden peony flowers continue to be very showy. Northern catalpa trees and Japanese tree lilacs bloom nicely. American crows are molting flight feathers. Field corn is knee high to a bit taller in the Fairmont area. The first cutting of Minnesota alfalfa is completed on about 74 percent of the acreage, well ahead of the five-year average of 18 percent.

- **June 7, 2005** - High temperature hit 91°, and the surface water temperature of Lake Waconia has warmed to 72°. Kentucky coffee trees begin blooming.

- **June 7, 2006** - Our sixteenth consecutive day of 80 degrees or above. Northern catalpa trees are loaded with clusters of bright, mostly white, flowers. Masses of white Dutch clover bloom on lawns. Dickcissels are heard singing in rural Waseca.

A Closer Look:
Summer Begins

Often summer is thought of as the season of sunlight and possibilities. Meteorologists in the Upper Midwest consider June 1 to be the first day of summer; astronomers wait until the June solstice on or next to the 21st for summer to begin in the Northern Hemisphere. However we look at June, there are discoveries to be made overhead, underfoot, and all around us.

There is a palpable rush of life in June, and it sometimes seems that all living things in our temperate zone, as if conscious of the limitations of the growing season, are forcing themselves to grow and renew. Every forest, every prairie, every wetland, every roadside ditch and every backyard is rich with green abundance—evidence that our planet is designed as a place for life, no matter what foolish acts people commit.

The long light of June affects all people and helps create a sense of well-being. Summer is the season for repairing the human perspective, for discovering once again that there are forces and rhythms at work to make life possible.

In the Grand Marais area, nature's calendar of summer events in early to mid-June include: fireflies, luna moths and Canada tiger swallowtail butterflies on the wing, the black-throated green warblers singing and ruffed grouse still drumming; and the showy blooming common purple lilac, crabapple trees, native mountain ash, wild lupine, twinflower, and bunchberry. In southern Minnesota, farmers harvest their first cutting of alfalfa as gardeners pick ripe strawberries and young northern cardinals leave their nests. In scattered spots in the north and south, bald eagles feed their offspring fish from waters near their nests.

A Closer Look:
The Western Meadowlark Sings

On the prairie, the western meadowlark replaces the American robin in leading the morning chorus. As a child, my mother lived on a farm in northwestern Minnesota, where she loved the clear flute-like jumble of gurgling notes of the meadowlark. Her enthusiasm for these sounds was so contagious that I have been able to recognize the voice of the western meadowlark and thrill to its unique character since I was a boy.

The distinctive pose of a meadowlark, perched on a fence post, facing the sun, its bright yellow breast with a bold, black V, its head thrown back in song, is familiar to many. One may judge how well the bird and its song have won people's affection by noting the states that have chosen the western meadowlark as

© Steve Byland | Dreamstime.com

their state bird. These include North Dakota, Nebraska, Kansas, Montana, Wyoming, and Oregon.

It is hard to describe the waves of melody making up the western meadowlark's songs. Although attempts to express the song in human words are inadequate, they, at least, indicate the rhythm and serve to recall them. Phrases like "now's the time to plant the corn" or "U-tah's a pretty place" help one to remember the songs are made up of seven notes.

A Closer Look:

Brake for Turtles

Pedestrian crossings and deer crossings you've seen. But a turtle crossing? Your eyes aren't deceiving you if you're driving and see a yellow diamond traffic sign bearing the silhouette of a shelled critter. Three Rivers Park District workers have, through funding by the Minnesota DNR's Nongame Wildlife Program, posted several Turtle Crossing signs at popular turtle crossing locations in and near its parks, located just north, south, and west of Minneapolis.

The idea is to make motorists aware that eight species of freshwater turtles lay their eggs in May and June and females are leaving wetlands and crossing roads in search of higher nesting grounds. The females are gravid (swollen with eggs) and seek a proper place on land to dig a hole in which to lay their eggs. A location chosen is usually in the open because warmth from the sun is important for the development of the young in their eggs. The choice of place is made with care so turtles will travel fairly long distances from water to find a suitable spot. It is at this time, when turtles slowly cross country roads and busy highways alike, that many are killed.

The female turtle uses her hind feet to dig out a hole as deep as her feet can reach. After the eggs are laid, she covers them with soil. Some turtles go to great pains to make the finished nest look as natural as possible so that it will not attract the attention of raccoons and other predators. When the job is done the turtle departs. She plays no further role in the future life of the eggs or the baby turtles when they

hatch. The two most common turtle species in Minnesota, the snapping turtle and the painted turtle, lay 20 to 40 eggs or 4 to 10 eggs, respectively, at a rate of about two per minute.

The time it takes for bird eggs to hatch is quite exact (for example, northern cardinal eggs hatch in 12 to 13 days), for they are kept warm by the warm-blooded parent bird. Turtles are cold-blooded and so cannot provide warmth for the eggs. The warmth turtle eggs receive comes from the surrounding earth, heated by sunlight and the local weather, so the time it will take them to hatch is quite varied. Usually as much as two to three months or more pass before they hatch. The hatchling turtles then are on their own to find a wetland and fend for themselves.

Each year, thousands of turtles are killed on roadways, especially during nesting season. Turtles might not reproduce until the age of fourteen, and they rely on nesting for many years to compensate for a high rate of predation on their eggs and young. A mature female killed on a roadway is a significant loss for the turtle population.

A Closer Look:
Listening to Loons

Common loon calls are captivating and memory-stirring for those of us who have spent time among the pines, firs, birches, and crystal waters of the north. What would our northern lakes be without the mournful cry and laughter of the wilderness? To appreciate loon calls you simply have to hear them in their natural setting. And as we listen, the variations of yodel, tremolo, wail, and other calls can tell us much about loon behavior.

The yodel-call, "oo-AH-ho," is used for territory advertisement and defense. It is given only by the male. The far-carrying wail-call, "ahaa-ooo-oooo-oooo-ooo-ahhh," is frequently used and helps the pair keep in contact with each other. This call is often heard at night and is considered the mournful cry of the wilderness.

The tremolo-call, a wild laugh, is probably the loon's all purpose call and can signal alarm, worry, or greeting. Usually the tremolo is coupled with a behavioral response such as a dive, a run on the water surface or a take off, and it's the only call loons can give while in flight. The presence of people often evokes the tremolo, especially when boaters approach too closely. But we must remember, the tremolo isn't reserved just for intruding humans. Millions of years before people appeared, the tremolo-call echoed across ancient lakes. Loon pairs frequently use a tremolo duet when something threatens their young. This splendid tremolo duet is also used in spring to reinforce pair bonds and to advertise territorial rights.

Week two (June 8-15)

Both common cattails and narrow-leaved cattails shed their pollen; Juneberry (serviceberry) fruit is ripe and good eating. Japanese tree lilacs have big showy clusters of creamy-white flowers. Gardeners harvest leaf lettuce, radishes, small onions, and buckets of strawberries. The gasplant, coralbells, oriental poppies and lupines bloom nicely in perennial gardens. Farmers in southern and western Minnesota work to finish harvesting the first crop of alfalfa.

Black flies may bother us. The large mint-green colored luna moths show up around lights. Fireflies add their magic to the evening landscape. The surface temperatures of southern and central Minnesota lakes are usually in the low 70°s, and in northern Minnesota in the mid-60°s. (The cut-off for safe swimming is 70°.)

scattered events

- **June 8, 2001** - The smooth wild rose begins blooming. Baltimore oriole parents are feeding nestlings. A hen wild turkey is seen with eight small young.

- **June 10, 2001** - First garden strawberries ripen. In the Walker area, red pines shed pollen, Indian paintbrush and columbine are showy blooming wildflowers, dragonflies are numerous and many are feeding on mosquitoes, pairs of tree swallows feed their newly hatched young, common loons and eastern wood pewees are vocal, and the surface temperature of Leech Lake is 64°.

- **June 10, 2005** - Both painted and snapping turtles are up on dry land, laying eggs. A gray catbird nest has four eggs. Tree swallows feed young nestlings. In Duluth, common purple lilacs, crabapple trees, and many tulips are blooming. Young bald eagles are now quite large in nests at Voyageurs National Park.

- **June 13, 2006** - Purple martin young now hatching.

photo: Christian Gilbert

Showy pink and white lady's-slipper

- **June 14, 1998** - Both hairy and downy woodpeckers bring fledglings to suet feeders. The Minnesota state floral emblem, the showy pink and white lady's-slipper, blooms nicely in Itasca State Park and area. Statewide, the average height of field corn is 19 inches; the 5-year average is 8 inches.

- **June 14, 2003** - Russian olive trees at bloom peak. Eastern cottonwoods are "spitting" much

cotton. Lake Waconia surface temperature is 74° F. The surface temperature of Lake Superior at Two Harbors is only 41°.

- **June 15, 2000** - Staghorn sumac at bloom peak with its yellow-green flowers in clusters. Baltimore oriole young fledged from their nest. Cedar waxwings, American robins, and many of us humans are eating ripe juneberry fruit.

A Closer Look:
Joys of Bird Watching

Right now we continue to see broods of small wood duck ducklings with their mothers, American robins are nesting for the second time, house wren and Baltimore oriole parents are busy feeding young nestlings, and indigo buntings and rose-breasted grosbeaks delight us with their presence at our feeding stations. Also, ring-necked pheasants and mourning doves enchant us with their vocalizations. The list of June bird happenings can go on and on.

Some enthusiasts call their engaging interest "birding" and other say "bird watching." Either way, the observing of birds is a worthwhile activity which helps keep people in touch with some of the living things that share the Earth with us. Sandra and I enjoy having a feeding station in our yard and watching the actions of

GARDEN ROSES AT OVERALL JUNE BLOOM PEAK			
UNIVERSITY OF MINNESOTA LANDSCAPE ARBORETUM			
Observations by Jim Gilbert			
2008 - June 25	2002 - June 23	1996 - June 27	1990 - June 19
2007 - June 13	2001 - June 22	1995 - June 25	1989 - June 22
2006 - June 10	2000 - June 20	1994 - June 17	1988 - June 10
2005 - June 20	1999 - June 18	1993 - June 22	1987 - June 12
2004 - June 22	1998 - June 14	1992 - June 18	1986 - June 19
2003 - June 23	1997 - June 22	1991 - June 16	1985 - June 12

about two dozen bird species in a year's time. But, I also take a couple of bird guides and a pair of binoculars on picnics and campouts, on trips throughout the United States, and further afield. Any vacation or outing away from home becomes more interesting if you can add the extra dimension of bird watching.

A Closer Look:
Rose Notes

Fossil discoveries tell us that roses, in some form or other, have been on the North American continent for at least 32 million years. The rose is known as the flower of love and the queen of flowers, and came to be selected by some poets as the emblem of beauty for its form, colors, and exquisite perfume. Since ancient times the rose has been more celebrated than any other flower.

Roses have an irresistible combination of elegance and charm, thorny vigor and captivating delicacy, and they bloom in an amazing variety of colors, sizes, and fragrances. It is the sensuous appeal of roses that has made them the best-known and most popular ornamental plant in the world and the most popular of cut flowers.

Many Minnesota gardeners are fascinated by roses and mix them in with flowering perennials, annual flowers, and ornamental trees and shrubs. A rose garden may sound romantic but it actually involves a great amount of care and willingness to contaminate yourself and the environment with the sprays necessary to keep the foliage and flowers in pristine condition. The best way to avoid harmful chemicals is to select roses that are relatively trouble free, and to tolerate a certain amount of blackspot and problems from insects and other tiny animals.

For me, rather than growing roses in our garden, I enjoy the fragrance and visual beauty of the pink flowers on the native smooth wild rose shrubs that grow on the banks above Lake Waconia. Sandra and I also visit the rose garden at the University of Minnesota Landscape Arboretum many times each growing season. These garden roses are cared for by professional gardeners and knowledgeable volunteers.

To see the greatest diversity and number of flowers, try to get to a rose garden several times during the month of June when they're at their peak. A good share of the garden roses (floribundas, grandifloras and hybrid teas) have good recurrent bloom and we can enjoy them through the summer and into fall. However, there is one date each year, as the chart above shows, when the garden roses are their finest and we call that the June peak.

About a week or 10 days after the peonies are at bloom peak, and during the time when the northern catalpa trees bloom, garden roses are at overall bloom peak.

A Closer Look: Nesting Warblers

Of the 427 species of birds that have been observed and officially recorded in Minnesota, over two dozen of these are warbler species seen here during the migration and nesting season. Most inhabit the woodlands, and this is prime time for warblers to be nesting. Since they feed almost exclusively on insects, they are highly migratory and thousands of miles frequently separate their summer and winter homes. Warblers are mostly nocturnal migrants whose long journeys in the dark over water and land expose them to many dangers.

To warble means to sing with trills and quavers, and this describes some of the songs of the group of birds called the warblers. Over 100 species are known of which 44 can be found in the United States, with twice as many in the eastern as in the western states. The wood warblers, the Parulidae family, are found only in North and South America.

Warblers are small (5 to 6 inches long from bill tip to end of tail), active, mostly colorful songsters with slender, straight, pointed bills. Colored in gray, olive or green, many warblers are brilliantly patterned with bright yellow, orange, red or blue with under-parts plain, streaked or striped, They are nervous little birds, flitting about in trees, thickets, or on the ground in their search for food, causing bird expert Roger Tory Peterson to call them the "butterflies of the bird world."

Learning to identify warblers is one of the more difficult tasks for beginning birdwatchers, but also very rewarding. Ornithologists and amateur birders have written volumes on warblers. In this entry I'll include a few observations on five quite common Minnesota nesting warblers.

The yellow warbler is one of the first that I learned to identify, and I have for many years enjoyed listening to their song, a cheerful swift musical "sweet, sweet, sweet, so-sweet." Yellow warblers winter from Mexico to Peru and are summer residents throughout the state. They are found in a variety of habitats, but appear to nest almost exclusively near water in shrubs or small trees.

The common yellowthroat is a very widespread and numerous summer resident throughout Minnesota. It's probably the most evenly distributed warbler breeding species in the state. This warbler has a rich yellow throat; in addition the male has a black mask. A clear rapid chant, "witchity, witchity, witchity, witch" is the voice of the common yellowthroat heard in just about any wetland area. Their winter home is from the southern U.S. to Panama.

From top: ovenbird; northern parula warbler; chestnut-sided warbler; black-throated green warbler. (photos: David Brislance)

Ovenbirds are summer residents through-out the wooded portions of the state, mainly in the northern, east-central and southeastern regions. They feed along the forest floor, and build their Dutch oven-shaped nests there too. The nest is a domed structure of leaves, grasses and stems, with a side entrance. Eggs, 3 to 6 in number, are incubated 11 to 14 days by the female. The young leave the nest about 10 days after hatching. Food for ovenbirds consists of insects, spiders, earthworms and snails. The ovenbird is more often heard than seen. Its powerful "teacher, teacher, teacher, TEACHER" call announces this warbler's location and leaves no doubt as to its identity. The winter territory of the ovenbird is from southeast United States to northern South America.

The black-throated green warbler sings from the upper canopy, so it's tough to get a good look at one, but its song, "zee, zee, zee, zoo, zee" clearly indicates its presence. The "zee" notes are all on the same pitch, the "zoo" notes are lower. Another set of words to the buzzy song, "trees, trees, trees, murmuring trees" may help an observer recognize this bird.

I really enjoy hearing black-throated green warblers singing on their nesting territories near the North Shore of Lake Superior on June days. Being a migrant and summer resident in Minnesota after wintering from south Texas to Columbia, the b-t greens, as these birds are affectionately called, nest in the northeast and north-central regions of the state. This species usually builds high up in a tree, but some nests are found only a foot above ground. Conifers are preferred but sometimes nests are built in birches, maples and others.

After wintering from Mexico to Nicaragua, the northern parula warbler is back in northeastern and north-central Minnesota for the nesting season. Their usual song is a buzzy trill or rattle that climbs the scale and then trips over at the top: "zeeeeeeeeee-up." In Minnesota, the northern parula warbler breeds mainly in forests where usnea lichen, also called beard lichen, hangs from the trees. Their nest, most often, is a loosely woven cup of beard lichen hanging from a branch 4 to 60 feet above ground.

A Closer Look:
Wild Lupines

In Minnesota the best place to see the wild lupine blooming in profusion is the North Shore of Lake Superior area, and the best time is June. A native species of the western states, when in bloom lupine lines roadsides with a dazzling display of blue, purple, and pink. A beautiful wildflower with elongate spikes of pea-like flowers, the lupine usually grows in sandy soils and reaches a height of over 2 feet.

Photo: Anders Bjorling

The deep green palmately compound leaves have 7 to 11 leaflets.

Its name is derived from *lupus*, the Latin word for "wolf," and is based on the ancient but mistaken notion that lupines impoverished the soil. Lupines often grow in open places where the soil is none too rich. That lupines have anything to do with creating the poor soil remains unproved.

Week three (June 16-23)

Red mulberry trees are loaded with ripe and ripening fruit; gray catbirds, American robins and many of us humans sure enjoy the berries. The northern catalpa trees have begun blooming; they share with the horse chestnut and Ohio buckeye the distinction of bearing the most showy flowers of all ornamental trees grown in the Upper Midwest. Shrub and garden roses flower profusely, and the first hollyhock flowers open. Common milkweed, Canada thistle, European bellflower, and tawny daylily all begin blooming.

Honey bees forage on yellow sweet clover, white Dutch clover and staghorn sumac flowers. Both deer and stable flies are on the wing. The first baby American toads and leopard frogs come up on dry land; they are leaving the water after being in the tadpole stage. Young 13-lined ground squirrels appear above ground and explore their new world. Striped skunk young travel about with their mothers.

From about June 10th to 20th each year, we have our earliest sunrises (5:26 in the Twin Cities and area), and birds start singing about 4:30 a.m. Young house wrens, song sparrows, blue jays, northern cardinals, and Baltimore orioles are fledging (leaving their nests). Common nighthawks incubate eggs and red-winged blackbirds feed their young. Adult Canada geese are particularly vulnerable now as they molt, losing their flight feathers and are grounded. At 9:20 to 9:30 p.m. most chimney swifts enter their chimney roosts. The last American robins and yellow-headed blackbirds are heard calling until forty minutes after sunset.

The green pea harvest starts in southern Minnesota, where farmers cultivate corn and soybeans, and the harvest of the second crop of alfalfa begins. In the northern part of the state, banded purple butterflies can be seen on the wing, eastern phoebes are vocal, and the white water lily and showy pink and white lady's slipper blooms. Tulips, crabapple trees and common purple lilacs bloom in Grand Marais.

scattered events

- **June 16, 1996** - Smooth wild rose first blooming. Poison ivy in bloom. Song sparrows and barn swallows are busy feeding their nestlings. Statewide, 52 percent of the first cutting of alfalfa has been completed.

- **June 18, 1998** - In Carver County, much of the field corn is knee to waist high. Butterfly-weed, black-eyed susan, northern bedstraw and prairie phlox are colorful blooming plants on the Linnaeus Arboretum prairie in St. Peter.

- **June 19, 1992** - American robins, gray catbirds, rose-breasted grosbeaks, and brown thrashers are eating ripe fruit from scarlet elderberry shrubs. Purple loosestrife begins blooming in wet areas.

- **June 21, 1992** - Scattered frost resulted in some damage to corn and soybean plants in southeast Minnesota and western Wisconsin.

The surface temperature of Caribou Lake, near Lutsen, is 62˚. In the forests nearby we hear red-eyed vireos, ovenbirds, winter wrens, and white-throated sparrows.

- **June 22, 2007** - First ripe garden raspberries (both red raspberries and black ones). Red admiral butterflies have become numerous. The prickly pear, a native cactus with its three-inch yellow flowers, blooms nicely in the Minnesota Landscape Arboretum and at Blue Mounds State Park.

- **June 23, 2005** - Eastern bluebirds feed second broods of nestlings.

A Closer Look:

Chimney Swifts Overhead

From late April or early May and on through the summer, chimney swifts chatter, glide, and feed on flying insects over Albert Lea, St. Peter, Excelsior, St. Paul, Benson, Alexandria, Park Rapids, Bemidji and other Minnesota cities and villages. Observing the fast erratic flight of chimney swifts across the sky is one of those things that "makes my day." Most people associate this species with urban areas where chimneys abound, but some swifts, particularly in the northern forested areas, continue to nest in hollow trees or on the walls of cliffs and little-used buildings.

Chimney swifts are soot-colored, five-inch swallow-like birds with very short tails and long, narrow curved wings perfectly adapted for rapid flight and quick turns. They feed exclusively on flying insects, pursuing them through the air with open mouths. Their wing span is about a foot. So rapid are the wing beats of the chimney swift that until fairly recently it was thought they beat their wings alternately. Slow motion photography proved they do beat their wings together as do other birds.

Except when roosting, chimney swifts spend most of their lives in the air. So perfectly adapted for aerial life are these "flying cigars" that they drink water and bathe by dipping into the water of a pond or stream as they fly over it. They even court and mate in flight. Since they never perch, chimney swifts gather nesting twigs in flight, snapping them off with their bill or feet as they pass by trees.

Nesting takes place in June, when four or five white eggs are laid in a small nest of sticks glued together with saliva and attached to the wall of a chimney or other surface. Both sexes share incubation, which takes about three weeks. Most often chimney swifts nest in colonies; sometimes there may only be two or three other pairs. The young take about four weeks to fledge.

During mid-May and again in August, when there are peak numbers of these social birds in a certain area, observers have reported large flocks of a thousand or more whirling in a huge circle as they funnel down for the night in a big chimney. A good share of the chimney swifts depart Minnesota by September 15. The breeding range of this swift includes the entire eastern United States from Texas north into southern Canada. A long-distance migrant, they are known to winter only in Peru, Chile, and Brazil.

A Closer Look:
Arboretum Reflections

The traditional definition of an arboretum is—a living museum of woody plants, each properly identified and labeled. More than a hundred arboretums are located in the United States. In the last fifty years or so, many of them have been expanded to include natural forests, wetlands, and prairies; or restored forests, wetlands, and other natural areas. Arboretums also often contain annual and perennial flower gardens, herb gardens, and even vegetable gardens and orchards, along with a representative sampling of plantings from other parts of the world. As a result, most

Photo: Jim Gilbert

arboretums are also botanical gardens. Both the Minnesota Landscape Arboretum and the much smaller Linnaeus Arboretum fit this broader definition of what an arboretum might offer the visitor.

Often described as gardening within a natural setting, the University of Minnesota Landscape Arboretum proper was founded in 1958, but its roots extend back to the Horticultural Research Center that was founded in 1908 in the same general area, and is now part of the same organization. This world-class northern arboretum is located a couple of miles west of Chanhassen on 1,047 acres of land that was once part of the Big Woods, and it includes extensive native forest areas of sugar maple, basswood, and mixed oak trees within its borders. The Arboretum property also contains natural and restored wetlands and a restored prairie. Major collections include crabapple, pine, and maple; and major gardens display herbs, perennial flowers, roses, annual flowers, hostas, and wildflowers. Over the years I (and no doubt millions of other people) have come to the Minnesota Landscape Arboretum to seek nature's beauty, to learn, and to be refreshed. What a resource! It has been my privilege to work with all three directors: Leon C. Snyder (1958–1976), Francis de Vos (1977–1984), and most recently Peter J. Olin. Each one provided the leadership needed to connect people of all ages to plants and the wonders of nature.

The Linnaeus Arboretum at Gustavus Adolphus College in St. Peter, Minnesota, is a living library provided for the college students and other people of the community and beyond. Founded in 1973 under the guidance of Charles and Harriet Mason, and covering a little more than 100 acres on the south and west sides of the campus, the Arb has plantings of woody plants—trees, shrubs, and vines—plus wetlands, a restored prairie and the likeness of both a deciduous and coniferous forest. There are also collections of linden trees, conifers, and maples; a pioneer cabin, perennial gardens, and a waterfalls garden. Along with the plantings are resident and migrant birds; several species of mammals such as 13-lined ground squirrels and red foxes; frogs and toads; many insect species, spiders, and other small animals. All this adds greatly to the biodiversity of the Gustavus campus, and provides opportunities for people of all ages to take pleasure in the beauty of the Earth; and hopefully be inspired to become better stewards. Carl Linnaeus, the famous Swedish biologist who taught in the 1700s, wrote, "Also, the small things deserve our attention." And, "Every form of life created by God is worth our attention."

Both of the arboretums have played a big part in my journey to develop as a naturalist. I'm grateful for the many people I have met at these two special places who have helped me interpret the landscape and gain some insights into how the world works.

Two questions that I often get when working in Linnaeus Arboretum or the Minnesota Landscape Arboretum are: "What is the best day of the year to visit the arboretum?" and "When is everything in bloom?" The answer to the second question is never, because some plants only bloom for a day or two each year. The answer to the first question is—every day of the year. But I would have to add that any June day would be an especially good time to walk an arboretum trial and take in the beauty. There is just so much to be discovered at the height of the growing season.

A Closer Look:

Summer Solstice

The June solstice occurs on June 20 or 21, when the earth's orbit is positioned so that the north polar end of its axis leans at the full 23½ degree angle towards the sun, giving all parts of the earth north of the Arctic Circle constant daylight. At this time astronomical summer begins in the Northern Hemisphere, and with it the year's longest span of daylight. From our summer solstice until December's winter solstice, the nights will slowly lengthen and the daylight hours diminish.

On June 20, 2008, summer began at 6:59 p.m. CDT. It's the longest day of the year, with 15 hours and 36 minutes of sunlight in the Twin Cities area. Winona, in southeastern Minnesota, will have 15 hours and 30 minutes of sunlight, and Hallock in the extreme northwestern part of the state, will have 16 hours and 15 minutes of sunlight. We in the Twin Cities actually have 15 hours and 36 minutes of daylight from June 17 to June 23; on June 24 we lose 1 minute of daylight.

Even though the sun is highest in the sky on the June solstice—68½ degrees above the horizon at noon in the Twin Cities—it will take about five more weeks until we get our warmest days. July 26 is statistically our warmest day of the year. This is due to the lag time it takes to heat the earth's surface to the maximum, for it is radiation given off by the surface, rather than the sunlight itself, which heats the atmosphere.

Yes, from the astronomical point of view the first day of summer here in the Northern Hemisphere is June 20 or 21, yet meteorologists and climatologists continue to point to June 1 as the critical date here in Minnesota, and this earlier date is in better accord with the normal course of plant development locally.

A Closer Look:
Bee Watching

Most honey bees live in artificial hives, but swarms regularly escape and establish wild hives, usually in hollow trees. Honey bees aren't native to this country; they were first introduced into New England about 370 years ago. Archaeologists recently found evidence that beekeeping was going on about 3,000 years ago in what is now northern Israel.

Nearly every day during the growing season I have the opportunity to bee-watch, sort of like bird-watching but without the binoculars. I like to move in within a foot of the handsome half-inch animals and observe their actions at flowers—those of clovers, alfalfa and roses at this time of year.

I even encounter honey bees in very urban areas. Some people wonder where they come from in such situations. It's not unusual for beekeepers to keep hives in major cities, and they often do so on rooftops. Honey bees are always colonial. A hive may contain up to about 60,000 bees at full strength. Most bees return to their hives occasionally during the day, and then remain there during the night. So honey bees seen in cities aren't strays. The bees usually fly less than 100 yards to forage, so the hives are close by.

I find honey bee lore almost as fascinating as watching bees. Listed below are just a few things I have learned over the years.

- Bees are quite speedy. They can fly about 15 miles per hour. In contrast, we walk about 3 MPH.

- About 1.1 pounds of honey is consumed per capita in the United States yearly.

- A single honey bee can produce only $\frac{1}{12}$ of a teaspoon of honey in its lifetime.

- Honey bees from the same hive visit approximately 225,000 flowers per day. They are the number one pollinators for vegetable crops and orchards.

Week four (June 24-30)

Gardeners harvest peas, Swiss chard, kohlrabi, broccoli, cauliflower, beets, and carrots. The native blackcap raspberry and garden raspberry plants have their first ripe fruit. Delicious! The native common elderberry shrubs are at bloom peak with big flat clusters of white flowers. New cattail flowerheads are dark brown and very showy in marshlands.

The first monarch butterflies of the new generation, since arriving in Minnesota, are on the wing. We listen for the first buzzing of the annual cicada and watch for the first flying Carolina grasshopper. The peak time to see fireflies (lightning bugs) is now in early summer. Look for these tiny lights over meadows and grassy ditches not far from woodlands, from extreme southern Minnesota up into Canada.

A trained observer can pick out two dozen different bird species in the morning chorus of singers. Waterfowl are mostly all in a flightless condition now. Purple martins are busy feeding young nestlings. Wild turkey hens can be seen with their small young (poults). On these summer evenings, watch for common nighthawks flying, calling and feeding over most of our cities and towns. They nest on rooftops. By 9:40 p.m. nearly all chimney swifts

Common nighthawk

are in their chimney roosting sites.

Southern Minnesota farmers begin cutting the second crop of alfalfa. Wild blueberry picking begins and fireweed starts blooming in northern Minnesota and Wisconsin, where young common loons are seen with their parents on many of the lakes.

scattered events

- **June 24, 2007** - Prairie areas in southern Minnesota have become colorful with such blooming wildflowers as Culver's-root, grass-leaved goldenrod, leadplant, purple prairie clover, ox-eye and black-eyed susan.

- **June 27, 1990** - Swamp milkweed begins blooming. Nanking cherry fruit is ripe. Between Hastings and Northfield, the green pea harvest is in full-swing.

- **June 27, 2005** - Carver County farmers begin cutting the second crop of alfalfa. Sweet corn is tasseling. North Star cherry fruit is ripe.

- **June 28, 1998** - The second crop of alfalfa is being cut in central MN. At Alexandria, cliff swallows build bulb-shaped nests of mud, chimney swifts and house finches are vocal, and native basswood trees have their first open flowers. First dewberries and wild red raspberry fruit now ripe at Finland, MN.

- **June 29, 2000** - Annual sunflower first blooming along highways. Native basswood trees begin to flower. Delphinium and lilium are very showy garden flowers.

- **June 30, 1996** - Statewide, field corn height averages 21 inches.

- **June 30, 2007** - The surface temperature of Lake Waconia and other southern Minnesota lakes hit a warm 80°F. Much of the field corn in Carver County is up 5 to 6 feet.

A Closer Look:
Dragonflies, the Superb Flyers

While working with my summer field biology students on the bog trail at the Minnesota Landscape Arboretum at the end of June a few years ago, a half-dozen dragonflies joined us and gobbled up mosquitoes that came close. We had biological control happening right in front of our eyes. Those colorful, winged creatures of the air, the dragonflies, are seen from spring well into the fall season, but it's now that their numbers and different species reach a peak. They rival the butterflies and moths in beauty, form, and color. Twelve-spotted skimmers, common whitetail skimmers, and green darners are some of the easy-to-identify dragonflies on the wing now. To get into the hobby of dragonfly watching or "dragonflying" it helps to have binoculars that focus under ten feet and a good field guide book such as *Dragonflies of the North Woods* by Kurt Mead.

Dragonflies, also known as darning needles or stingers, are relatively large and often beautifully colored insects that spend much time on the wing in darting and rapid flights. An expert hunter, the dragonfly has a streamlined body and glistening wings that carry it through the air at speeds of 30 miles per hour or more; each pair of wings strokes alternately, the front pair going up while the hind pair is going down, at a rate of 30 or 40 strokes per second. The motor muscles that operate a dragonfly's wings comprise approximately one-quarter of its weight. Like hummingbirds, dragonflies can hover in the air or suddenly dart upward, downward, or to one side. While sunning and resting, they extend both wings as if in flight.

Photo: David Brislance

Dragonflies are reported to be dangerous, and they are, but only to smaller insects such as midges and beetles which they can catch and eat on the wing.

We look for adult dragonflies near lakes, ponds, streams, and wetlands, but they are strong fliers, and their many-veined transparent wings can take them miles away from water. Often we see them flying in tandem, the male holding the female by the back of the head with the appendages at the end of his abdomen. Eggs are generally laid in aquatic vegetation or are washed off the end of the abdomen when the female flies low over water. Eggs hatch into nymphs that live in ponds or streams where they are ferocious predators, feeding on daphnia, tadpoles, tiny fish, and insects (including other dragonfly larvae). Most dragonfly larvae mature to adulthood in one to three years. There is no pupal stage in the life of a dragonfly. Incomplete metamorphosis consists of the egg, the larva (nymph) and the adult.

Both the nymphs and adults of the dragonflies are enemies of mosquitoes. They wolf them down as mosquito wigglers when they are nymphs and snatch them out of the air as flying mosquitoes when they are adult dragonflies. Sometimes a dragonfly catches so many mosquitoes that there will be a hundred or more in its mouth at one time. Another common name for the dragonfly is the mosquito hawk.

A dragonfly is capable of eating its own weight in food in half an hour. Occasionally they may sweep some insect resting on a leaf into their jaws, but mainly their food consists of insects caught in flight. Sometimes the mosquito hawk catches its victims in its jaws but more often they are scooped from the air by means of its legs. The six spiny legs form a kind of insect net in which to capture its victims, some as large as bees, moths, and even butterflies. Once prey is caught in the basket of its spiny legs, the dragonfly transfers the captured insect to its mouth with the forelegs.

Photo: David Brislance

A Closer Look:
What is a Bird?

Birds belong to the animal kingdom. They are vertebrates—animals having a definite head, a backbone, and a well-developed brain. In addition, they are warm-blooded, have forelimbs modified as wings—though some birds such as penguins don't fly—and skin covered with feathers. The number of feathers a bird has increases with its size. For example, hummingbirds have about fifteen hundred feathers, black-capped chickadees around two thousand, American robins almost three thousand, and tundra swans more than twenty-five thousand.

Birds are interesting. They are the "litmus paper" indicators of how healthy our environment is at most any time and place.

A hundred billion birds live on Earth; that's about fifteen times the human population. They range in size from the 300 pound ostrich, standing nearly 8 feet tall, to the bee hummingbird, measuring a tiny 2.2 inches in length. A majority of small land birds travel at speeds between 20 and 30 miles per hour, while the flying speed of ducks and geese ranges from 40 to 55 mph. A peregrine falcon pressed by an airplane went into a dive at 180 mph.

Birds have ears on the sides of their heads but no trumpets or lobes so as to be more streamlined. All the same, their sense of hearing is very good. It is believed that birds have relatively poor senses of smell and taste as witnessed many times by watching American crows feasting on road-killed skunks. The fact that birds see colors should be no surprise, for of all forms of animal life, birds are among the most colorful.

There are about 9,700 species of birds living on the planet now. (Birds that look alike and interbreed are called a species.) About 650 species of birds are found in North America, and of these close to 300 could be observed during any one year in the state of Minnesota, where about 240 species are known to nest. However, only about 60 species spend their winters in Minnesota, and of these only a dozen or so come regularly to snowy backyard feeding stations. During

June and July a person can observe up to 20 species coming to a feeding station, with the added reward of watching adults bring their young to feed.

A Closer Look:
Basswoods Blooming

The basswood, also called the American linden, is one of the prominent trees of deciduous forests throughout the Upper Midwest. Here in Minnesota we can see them growing from the Iowa border north to the Canadian border.

Basswood leaves are easy to recognize. They are large and heart-shaped, four to six inches long, sometimes longer. They are dark green above and light green below, and edged with course teeth. The basswood forms a handsome, symmetrical tree that grows from 50 to 100 feet tall. In late June, when it come into bloom, the trees are loaded with clusters of fragrant, creamy-white flowers that perfume forest areas and our neighborhoods, and attract honey bees and other insects. When the basswood blooms, for about two weeks, it can be an excellent source of honey which to many of us has a great flavor.

Basswoods not only shade us, but also provide visual beauty and sweet-smelling flowers, while also playing a very important

Photo: Jim Gilbert

role in the forest ecosystem. Their wood is used for home building, furniture making, wood carving, and as pulp for paper.

A Closer Look:
Birds on Hot Days

Although birds do not have sweat glands, on hot days they are able to lose some of their body heat by vaporization of the moisture from their skin. However, birds are pre-eminently "panting animals" and their evaporative cooling comes mostly from the moist membranes lining the respiratory tract. During hot afternoons it's not unusual to see American robins, American crows, or other birds perched quietly in the shade with their bills wide open, panting.

July

Historically, July is our warmest and sunniest month, heating the lakes up for the best summer swimming conditions and allowing corn to grow tall. House wrens are very vocal. Annual cicadas buzz loudly on hot days. Farmers harvest small grains. Gardeners pick cucumbers, zucchini and tomatoes, and dig new potatoes. In the northern parts of Minnesota, fireweed is blooming and wild blueberries are ripe for picking.

READING THE LANDSCAPE

Week one (July 1–7)

The Sound of a Wren
Fireflies Light Up the 4th
The Danger of Lightning
Prairie Bloom

Week two (July 8–15)

Field Corn Silking
Hollyhocks
Bird Migrations Start Early
Purple Martin Nestlings

Week three (July 16–23)

Sweet Corn
Wild Bird Longevity
Birds Bathing
Bumble Bees are Humming

Week four (July 24–31)

Music in the Darkness
Roadside Wildflowers
The Warmest Day
The Birds of Coney Island

first week in july

The normal high temperature for July 1 in the Twin Cities is 82° and the low 61°F. The record high is 100° set in 1883, and the record low is 46° set in 1852 and 1995. Expect lake surface water temperatures to be in the 70s, but many will rise above 80° during hot spells.

Gardeners dig the first new potatoes and try to beat the birds to the ripe raspberries. Pie cherries are at the peak of ripeness.

Purple loosestrife begins blooming in wetlands. Red-osier dogwood is at its second bloom peak, as staghorn sumac fruit clusters turn red. Wild gooseberries are ripening and perfect for picking. It's time to snack on wild blackcap raspberry fruit and red mulberries.

Fifty to 95°F is the temperature range at which honey bees forage. Sight and smell enable bees to locate sources of pollen and nectar. This week honey bees are foraging on the fragrant flowers of the native basswood tree, and on butterfly-weed, swamp milkweed and many blooming garden plants. Mosquitoes become bothersome around sunset. Young raccoons are out and about with their mothers.

American goldfinches feed on Canada thistle seed heads. Black-capped chickadee parents come to feeding stations and pick out sunflower seeds to feed their young perched nearby. Baltimore orioles visit grape jelly and sugar water feeders, and bring their young. Barn swallow young leave their nests. The second broods of eastern bluebird nestlings are being fed by their parents.

In southern Minnesota, we expect field corn to be at least knee high, but often in the last few years it's four to five feet or taller. Spring wheat is turning color and soybeans are starting to bloom. Along the North Shore the surface temperature of Lake Superior is in the 40s, rugosa roses and double peonies bloom nicely, and showy blooming roadside plants include wild lupine and cow-parsnips.

scattered events

- **July 1, 2006** - Tawny daylily at bloom peak. Last of the eastern cottonwood tree cotton is falling. The surface temperature of Lake Waconia is a warm 78° F. Deer flies are bothersome. Red-necked grebes at Mott Lake in Waseca County continue incubating eggs.

- **July 3, 1999** - In the Walker area, the native basswood trees are first blooming, purple martins are busy feeding their nestlings, and the surface water temperature of Leech Lake is 70°F, the cut-off for safe swimming. Also, Baltimore orioles, red-headed woodpeckers, yellow-bellied sapsuckers, and ruby-throated hummingbirds come to sugar water feeders.

- **July 3, 2005** - First ripe garden tomato. Garden raspberry picking is good.

- **July 6, 2005** - At Grand Marais, the surface temperature of Lake Superior is a cold 48° F, and the common purple lilac shrubs are blooming and very fragrant.

A Closer Look:
The Sound of a Wren

One of my favorite sounds of summer is the clear, loud, bubbling notes of the house wren. The full-throated song is sort of like the syllables "tsi, tsi, tsi, tsi, oodle, oodle, oodle," the pitch rising at the beginning, falling at the end. Through our screen windows I listen to the gurgling song repeated over and over in our yard, on the shore of Lake Waconia. These wrens also give out chattering, scolding notes.

At this time, in very early July, young are often still in the nestbox in the backyard and the adult pair is very busy bringing in the insect and spider food. Two broods of five to eight young can be expected each summer. The second nestings typically occur between early July and mid-August. After the nesting season we no longer hear the house wren music.

Despite its tiny size, about 4½ to 5 inches, and its drab gray-brown plumage, the house wren is as well known as the American robin, for what it lacks in size and color is made up

© Michael Woodruff | Dreamstime.com

migration and the hazards of life on his winter territory, he will indeed return to sing in our yards and attract a mate, possibly the same one he had the previous year. This bird species is attracted to the site of his hatching as if by a magnet. He returns over and over as long as he lives. Eight house wrens banded at a station near Lake Minnetonka returned and were recaptured one or two years after being banded. If a male of the previous summer does not return, the singer in the yard would likely be one of his offspring. Females also return but could go to a new territory if a male's singing entices her there and she approves of a nest site, and if protein-rich spider and insect populations are high.

We usually observe the first house wren in our yard about May first. The male arrives about nine days before the female and as soon as he appears on the breeding ground he announces his arrival by singing. The male advertises and defends a territory of about ¼ to 3½ acres by much singing. He also begins immediately building dummy nests of twigs in all or most of available nest sites. The male likes to leave one twig sticking out of the entryway, maybe as a way to promote his handiwork to prospective females. A female then may choose one of the pre-chosen sites. On the base of twigs she builds a cup of grasses, plant fibers, feathers and hair.

for with voice and energetic activity. The house wren is a summer resident throughout the entire state, and true to its name, it is often found near human dwellings in suburban and rural communities. The house wren can be found in burned-over northern forest areas but are uncommon in areas of heavy urban development, intensive agriculture, or in dense forests. House wrens from the Upper Midwest winter in the Gulf states, eastern Texas, and down into Mexico. On winter territory they are silent as they search through dense thickets for food. Both sexes look alike.

Banding has proved that if the male survives

Nestboxes that are set out in yards near our homes are often used. So are natural cavities or woodpecker holes in trees. The house wren also uses its share of unusual spots for nesting sites, including abandoned paper nests of hornets, old hanging automobile tires, flower pots, nests previously used by swallows or phoebes, localities over doorways, in overalls and pants left hanging by deserted buildings, in old boots, and in iron pipe railings.

A Closer Look:
Fireflies Light Up the 4th

On July 4, 2007, environmental educator Julie Brophy wrote: "We set out to watch fireworks of the natural kind tonight; we visited Spring Peeper Meadow at the Minnesota Landscape Arboretum and saw thousands of fireflies filling the night sky and meadow—it was magical!" Yes, fireflies, also known as lightning bugs, do give special charm to warm nights.

The common names firefly and lightning bug, used for insects that communicate silently with pulsating flashes of cold light, are both incorrect from an entomologist's point of view. Fireflies are not flies or bugs but beetles—the dominant life form on this planet, at least in terms of numbers of species. It is a generally accepted fact that there are more species of Coleoptera, the order of beetles, than in any other group of life forms on earth. There are some 300,000 described species (kinds) of beetles and no doubt a huge number that have not yet been specifically identified. The diversity and vast numbers of insects may be difficult for us to comprehend. There may be as many as 20 million insect species, rather than the mere million or so currently known to science.

Fireflies are actually elongate soft-bodied beetles possessing "taillights"—segments near the ends of their abdomens with which the insects are able to produce light. There are 136 species of beetles known as fireflies in eastern North America. Here in Minnesota we ordinarily see these tiny lights in the dark from late May through July. Wetlands, wet ditches, tall grassy spots, old fields, forest edges, and sometimes lawns near these more natural areas, are good places to observe them.

The flashing is a recognition signal enabling the sexes to find each other. Each firefly species has a characteristic flashing rhythm. Typically a male emits flashes of yellowish light at intervals of 5 to 10 seconds while he flies a few feet above ground. Females wait on top of low vegetation and if a flashing male comes within about 6 feet she flashes back. The exact number of seconds between flashes serves to distinguish the species. So the male will only approach a light if it blinks at the proper intervals.

The light emitted by these insects is unique in that it generates no heat. Nearly l00 percent of the energy is devoted to the light itself, which is produced by the oxidation of a substance called luciferin, manufactured in the cells of the light-producing organ. Fireflies control the blinking by controlling the amount of air they take in through tiny openings in their abdomens. When air is admitted, luciferin in the presence of an enzyme called luciferinase is almost instantly oxidized, releasing the energy as light.

Adult females of some firefly species are wingless glowworms. The larvae of many species glow as well. These larvae are predators of ferocious intent, seeking prey and devouring it. They feed on various small insects, snails, and earthworms.

© Stoica Alexandru | Dreamstime.com

A Closer Look:
The Danger of Lightning

Lightning is a visible electrical discharge produced by thunderstorms, cloud-to-cloud, cloud-to-earth, or cloud-to-air. Hundreds of people are hurt or killed by lightning every year in the United States. Lightning kills more people than tornadoes. It also starts forest fires, disrupts electrical service, and occasionally even burns our homes. Yet lightning also plays an important role in natural processes. An estimated sixteen million thunderstorms rage annually over the Earth and the thunderbolts involved create a hundred million tons of fixed nitrogen compounds by breaking down the air, which is composed of roughly four parts of nitrogen to one part of oxygen. This nitrogen is deposited on soil and plants with the rain and acts as a valuable fertilizing agent.

Lightning is essentially the completion of a huge electrical circuit. Positive electrical charges pile up in the top of a thunderhead while negative charges build up at the base of the cloud, probably because of distribution of liquid water drops at the base and ice crystals near the top. The negative charges at the base of the thundercloud upset the usual neutral distribution of positive and negative electrical charges on the ground below. Because like charges repel each other, the negative charges in the cloud base push the negative charges on the ground deeper into the ground. This movement leaves the ground with an excess of positive charges. Then, because opposite electric charges attract each other, the stage is set for lightning. When a stream of negative charges from the cloud, called a step leader, meets the stream of positive charges streaming up from the ground at more than 50,000 miles per second, the circuit is complete and there is a lightning bolt.

The booming sound known as thunder is generated by rapidly expanding gasses along the channel of a lightning discharge.

While driving home from work one late June evening, I witnessed once again a common summer custom. It was about 9:45 and the sky was lit up with one lightning strike after another. Thunder was loud, we were in a tornado watch, and yet there was a youth baseball game going on in a local park!

All of us need to think about the danger of lightning. When you first see lightning or hear thunder, head for shelter. I would encourage teachers, parents and coaches to call a game, or any outdoor activity, at the first sound of thunder. Deadly lightning can shoot out from even very small thunderstorms.

Listed below are a few lightning safety tips. Hopefully this information will help you to decide what to do when a thunderstorm (which always has lightning) approaches. These ideas could save your life or the lives of people around you.

- **Take shelter in a building or in all metal vehicle with rubber tires.** The practice of seeking refuge in small isolated buildings such as beachhouses, sheds or ticket booths should be avoided. Hurry to a sizable building such as a house or school. Roofs and walls of buildings make a better path than the human body for lightning to reach the ground.

- **In a house, avoid using the telephone, television, and electrical appliances.** Stay clear of stoves, fireplaces, attics, doors, and windows. Keep out of a bathtub or shower.

- **You certainly want to avoid being on an open area such as a golf course, beach,** or athletic field. And don't take shelter under a tall tree. The step leader of negative charge from the thundercloud seeks out the shortest path to positive charges on the ground, and tall objects such as trees are definitely the shortest path. For the same reason you want to avoid being on a hill.

- **Get out of and away from open water, whether swimming or boating.** While the chances of a swimmer being hit directly are slim, the flow of current carried by the water from a bolt striking at some distance can cause electrocution.

- **Get away from tractors and other metal farm equipment.** Get off of and away from motorcycles, scooters, golf carts, and bicycles. Also, put down all golf clubs.

- **Stay away from wire fences, clotheslines, metal pipes, rails, and any metallic paths that could carry lightning from a distance.**

- **In a forest, seek shelter in a low area under a thick growth of small trees.**

- **If you are caught outside in a thunderstorm, the best thing to do is to get into a depression or a ditch.** Then crouch into a ball in order to be as low as possible yet minimize the amount of ground contact for a bolt of lightning to hit.

- **When you are forced to seek shelter from lightning, wait a good half hour before you head back out, as lightning can still be around after the rain ends.**

A Closer Look: Prairie Bloom

Some showy blooming prairie plants at this time include ox-eye, prairie phlox, black-eyed susan, and both purple prairie clover and white prairie clover. Another is the butterfly-weed, one of the brightest and most conspicuous of the northern wildflowers. It is topped with blazing orange flowers that monarchs and other butterflies desire.

A prairie is defined generally as a natural grassland composed of herbaceous plants and native perennial grasses such as big bluestem and prairie cord grass. This primeval vegetation that occupied the land for thousands of years is mostly gone; its accumulated productivity now supplies food for many hungry people of the world.

Before European settlers arrived on the plains of the Midwest and West, prairie grasses and wildflowers stretched as far as people could see. In Minnesota more than one-third of the state, or about 19 million acres, were covered with prairie vegetation. Hundreds of thousands of square miles in the United States are known today as farmland but were at one time the prairie.

Remnant prairies do still exist. They have been saved through the initiative of a relatively few individuals and conservation groups such as the Nature Conservancy. Yet in spite of these efforts, remnant prairies are still being destroyed. Some are plowed up and planted to crops; others are sprayed with herbicides or ruined by over-grazing or continuous mowing. These remnants must be guarded since they are our remaining link to a world that lived ten thousand years ago. Prairies are too few to make prairie plants common, but the remaining plants and the animal life they support need our protection.

Week two (July 8-15)

Geraniums, petunias, snapdragons and marigolds flower gloriously in annual gardens. The first giant sunflowers bloom. Apricots have ripened. Gardeners pick their first ripe tomatoes. We could be enjoying our first meals of locally grown sweet corn.

A few yellow leaflets can be seen on butternut trees, as this is the first woody plant species to show fall color each year. Tartarian honeysuckle shrubs have shiny bright red or orange fruit. Showy blooming roadside plants include swamp milkweed, white sweet clover, butter-and-eggs, and common mullein. A few common sunflowers have begun blooming along highways, their flowers facing east.

The first of the second generation of eastern tiger swallowtail butterflies have emerged. Monarch butterflies lay their eggs on common milkweed leaves.

Bird song decreases dramatically after July 4 since the nesting season is over for many species and there is no further need to attract a mate or to defend territory. Shorebirds such as lesser yellowlegs and least sandpipers have begun migrating through from the arctic. They are probably adults that were unsuccessful in nesting, but this still marks the beginning of fall migration. Hosta blossoms now provide a new source for nectaring ruby-throated hummingbirds. Osprey young have grown quite large but remain in their nests. Red-winged blackbirds and common grackles are in large flocks; their nesting is done for this year.

In southwest Minnesota and into South Dakota the combining of wheat begins On southern and western Minnesota prairies there is a profusion of blooming wildflowers, including wild bergamot, leadplant, ox-eye, and white prairie clover. In the Arrowhead region, northern parula and black-throated green warbler young have begun leaving their nests, and both dewberry and wild strawberry fruit is ripe.

scattered events

▪ **July 9, 2000** - Juvenile green herons leave their nest. The surface temperature of Lake Minnetonka has warmed to 80°F .

▪ **July 10, 2006** - Lilium (the true lilies) at overall bloom peak and very colorful at the Minnesota Landscape Arboretum.

▪ **July 10, 2007** - The first locally grown sweet corn is now available.

▪ **July 11, 1999** - Statewide, 5 percent of the field corn is tasseling, compared to 11 percent for the 5-year average; soybeans are blooming on 24 percent of the planted acreage versus 27 percent for the five-year average.

▪ **July 13, 1998** - Canada thistle casts off seeds on silver-white carriers in huge numbers. Garden daylilies very showy. Pods on female Kentucky coffee trees are four to six inches long and still green. Squirrels eat white oak acorns which are still a green color. First snowy tree crickets chirping.

▪ **July 15, 2006** - First Canada geese flying after their molt. Both Sungold and Moongold apricots are ripe. High of 102° in both Duluth and Ortonville, 99° in the Twin Cities, and 94° at Grand Marais. The surface temperature of Lake Nokomis in Minneapolis is a warm 82°F.

A Closer Look:
Field Corn Silking

The pollen shed and silking of the corn plant usually takes place during the hottest days of the growing season, and that's July here in the Corn Belt. By now all major vegetative growth of the plant has taken place. The leaves and the stalk have reached their full size, and plant tissue metabolic activity is at peak level. The flowering parts emerge, fertilization of the silk is completed by pollen, and kernel development starts while all activities of the plant are at their maximum rate and capacity.

Corn tassels

It's interesting to note that with plenty of moisture the optimum growing temperature for corn is likely to be 90° to 95° F. However, Studies have shown that when the air temperature rises above 86°, corn roots have an increasingly difficult time taking in water fast enough to keep the plant cells full of water and working at top speed.

The tassel on top of the plant is the male flowering structure of corn. Its only function is to produce ample quantities of pollen to fertilize the female structures (ears). The number of pollen grains produced by a healthy tassel is probably somewhere between 2 million and 5 million. This means that there are about 2,000 to 5,000 pollen grains produced for each silk. The tassel normally emerges a few days before the first silks appear. Pollen shed is not a continuous process. It stops when the tassel is too wet or too dry and begins again when temperature and moisture conditions are favorable. Typically the peak pollen shedding is between 9 and 11 a.m.

The corn ear, or female flowering structure, is located on the side of the plant down from the tassel. The ear itself is a central cob with a group of flowers in rows in a cylindrical form. On a well-developed ear of corn there are 750 to 1000 potential kernels (ovules, individual female flowers) arranged in an even number of rows around the cob. Each of these ovules produces a long slender tube called the silk which receives the pollen and conducts the contents of the pollen grain down to the female flower on the cob.

The most interesting part of this pollination process to me is the fact that there is one silk for each kernel of corn produced on

FIRST FIELD CORN SILKING
(Carver County)

2008 - July 17	2002 - July 14
2007 - July 3	2001 - July 19
2006 - July 11	2000 - July 11
2005 - July 16	1999 - July 13
2004 - July 19	1998 - July 7
2003 - July 16	

a cob. Each silk is a long slender tube attached to the potential kernel (ovule) on the ear. Pollen grains fall on the silk and are held by tiny hairs on a sticky surface. They germinate and send a pollen tube down the silk to the ovule where the pollen nucleus fertilizes the egg and then the new kernel begins to develop.

A Closer Look:
Hollyhocks

Hollyhocks have begun blooming. As a child growing up in Minneapolis, I noticed these tall, stately garden plants with colorful flowers and accepted them as part of what makes mid-summer interesting. For many years I have recorded the date we first see hollyhocks in bloom. I do this just to see how summer plant development is unfolding and to assure myself that much is still OK with the world. Examples of my observations:

Hollyhocks starting to bloom in Carver County

July 7, 1983	June 28, 2005
July 9, 1985	June 22, 2006

The hollyhock had been cultivated in China

Photo: Jim Gilbert

for a thousand years before it was introduced into England in 1573. The plant quickly won favor because of its long blooming period, from midsummer to early fall. Typically a short-lived perennial, it is now grown as a biennial or even as an annual in temperate regions. Records show that soon after colonists reached America many of them cultivated hollyhocks in their simple gardens. These were mostly red, pink, or white varieties with single flowers. Then as now, hollyhocks were especially attractive under windows, along fences, or against the walls of houses or other buildings.

Hollyhocks need full sunlight, moist but well-drained soil, and staking to support the fragile stems in windy locations. New plants are best started from seeds sown in summer for flowering the next year. Once established in a garden, hollyhocks often grow spontaneously from seeds dropped during the summer.

Plants grow in clumps with stems usually 5 to 9 feet tall. The rough leaves, 6 to 8 inches across, have 5 to 7 lobes. The flowers are borne on the top 1½ to 2 feet of each stem. Blooming begins at the bottom of this area and moves progressively upward. The blossoms are 3 to 5 inches across and range in color from white through shades of yellow, pink, purple and red to nearly black. In addition to the time-honored single hollyhock flowers there are new strains whose petals are ruffled or doubled. I like the singles best.

A Closer Look:
Bird Migrations Start Early

© Norman Bateman | Dreamstime.com

It's only July, and the fall season seems far away, but bird migrations have already started! Here in Carver County avid birder Bob Dunlap counted seven lesser yellowlegs and thirteen least sandpipers on the mudflats of a Chaska lake on July 6.

These birds and about twenty-five other shorebird species can be observed in the Twin Cities and Waconia area, some for only a few days each year as they migrate through. We consider these highly migratory species "water" birds because they spend a large part of their lives around the shores of lakes, streams, or seacoasts. They typically have pointed wings and slender, fairly long bills, which are suitable for searching in shallow water or probing in mud for food. These birds typically have waterproof plumage, long legs, and partially webbed feet that are well-adapted for wading.

The early migration that is taking place now is related to the shorebirds' nesting habits. Most nest in the far north, arriving on the tundra usually in May while snow still covers about two-thirds of the ground. As soon as the snow melts in the arctic and the dark ground is exposed to the warming sun, vegetation breaks out and great swarms of insects appear. The major obstacle to life in the far north is the brevity of the summer season, which causes the nearly explosive blooming of the flowering plants, the hurried development of insects, and the short nesting period of the shorebirds. Almost all northern birds are primarily insect predators, and the insect swarms in the arctic are their food. The hatching of millions of shorebird chicks is, no doubt, synchronized with the peak of the insect cycle.

Nearly all shorebirds nest on the ground, and the usual clutch size of four large eggs seems to be the maximum number successfully incubated. The young are precocial (capable of a high degree of independent activity from birth), covered with down, and able to leave the nest the same hour they hatch. All adult birds leave the far north before the young are able to follow them. Some biologists think this may be an adaptive trait designed to lower the population size and reduce competition for food. In any case, the young are left to fend for themselves after their parents leave, and they migrate south later. How they find their way southward, many traveling as far as Argentina, is a migration mystery.

By mid-July the migration of several shorebird species through Minnesota is well under way, reaching a peak in mid-August. A second peak occurs again in September when the young birds follow the migratory paths of their parents.

The early return of small numbers of adults to our area now is probably correlated with the abandonment of their nests during severe weather in the arctic. Mudflats along the edges of water are places to look for migrating shorebirds as they fly through Carver County.

from *The Waconia Patriot*
– July 12, 2007

A Closer Look:
Purple Martin Nestlings

From April to September, many of us in Minnesota enjoy the bubbling chirps and trills of purple martins in and over our neighborhoods. This was especially true for our family when we spent time at our cabin on the shore of Leech Lake. Some of us provide apartments, thoughtfully placed and maintained for the martins. In return, these largest members of the swallow family give us pleasure with their aerial displays and songs.

Native Americans formed a friendship with purple martins long before Europeans arrived, hanging hollow gourds near their lodges in order to entice the birds to nest nearby. Purple martins are summer residents throughout Minnesota, but most numerous in the Mississippi River Valley and in the central and western regions of the state, mainly in and around towns and cities.

At this time of year both male and female martins are busy feeding their young. The diet of the purple martin could almost be covered by one word—insects—but this is not quite true, as they also eat a few airborne spiders. Dragonflies are a favorite insect food. Their food is generally procured on the wing and in the usual swallow fashion by darting, swooping, and wheeling in streamlined flight. Sometimes they can be seen flying close to the surface of lakes or rivers, dipping down for drinks.

Purple martins, like other insect-eating birds, are susceptible to pesticides. Martin landlords have reported finding whole colonies dead or dying in their yards or nesting boxes for no apparent reason. It's likely these birds were foraging in areas where pesticides had recently been applied for mosquito or other insect control.

One brood of young is raised each summer by martins in the Upper Midwest. The nest is started about a month before the eggs are laid, with both sexes building the nest. Usually four or five eggs are laid, and incubation apparently is performed by the female only. She is similar in color to the dark steel-blue males but has a light-colored belly. The eggs hatch in about fifteen days and the young remain in the nest for nearly a month.

After the nesting season has ended each summer, martins gather into assembly groups before leaving the area. The early migration of martins comes to a peak the second half of August in Minnesota as the birds leave for their winter home in Brazil. While there they feed on insects in the air, as usual, but they do not nest. Their homing instincts are strong, and a good share will return to the same nesting area the following spring.

Week three (July 16-23)

Garden perennials such as daylilies, purple coneflowers, phlox, and hollyhocks have magnificent flowers. Glads and giant sunflowers start blooming. Among wildflowers Joe-pye weed, boneset, arrowhead, blue vervain, and water-plantain are blooming in wetlands. Long-horned milkweed beetles can be seen on the flowers of common milkweed. Garter snake young are being born.

The first Canada geese are flying; the adults have been flightless since about mid-June, when they molted their wing feathers. The young geese test their new flight feathers. Mallards are also now starting to fly after their molt. Purple martin young fledge.

Chokecherry fruit is ripe with clusters of deep red to dark purple fruit. These cherries are popular for jelly-making, and very important as food for wildlife.

In northern Minnesota, fireweed, a four-foot-tall wildflower, has clusters of rose-purple flowers. Fireweed rapidly invades sites after forest fires. Also in the north, chipping sparrows, white-throated sparrows, and red-breasted nuthatches are busy feeding their young. Along the Superior Hiking Trail, wild blueberries, raspberries, and strawberries are ripe.

scattered events

- **July 17, 1998** - First bull thistle flowers opened. European mountain ash fruit is light orange. Purple prairie clover, gray-headed coneflower, and big bluestem grass all bloom nicely on southern Minnesota prairies.

- **July 17, 2006** - Sixth consecutive day with a high temperature of 90° or above in the Twin Cities. First noticed yellowjackets coming to our picnics. This evening we heard the first snowy tree crickets calling. Most field corn over the southern part of the state is pollinating.

- **July 20, 1997** - The daylily collection at the Minnesota Landscape Arboretum is at overall bloom peak. Other very showy blooming perennials there include lilium, phlox, roses, clematis, and monarda. Statewide, field corn height gained 16 inches in the last week to reach an average of 59 inches, surpassing the five-year average by 6 inches.

A Closer Look:

Sweet Corn

Corn is native to the New World and has been a valuable food crop at least since the Incas cultivated it. Modern corn is actually a tall annual grass, and all kinds, including ornamental corn, popcorn, field corn, and

Photo: Arlene Gardinier

sweet corn, are varieties of a single species—*Zea mays*. *Zea* is the Greek name for a cereal.

Sweet corn, also called sugar corn, is *Zea mays var. rugosa*, and is one of the most delicious of American vegetables. Nothing tastes like an ear of corn cooked as soon as it is picked. Sweet corn with yellow kernels is a favorite, but in parts of the U.S. white kernels are preferred. There are now ultra-sweet and super-sweet hybrids, as well as bicolor hybrids with one super-sweet parent that are bred for enhanced sugar. The sugar in these sweeter hybrids does not convert to starch as rapidly as in standard hybrids.

Sweet corn is among the easiest vegetables to grow provided it is given a sunny location and really fertile soil. However, most of us don't have the yard space or the time and energy to grow our own, so we can hardly wait for the commercial producers to have the first corn ready for sale. Sweet corn is strictly a warm-weather crop. From mid-July to mid-September we bring it home to our kitchens to cook and then enjoy its natural sugars and savory flavor.

First sweet corn available from local growers, Carver County:

2008 - July 24	2005 - July 17
2007 - July 10	2004 - July 16
2006 - July 13	2003 - July 20

A Closer Look:
Wild Bird Longevity

How long do wild birds live? This is a question I'm often asked. The general answer, for songbirds, is four or five years, if the bird survives its first year of life.

Until we began banding birds methodically in the 1950s, our only information on their ages came from captive birds. All wild native birds are now protected by federal law; it is illegal to keep them in captivity except for scientific study. Cardinals were popular cage birds until well into the twentieth century. A caged northern cardinal is on record as living for 28½ years whereas in the wild the extreme upper longevity record is 13 years and 8 months.

A captive bald eagle lived more than 48 years. Ten years in the wild is a record for this magnificent species, our national bird. Other big birds, hawks for instance, live a long time in zoos where they are fed and protected. One red-tailed hawk survived for 29 years in captivity, while in the wild the record for these raptors is 16 years.

The record for the tiny, jewel-like ruby-throated hummingbird (the only common hummingbird east of the Rockies) is five years. This species is a summer resident in Minnesota. A male banded at Oklahoma City in August of 1964 was recaptured at the same location five years later, so probably the hummingbirds we are seeing in our yards are birds that were here last summer or maybe several summers ago.

Listed below are a few banding reports for some of our commonly observed birds. These may not be longevity records but at least they give us some idea of the length of life for our feathered friends in the wild.

- Red-winged blackbird–14 years
- Black-capped chickadee–caught and released when 12 years and 5 months old
- Mourning dove–10 years
- Mallard duck–29 years

- American goldfinch–caught and released when 8 years and 10 months old
- Great blue heron–21 years
- Purple martin–some more than 7 years old when retrapped
- Baltimore oriole–one banded in Fargo, ND, retrapped and released at same place 7 years later.
- American robin–11 years and 8 months
- Barn swallow–16 years
- House wren–7 years and 2 months

Shaday365 | Dreamstime.com

A Closer Look:
Birds Bathing

Among the wild birds there are three main kinds of bathing—the water bath, the sun bath, and the dust bath. A bird bathes in water to facilitate oiling and preening, and secondly to clean the plumage. During hot weather water bathing no doubt also has a cooling effect. Probably most land birds take water baths. Birds that I have observed water bathing include common grackles, American robins, gray catbirds, blue jays, northern cardinals, and American goldfinches. Even the larger birds such as eagles, hawks, owls, and crows bathe in shallow pools along the edges of streams, in shallow ponds, and in puddles of rain water and melted snow.

Typically a songbird wades into the water to a depth of about 1 to 3 inches. In bathing, a bird ducks its head into the water, quickly raises it up, and then beats the wings, splashing water over the back. Immediately after bathing, a bird usually flies up from the birdbath or other bathing place to a tree or other safe perch, where it preens its feathers or spreads them to dry in the sunshine.

Preening is the most important act that a bird performs in the care of its feathers. A bird preens its plumage by pulling individual feathers through its beak to remove oil, dirt, and parasites. The preening movements also smooth the feather barbs so they will lock together. Also, worked into each feather is fresh oil from the oil gland at the base of its tail.

Aerial birds such as swifts and swallows bathe while in flight, splashing repeatedly into the surface of a pond or stream. Some of our so-called lawn and garden birds such as the ruby-throated hummingbird and the American robin will bathe in the spray of a lawn sprinkler.

Birds and humans receive the same benefits from sun bathing—the stimulation of vitamin D production. For birds, this vitamin benefits the skin, feathers, and oil gland.

Birds carry minute parasites called mites which can be very annoying. They cause itching and the bird responds by scratching. In fluffing the feathers and exposing the skin to the sunlight, a bird causes the mites to move to the close feathers on its head where they can be scratched easily. To escape the sun's rays, the parasites also hide under the wings. There they can be more easily removed by a bird's bill.

Common birds seen sun-bathing include American robins, northern cardinals, and house sparrows. There are probably dozens more. Hawks and owls also sunbathe by facing the sun and holding their wings spread wide.

Birds also take dust baths. A dusting bird squats or lies down in a sunny dusty spot on a dirt road or at the edge of a field or garden. An energetic flicking of its wings causes the dust to rise through its plumage, absorbing the excess oil in the feathers, and also ridding the feathers of mites, other parasites, and dandruff. In other words, dust bathing is another type of preening,

keeping the feathers in top shape. After bathing in the dust, a bird vigorously shakes the dust from its feathers. Birds of the open country, such as larks, ring-necked pheasants, and wild turkeys are dust bathers. So are certain hawks and owls. On many occasions I have watched house sparrows bathing in dust.

A Closer Look:
Bumble Bees are Humming

Listen carefully as you watch bumble bees going about their chores and you will hear them humming. It was this humming that gave them the name of bumble bee, from the Middle English word "bumblen," which means "to hum."

On observing bumble bees in flight, people are surprised that these burly giants can actually make progress through the air on such small wings. Antoine Magnan, a French zoologist, made some very careful studies of bumble bee flight in 1934 and came to the conclusion that because of their size they should not be able to fly.

There are many species of bumble bees. The most common kinds usually can be recognized by their robust shape, hairy bodies, and black and yellow markings, with a few having orange markings. Most of them are three-quarters of an inch long or longer. They live in colonies,

© Ruta Saulyte | Dreamstime.com

usually in the ground, and most often in an animal's deserted burrow.

Bumble bees collect pollen and nectar at the same time, making them very good pollinators and the busiest of all bees. They are said to visit twice as many flowers in an equal amount of time as other bees. The pollen grains are transported in the so-called pollen baskets, which are smooth, shining hollows on the outer surface of the hind legs, with long, overhanging hairs on the sides. Both pollen and nectar are food and are brought back to the nest to feed the larvae and queen.

It's during these countless trips to flowers that bumble bees transfer pollen on their bodies from the male flower parts to the female flower parts, where fertilization takes place. Before a plant can produce fruit or seeds, the flowers must be pollinated.

Many important plants, such as grasses, are pollinated by wind, but many others depend upon insects. Every year we have a multi-billion-dollar job performed for us, free of charge, when this pollination job is done by bees and other insects. We have fruits and vegetables because insects carry pollen. Of the insects, bumble bees are very important as they readily visit orchards and gardens, fields and meadows. The flowers of red clover are solely dependent on bumble bees, which are the only insects with tongues long enough to reach the nectar and at that time transfer pollen so seeds can form.

Week four (July 24-31)

Purple coneflowers attract numerous butterfly species including the painted lady, red admiral, and monarch, all of which come for nectar. The flying Carolina grasshoppers are the dominant insect in terms of both size and numbers on bike trails and along country roads. Annual cicadas sing on warm days and can be heard until about one-half hour after sunset. Their song is produced only by the males and is a loud, sometimes pulsating buzz.

Both pale touch-me-not and spotted touch-me-not have begun blooming in wetlands. The ragweeds, great and common, could start shedding pollen. Some acorns from bur and red oak trees have begun to fall.

Baltimore orioles come readily to feeders offering grape jelly mixed half-and-half with water, or a sugar and water solution. It's hatching time for the second broods of barn swallow young.

Early season apples such as Quinte and Lodi can be picked. Watermelons, muskmelons, and other garden melons are ripe.

A good share of Minnesota's lakes are considered to be warm water lakes so their surface temperatures can be expected to rise to 80° or higher at the end of July. Southern Minnesota farmers harvest the third crop of alfalfa. Fields of oats are ripe and golden-brown. Wild rice is in full-bloom in the central and northern parts of the state; by early autumn the grains of rice will be ripe.

scattered events

▪ **July 24, 1999** - Both Lake Waconia and Lake Minnetonka reached a surface water temperature of 85°F. That's very warm! The water temperature of Green Lake at Spicer is 82°, and Portage Lake at Park Rapids hit a high of 86°.

▪ **July 26, 1995** - At Wolf Ridge Environmental Learning Center, located near Finland and close to the North Shore, the students and I enjoyed finding, picking, and eating ripe wild red raspberries, thimbleberries, pin cherries, june berries, and blueberries.

▪ **July 28, 1995** - At Gooseberry Falls State Park, many wild gooseberries are ripe but even the green ones are good-eating.

▪ **July 30, 2006** - Great ragweed starting to shed pollen. Pumpkins turning orange.

▪ **July 31, 1996** - In the Park Rapids area, white water lilies are in full bloom, and some cliff swallows continue to feed young in bulb-shaped mud nests.

▪ **July 31, 2006** - Common ragweed begins shedding pollen. Eight species of birds, including Baltimore orioles and house finches, come to the birdbath on this hot day. The surface water temperature of Lake Waconia is 83°F. High temperature today reached 101° in the Twin Cities. July 2006 ended up being the warmest July since 1936 in Minneapolis/St. Paul.

A Closer Look:

Music in the Darkness

I enjoy the insect chorus heard through our open windows in the Waconia countryside. Late summer nights are best. The insect population is at its height and most of the individuals have reached their maturity, so by nine o' clock the activity of the night insects is in full swing. One can locate these nighttime singing insects by carefully searching with a flashlight. A beam swinging downward into the lawn may reveal musicians such as the black field crickets with their chirping sounds.

A cricket sings with the front or upper set of his two sets of wings. These upper wings have tiny ridges like the ridges of a file on their undersides, and also a thickened area, like a scraper, on the edge. The cricket moves his wings rapidly from side to side, rubbing them across each other so that they vibrate and make a rasping noise—the "chirp." Female crickets don't sing, but they listen with eardrums near their knees.

Temperature has a great deal to do with the way a cricket behaves, just as it does with other insects. Since July 18 (2007) we have been hearing the enchanting sound of the snowy tree crickets in the Waconia area. Last year I heard the first ones singing July 17, and in 2005 it was July 19.

The snowy tree cricket, a relative of the black field cricket, is also called the temperature cricket because it is a rather accurate thermometer. This cricket chirps more times per minute when it is warm than when it is cool. To produce their music, the males raise their wings straight above their backs and vibrate them rapidly from side to side. The females are silent. Males often sing in a chorus, and if the sound seems to be coming from all around, it often is. Snowy tree crickets chirp with a shrill tuneful and persistent "chee-chee-chee," also described as "waa-waa-waa," or "treat-treat-treat"—sleigh bell-like sound. If you count the number of chirps in 15 seconds and add 40, you will have a good approximation of the air temperature in degrees Fahrenheit.

Looking carefully with a flashlight into a shrub you may catch sight of this shy, pale-green creature hardly an inch in length. Hawthorne described this melodious night singer as having music like "the sound of moonlight." The snowy tree cricket is commonly heard but seldom seen.

A Closer Look:
Roadside Wildflowers

It has been said that travel is an enriching experience, and this experience can be broken down into many small enjoyments and encounters. One part of each automobile trip that I enjoy, whether across the state or just to and from work, is the chance to catch quick glimpses of the plant life in roadside ditches, or a little beyond, where there is a wealth of material to observe.

At the present time, tansy, black-eyed susans, and some early blooming goldenrods are yellow, wild bergamot has lavender flowers, and wild cucumber has tall clusters of white blossoms. Although I know these wildflowers well enough to spot them while cruising at 50 miles-per-hour, they can be more fully enjoyed and appreciated at slower speeds.

Photo: David Brislance

Common tansy

I would recommend that you stop to get a better look. With the aid of a good field guide to wildflowers, you'll soon be on your way to learning more about this very special resource, roadside plants.

Some of the wildflowers that we enjoy seeing are nonnative species and they could be put in the weed category—a plant out of place. They do bring shade and stability to soils in need, and they are colorful, but nonnative species can be invasive. Common tansy is a good example. Tansy was once favored as a garden flower. It was cultivated in Europe during the Middle Ages for its reputed medical value. Unfortunately tansy, also called golden buttons, is poisonous, and deaths have been caused by drinking too much of a tea made from the leaves. The tea was described by one observer as "perfectly vile tasting and worse than the ailments it was intended to cure." Tansy was thought to cure rheumatism and the measles, to kill intestinal worms, and help with nervousness. (Because of the plant's bitter taste, animals seldom eat it.)

Tansy has long since become a weed, albeit a very handsome three-foot-tall one, spreading along roadsides, vacant lots, and open fields. It forms large patches. The finely divided leaves release a fragrance when crushed. The button-like, yellow flower heads form a flat-tapped inflorescence.

Attempts are underway to eradicate tansy from some parts of Minnesota so that native species can flourish.

A Closer Look:
The Warmest Day

During July the central part of North America heats up with sunny skies and southwesterly or westerly winds providing the hottest temperatures of the year. The Atlantic Ocean high pressure systems move inland to clear the skies and diminish rainfall. July is the warmest and sunniest month of the year everywhere in the Upper Midwest except for a few locations along Lake Superior.

Using pioneer records going back to 1819 at Fort Snelling, the average high temperature for July 26 is 86°, and that marks the date as statistically our hottest day of the year in the Twin Cities. It's the peak of summer. The warmest air temperature ever recorded for the Twin Cities was 108° Fahrenheit on July 14, 1936. On July 6, 1936, the temperature rose to 114° in Moorhead. On July 29, 1917 the temperature hit 114.5° in Beardsley; the highest ever recorded in Minnesota. Bad Water, California, in Death Valley at 282 feet below sea level, is where the record high temperature for North America, 134°F, was measured on July 10, 1913.

A Closer Look:
The Birds of Coney Island

Anyone who goes boating on Lake Waconia cannot help but notice the many great blue herons and double-crested cormorants perched in the upper branches of tall trees around the northwest side of Coney Island. A closer look with binoculars will also provide views of the white-colored great egrets, plus many nests. All three bird species build platform nests of sticks, usually placed in trees. A fourth species, the more secretive black-crowned night heron, might also be nesting in the colony. During the nesting season, from spring to the first part of August, people should view this interesting colony from boats and refrain from walking in the area. There are close to eight-hundred nests in this healthy, successful colony.

The Coney Island nesting colony has an impact on a very large area because these birds go out from the lake ten to fifteen miles in all directions to forage for food. People like to watch them feeding. Great blue herons are often seen hunting on lakeshores, where they stand still or walk slowly, then suddenly extend their necks to grab small fish, frogs, birds, and aquatic insects with their bills. They can feed in deeper water by plunging or swimming, and can also hunt on land for small mammals such as mice and chipmunks.

Great egrets feed mostly in ponds and wetlands. They forage in shallow water for small fish and amphibians, but also on dry land for insects, reptiles, and small mammals. Cormorants feed in lakes, diving and swimming underwater to catch fish, and can stay submerged up to seventy seconds.

The most important rookeries, or nesting colonies, for the above mentioned species in the seventeen-county region between the Twin Cities and the St. Cloud area are at Pigs Eye Island, on the Mississippi River south of St. Paul; near Shakopee in the Minnesota Valley National Wildlife Refuge; and on Coney Island.

© Susan Gottberg | Dreamstime.com

August

August is the month of light winds. It is normally a sunny month and most often lacks the extreme heat of July. It's when we feast on sweet corn and garden-ripe tomatoes, listen to cicadas buzzing on warm days, pick ripe wild chokecherries, and watch the swallows line up on utility wires in preparation for migration. Garden plants now blooming nicely include phlox, hostas, giant sunflowers, canna lilies, cosmos, and zinnias. Canoe trips, tubing in streams, swimming, and pontoon-boat excursions are all enhanced by the warm water conditions.

READING THE LANDSCAPE

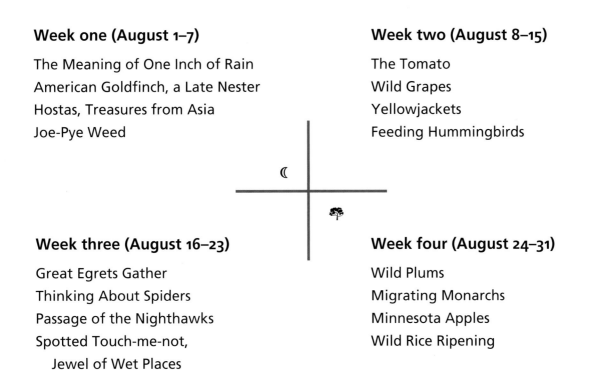

Week one (August 1–7)

The Meaning of One Inch of Rain
American Goldfinch, a Late Nester
Hostas, Treasures from Asia
Joe-Pye Weed

Week two (August 8–15)

The Tomato
Wild Grapes
Yellowjackets
Feeding Hummingbirds

Week three (August 16–23)

Great Egrets Gather
Thinking About Spiders
Passage of the Nighthawks
Spotted Touch-me-not,
    Jewel of Wet Places

Week four (August 24–31)

Wild Plums
Migrating Monarchs
Minnesota Apples
Wild Rice Ripening

first week in august

For August 1 in Minneapolis/St. Paul the normal high temperature is 83°, and the normal low is 63°F. The record high is 101° set in 1988, and the record low is 46° set in 1842. The surface water temperatures of most Minnesota and Wisconsin lakes are in the 70s to low 80s.

Ragweeds, both common and great, with their green flowers begin shedding pollen into the air to be carried by the wind. In our part of the country, these ragweeds probably account for more hayfever symptoms than all other plants put together. Fields of blooming Canada goldenrod are becoming showy. Goldenrods do not cause hayfever as their pollen is heavy and sticky and is carried on the sides of insects rather than in the air. Purple loosestrife is at bloom peak in wetlands and wet ditches. Small pods are seen on common milkweed plants. Muskmelons and honeydew melons are ready to pick.

Raccoons, eastern chipmunks and gray squirrels take green acorns from bur oak trees. Flocks of Canada geese are flying and honking. House wrens continue to sing. Mourning doves now on their third clutches of eggs. Eastern bluebirds and American goldfinches feed their young nestlings. Birds commonly seen at birdbaths include house wrens, blue jays, Baltimore orioles, American robins, black-capped chickadees and gray catbirds. Northern cardinals sing until thirty minutes after sunset.

Beekeepers begin extracting honey. Monarch and eastern tiger swallowtail butterflies nectar on blazing-star and purple coneflowers. Soldier beetles appear on flowers of Canada goldenrod, black-eyed susan and more. When on a picnic or out in a boat, the fly that gives us the painful bites about our ankles is a stable fly, not a house fly. House flies have lapping mouth parts and so can't bite, though they are the infamous germ carriers. Insect sounds from snowy tree crickets, katydids, and black field crickets fill the night air.

Soybean fields across the southern third of the state have flowers and new pods, and sweet corn is being harvested for commercial processing. In southern and western Minnesota, potato farmers have begun the harvest, and big fields of sunflowers are in full-bloom. Wild rice, which grows naturally in the shallow lakes and streams of central and northern Minnesota, is in bloom. Black bears are feasting on ripe wild red raspberries and blueberries. Along the North Shore of Lake Superior, juneberries, pin cherries, red raspberries, and thimbleberries are ripe and offer us a taste of the wild; and showy blooming wildflowers include fireweed, pearly everlasting and flat-topped white aster.

scattered events

- **August 1, 2007** - There is drought over Minnesota. The most severe dryness is in a wide band running from southwest to northeast, and including northwest Wisconsin. The water level of Lake Minnetonka is down 15 inches from 3 months ago. The Mississippi River at Anoka has only 25 percent of its normal flow. Lawns are tan-brown and field corn is very stressed.

- **August 3, 1999** - At Walker, the surface temperature of Leech Lake is 76°, the second generation of banded purple butterflies is on the wing, common ragweed is starting to shed pollen, and fireweed and evening primrose are among the showy blooming roadside plants.

- **August 4, 2007** - We see some yellow foliage on boxelders, silver maples, eastern cottonwoods, native basswoods, and both black walnut and butternut trees. No doubt mostly from drought stress. Some yellow leaves are falling, a defense to survive drought.

- **August 6, 2006** – The first wild grapes are ripe; dozens of bird species relish this fruit. In south and central MN, the wild cucumber, an annual vine, has mounds of white blossoms.

This vine is a wildflower which grows up into trees and shrubs, and on fences.

■ **August 7, 2002** – Clusters of highbush cranberry fruit show much red. Monarch butterflies now aggregating in flower gardens and trees near Christ Chapel at Gustavus Adolphus College in St. Peter.

A Closer Look:
The Meaning of One Inch of Rain

© Stokerphoton | Dreamstime.com

Official daily precipitation records for the first week of August in the Twin Cities are all in the two-inch range. When we see parched corn and soybean fields, walk on crunchy lawns, and watch ponds drying up, most of us react by saying "what we need now is a good all-day soaking rain." That can happen but much of our growing season precipitation occurs during thunderstorms.

In an average year, thunderstorms will develop on 45 days in southern Minnesota and on about 30 days in northern Minnesota. The majority occur from May through September when 65 to 75 percent of our annual precipitation usually falls. Thunderstorms can bring high winds, hail, heavy downpours causing flooding, and even tornadoes, but most often they bring moderate amounts of rain to sustain natural communities, agriculture, and our city lawns and gardens.

About 90 percent of the moisture that falls on Minnesota is carried from ocean sources by moist air masses. The greatest amount of it comes from the Gulf of Mexico but a small portion originates in the Pacific Ocean. Local moisture sources, such as evaporation off lakes and transpiration from vegetation, are of less importance. We know that the annual precipitation in Minnesota varies from about 20 inches in the northwest to 32 inches in the southeast, and we are aware that our precious water resources are used over and over again because of the hydrologic or water cycle. So when its dry and our landscape needs "a good drink" we keep hoping that atmospheric conditions will come together to give us a good rain—one inch would be great.

Looking at the numbers, it's interesting to see what 1 inch of rain amounts to on an acre of land. An acre of ground contains 43,560 square feet—that's about one football field of surface. A rainfall of 1 inch over 1 acre would mean a total of 6,272,640 cubic inches of water. This is equal to 3,630 cubic feet of water. A cubic foot of water weighs about 62.4 pounds, so the weight of 1 inch over 1 acre of land would be 226,512 pounds. The weight of 1 U.S. gallon of pure water is 8.345 pounds. Therefore a rainfall of 1 inch over 1 acre of ground would mean 27,143 gallons of water.

A Closer Look:

American Goldfinch, a Late Nester

Widespread and numerous summer residents throughout most of the state, American goldfinches are also with us in winter flocks. Their natural range is large, extending from coast to coast and from northern Mexico into southern Canada. American goldfinches add a definite liveliness to open country with their yellow and black coloring, their roller coaster flights through the air, and their sweet songs of "Just-look-at-me! Just-look-at-me." The familiar "wild canary" is mostly a seed eater, but also eats some berries and insects. They come to our feeding stations for sunflower seeds and thistle seeds. For a number of years up to 1964, when the common loon was selected as the symbol of the northwoods and our lakes, the American goldfinch was the Minnesota state bird.

Photo: David Brislance

The American goldfinch waits for nesting until July or August, when most other songbirds have finished raising their young and some species have begun their southward migrations. Then a good supply of wild seeds, especially thistle seeds, can be counted on. Nearly all seed-eating birds feed their nestlings insects, but these goldfinches nourish their 4 to 6 young with seeds that have been shelled and partially predigested. Both parents fill their crops with seeds and maybe a few insects. After a while they regurgitate them into the open mouths of their hungry babies. Carrying such a "mouthful," a parent can feed every nestling, instead of the usual one or two, with each return to the nest.

The female selects the nest site, usually bordering on or in a field. She builds a nest of woven plant fibers lined with thistledown or milkweed down, 1 to 60 feet off the ground in a shrub or tree. Some nests have been found close to the ground in thistle plants. The female incubates the eggs for about 13 days and the young leave the nest 11 to 16 days after hatching.

A Closer Look:
Hostas, Treasures from Asia

Numerous hostas are now blooming and some of the stalks of flowers are very

Photo: John Toren

showy, based on color, size and quantity of individual flowers. Hummingbirds are often attracted to the flowers. A few of the hosta plants are known for their fragrant blossoms. In general, hostas are hardy herbaceous perennials for cool, moist, shady places. Also known as funkia and plantain lilies, hostas are probably best known for their foliage, which rises 6 inches to 3 feet from a central crown in a remarkable range of colors, forms, sizes, and textures.

Hostas are native to China, Korea, and Japan, and have for centuries been an important element in Japanese garden architecture. They were first imported to Europe in the late 1700s and made their way to North America by the mid-1800s. Belonging to the lily family, Liliaceae, the genus name Hosta commemorates Nicolaus T. Host, an Austrian physician. Today there are more than fifty known species and thousands of cultivated varieties (cultivars) of hostas, many of which are available to Minnesota gardeners. If you want to see a wide range of species and cultivars showing their long spikes of funnel-shaped lilac-blue to white flowers, this is a great time to visit the Hosta Glade at the Minnesota Landscape Arboretum. You'll also enjoy the many types of leaves, from cool-green to blue, and from small and rounded to very large and lance-shaped; and get ideas for companion plantings of perennials in the huge hosta display garden.

If you are a beginning gardener or just thinking about planting a few hostas in your yard, it may be interesting for you to know that most hostas are sturdy, long-lived (25 years plus) reliable plants that grow quite rapidly and are relatively maintenance free. Hostas are easy to grow. They like light to medium shade. Most hostas will survive in deep shade, but the plants and individual leaves will be smaller. They thrive in rich, well-drained soil, are quite resistant to disease, and almost pest free. Also, they are extremely easy to propagate through division.

Plant hostas any time during the growing season, especially if they are potted. Be sure to water thoroughly each week. Planted clumps can be left undisturbed for years, or can be divided annually to increase quantities of plants. Divide hostas in the spring just before or as growth starts.

A Closer Look: Joe-Pye Weed

Joe-Pye weed, *Eupatorium maculatum*, a native wildflower, has made its way into home gardens and landscapes where tall plants are desired. This robust perennial can grow to a height of about 7 feet, but usually we see 3 to 5 foot Joe-Pye weeds growing in wetlands, especially  wet meadows near ponds and streams. The purplish flowerheads are in a flattish cluster. One guide book likens the flower color to crushed raspberries. The toothed leaves are generally in whorls of 4 or 5, and the stem is often spotted with purple.

After looking through piles of wildflower books, I finally found a likely answer to the question: Who was Joe Pye? He was probably a Native American living in New England who used the "weed" in some concoction as a treatment for typhoid fever, possibly because the plant could make people sweat profusely. He must have had some success for the plant has borne his name for more than three centuries.

Joe-Pye weed is blooming nicely in wetlands now, along with boneset and spotted touch-me-not. It is thought of as a transition plant from the midsummer's white of cow parsnip and Queen Anne's lace and rose-pink of swamp milkweed to the golden-yellows of goldenrods. So it serves almost as a harbinger of the cooler weather to come. If you mark the seasons with the progression of blooming wildflowers, like I do, you might shiver a bit in the heat of August when you see Joe-Pye weed. But actually Joe-Pye weed's season is quite long and they start to bloom in the last part of July.

Week two (August 8-15)

Ripe wild grapes offer hikers a refreshing snack. Wild chokecherries are at their peak of ripeness. It's the height of bloom for wild cucumber, the annual vine with upright clusters of white flowers. Joe-pye weed and boneset bloom nicely in wetland spots. On prairies, both Indian grass and big bluestem grass have grown to 5 or 6 feet and are shedding pollen. Both butternut and black walnut trees are showing some yellow leaflets as in an early preview of fall color. Bur oak acorns fall in numbers, and people report hearing them hitting rooftops.

It's time to look for more ruby-throated hummingbirds visiting area flower gardens and sugar water feeders. These are early migrants coming from up-north. Purple martins, the largest member of the swallow family, are lined up on utility lines as they prepare for migration.

The nests of the bald-faced hornet, the original paper-maker, are growing, layer by layer. These nests look like gray footballs up in trees. The second generation of monarch butterflies is on the wing.

Garden roses continue to bloom in profusion. It's the peak time for sun-ripe tomatoes. Gardeners are busy harvesting celery, green peppers, onions, carrots, beets, potatoes, tomatoes, muskmelons, cucumbers, acorn squash, zucchini, cabbages, watermelons, and sweet corn. Spinach, radish, and leaf lettuce seeds may be planted in gardens for a fall crop. Early season apples now ripe include Williams' Pride, Oriole, Viking, Mantet, and Zestar.

The third crop of alfalfa is being cut in southern Minnesota. In the southern and western part of the state the harvest of oats and winter wheat is at its peak.

scattered events

- **August 8, 1998** - Families of barn swallows line up on wires. State Fair apples and Parker pears are ripe. The surface temperature of Gull Lake, near Nisswa, is 74°F.

- **August 9, 2007** - A Park Point in Duluth, 16 migrating warbler species, including Nashville, yellow, and golden-winged, were observed. Lake Superior water level is down about 18 inches from normal.

- **August 13, 1995** - The first ripe Red Baron apples can be picked. Dahlias and morning glories bloom in gardens. The surface water of Lake Waconia is 80°F. Evening grosbeaks returned to a Grygla area feeding station after being gone all summer. Statewide, 56 percent of winter wheat and 46 percent of oats have been harvested.

- **August 15, 1999** - White snakeroot begins blooming. Common grackles and red-winged blackbirds are now in large flocks. First ripe Red Baron apples. The wild common elderberry shrubs have ripe fruit which is an important source of summer food for gray catbirds, brown thrashers, and dozens of other bird species. The purple martins left Stony Point, Leech Lake, headed for South America.

- **August 15, 2006** - Large numbers of migrating common nighthawks were observed between Britt and Virginia, and over Ironton.

Photo: Jim Gilbert

A Closer Look:
The Tomato

Like corn, potatoes, peanuts, and the pumpkin, the delectable tomato is an American gift to the world. Tomatoes are the most versatile, prolific, and easiest to grow of all vegetables. "Tomatoes can be prepared in so many delicious ways that one can eat them every day and not get tired of them," George Washington Carver wrote. They can be fresh-sliced, juiced, stuffed, boiled, baked, fried, canned, frozen, or dried. They can be served as appetizers, desserts, or main courses, and made into pizza and spaghetti sauce. The U.S. Department of Agriculture reported in the

1970s that four out of five people preferred tomatoes to any other home-grown food. The same is probably still true. It's no wonder people are planting tomatoes everywhere—on front lawns, on patios in pots, in window boxes, and even high up on apartment rooftops and on houseboats.

A ripe tomato has mature seeds, so it's technically ripe from the plant's point of view. It's also at its peak of juiciness. A garden-ripe tomato still warm from the sun is a taste treat no one should miss. It should be noted that tomatoes are low in calories but rich in vitamins. Only sweet corn equals the tomato in taste when picked fresh from the garden. All vegetables are better fresh-picked, but fresh-picked corn and tomatoes taste like different species related only by name to the usually bland store-bought versions.

Any good garden soil will grow tomatoes. Experienced gardeners know that too much fertilizer or manure close to the plants makes them more likely to produce more foliage and less fruit. The tomato is a lover of sunshine and warm weather. It is grown as a tender annual and is one of the first plants to be damaged by a fall frost. With comparatively little care the tomato plants yield well and produce, over a fairly long season, a succession of delicious fruits. The fruits are usually red, but varieties with yellow, pink, and white fruits are also grown. Tomatoes come in a medley of tastes and sizes, and even some of the old-fashioned varieties that have the best flavors are becoming more readily available. There are several hundred varieties, in fact, some having marble-size fruit and others with fruits weighing a pound or more. A single tomato plant can produce 6 to 50 pounds of usable fruits, depending on the size and health of the plant and on whether the local temperatures are favorable for pollination.

The parent species or wild ancestor of the common garden tomato is *Lycopersicum esculentum,* a perennial that's native to western South America. It's a member of the the potato family with strong-smelling foliage. This native tomato was a staple of Central and South American Indians long before it was introduced to southern Europe in the early part of the sixteenth century. Tomatoes were grown in Virginia by Thomas Jefferson in 1781, but they were largely unknown in North America as an edible vegetable until the 1820s, probably because people thought the fruit was toxic. It is true that all parts of the tomato plant *except* the fruits are toxic, containing dangerous alkaloids that cause severe digestive upset.

Some people argue about whether the tomato is a fruit or a vegetable. It is commonly grouped with the vegetables because of its use in salads and soups, but botanically it is a fruit or berry.

A Closer Look:
Wild Grapes

At this time and through September, ripe wild grapes offer hikers and other outdoor enthusiasts a refreshing snack. These grapes are eaten by more than sixty species of birds including wood ducks, ruffed grouse, and northern cardinals, plus such mammals as opossums, raccoons, and black bears. The wild grape fruit serves as a very important wildlife food.

The wild grape (*Vitis riparia*), also called frost grape or river-bank grape, is found throughout Minnesota. It is a vigorous, woody climber with forked tendrils. It's native on riverbanks and in moist rich woodlands, often climbing into tall trees. The leaves are large, heart-shaped, usually three-lobed, and have coarse teeth. The natural range of wild grape is from Montana to Nova Scotia, south to Texas and Tennessee. It is frequently planted to cover fences and arbors, or for fruits that are prized for jellies.

The fruits are in dense bunches of berries, each about ⅜-inch in diameter, and dark purplish-blue in color. In addition to fresh eating and jelly-making, the berries can be used to make juice, preserves, pie, and wine. Actually, wild grapes can be used in any recipe that calls for grapes, although they usually need more sweetening than cultivated grapes. Young leaves are also edible, as are the tendrils that my students call monkey tails.

A Closer Look:
Yellowjackets

By mid-August yellowjackets have become very numerous. They can be bothersome, especially when we eat outdoors. These black-and-yellow paper wasps often gather as soon as food is spread out on a picnic table. They will also alight on a peach, an apple, or a cup of sweet lemonade you may be enjoying outside. Besides sampling our food, they may sting us if we're not careful. It's best not to swat them but rather play "like a tree" and move slowly.

I once attended a potluck lunch in late summer at a senior center. Food dishes were spread out on two long tables positioned

end-to-end, covering about 16 feet. Almost immediately, yellowjackets arrived to taste the potato salads, ham sandwiches, and other foods. An intuitive woman brought out a portable electric fan, hooked it to a long electrical extension cord, and set the fan on one end of the long line of food. The fanned air sent the food fragrances—and the yellowjackets—away.

These small animals are social insects, and their nests are in underground holes, in burrows made by chipmunks or other animals, or at least near the ground in stumps or decaying logs. The nests are made of paper. Long before humans discovered how to make paper, yellowjackets and other vespid wasps made their own by chewing up wood very finely and mixing it with their saliva. Try to encourage neighbors not to destroy these very active underground nests we observe in August. The wasps will not do

anybody harm if we respect them, and they will patrol our yards for what we may call "pests"—other insects. Also, they sip sweet nectar from flowers and so are pollinators.

The yellowjacket life cycle is much like that of the bumble bees. A mated female overwinters under loose bark or in some other cranny, comes out when the weather warms in spring, and makes the beginning of a nest. She rears a few not-to-be-mated daughters who then gather food (usually flies, caterpillars and other insects) and attend to household chores while the mother devotes herself largely to laying eggs from which hatch more females that do not mate. Toward the end of the season more daughters are produced, and also sons. Then the mother dies, the not-mated daughters die, the sons die, and the mated daughters go into hibernation to repeat the cycle.

A Closer Look:
Feeding Hummingbirds

Over a large part of Minnesota, ruby-throated hummingbirds have begun their feeding frenzy; it's time to put out several feeders, widely spaced. The nesting season is over for this species and the population is nearly double what it was in June. Also, we in the southern part of the state are noticing more than twice as many ruby-throats nectaring in our gardens on hollyhocks, petunias, and fuchsias, and coming to feeders. These are no doubt migrants coming from up north.

If you see a hummingbird in your yard, try hanging a sugar-water feeder near a bed of flowers and another one in some other location. Studies of hummingbird feeding habits show that they gather sizable numbers of small insects from the flowers they visit for nectar. Insects are an important part of their diet. Feeders for hummingbirds are available at wild bird stores and lawn and garden centers. Homemade feeders need be no more than a glass jar tilted at a 45° angle, hung in a tree or from a post, and filled with sugar water. You may be surprised at the other species of birds that drink sugar water. Baltimore orioles, some woodpeckers, and some warblers are among those fond of the sweet liquid.

The recommended mixture is one part granulated white sugar to four parts water. Boil for two or three minutes. Boiling helps retard fermentation and makes the syrup a proper consistency. Store the sugar water solution in a refrigerator. Pour in fresh solution to feeders that are empty and have been cleaned. Rinse the feeder inside and out with water and scrub with a stiff brush to remove any dirt or sticky spots to help halt fermentation and mold growth. No need to add red food-coloring, some of which is not safe. It is believed that red color helps

attract the birds' attention, but some observers say you can't prove it. Hummers are also drawn to orange, yellow, and other colors, so use a feeder constructed with red or other colorful materials.

Week three (Aug 16-23)

We have reached the time of year when buckets of zucchini, cucumbers, and tomatoes appear on our back steps, put there by some unknown benefactor. Backyard and wild plums are ripening. Cultivated grapes are in their ripening stages. The best time to seed a lawn in Minnesota is between August 15 and September 10. Petunias, geraniums, cosmos, marigolds, snapdragons, and zinnias are some of the showy blooming garden annuals.

Watch for aggregations of monarch butterflies clustering on trees, a sign that their migration is beginning. Snapping turtle eggs are now hatching. White-tailed deer bucks are still in velvet. Cloth strips about 4 inches wide and 2 feet long, soaked with perfume and tied to tall stakes, will help keep deer away from vegetable and flower gardens. During warm nights the snowy tree crickets sound like sleigh bells.

Canada goldenrod and Jerusalem artichoke are showy blooming wildflowers. Both great and common ragweeds shed big quantities of pollen; we have arrived at the peak of the ragweed pollen season.

Migrating birds observed include chimney swifts, common nighthawks, red-breasted nuthatches, Franklin's gulls, and several warbler and shorebird species. Swallows line up on utility wires, sometimes by the hundreds, as they stage for migration.

Pagoda dogwood fruit is ripe and relished by robins, cedar waxwings, and other birds.

The harvest of southern Minnesota sweet corn for processing is in full-swing. About thirty-thousand black bears live in the northern part of the state. They are now feasting on ripe wild raspberries, blueberries, sarsaparilla berries, and other native fruits.

scattered events

■ **August 16, 2005** - In the garden, fall-bearing raspberry canes now producing ripe fruit. Common nighthawk migration begins.

■ **August 16, 2007** - In the Lutsen/Grand Marais area, large-leaved asters bloom, wild red raspberry and juneberry picking is good, and there is some fall color on paper birches (sunny-yellow) and mountain maples (reds and yellows).

■ **August 19, 1998** - Beacon, State Fair, Red Free, Paula Red, Williams' Pride, and Wealthy are some of the apple varieties which are being picked. The surface temperature of Green Lake at Spicer is 75˚F.

■ **August 20, 2006** - At Linnaeus Arboretum on the Gustavus Adolphus College campus in St. Peter, highbush cranberry shrubs have clusters of mostly bright red fruit, the first wild plums are ripe, and both annual cicadas and scissors grinder cicadas call.

■ **August 21, 2007** - After four days with good rains and cool temperatures, lawns have turned from tan-brown to lush green.

■ **August 22, 1998** - Among the many flowers attracting ruby-throated humming-birds is the wild spotted touch-me-not of wet places. Thousands of monarch butterflies gather in a green ash tree grove near Cologne.

A Closer Look:

Great Egrets Gather

In the heron family the terms "heron" and "egret" are applied loosely, although most egrets are white. The great egret is a sleek, long-necked, snow-white wader, about forty inches long with a pointed yellow bill and black stilt-like legs and feet. Wingspan is about 4½ feet. Great egrets are a foot shorter than great blue herons but both fly with their necks folded onto their backs and both nest in colonies.

© Arindom Chowdhury | Dreamstime.com"

During August and early September we often see a dozen or two, or even more of these majestic birds together, standing like statues along the edges of lakes, marshes, and swamps. Concentrations of a hundred or more birds have been reported during late August in southern Minnesota. But it wasn't always that way. The range of the great egret continues to expand. Historically, it was listed as a casual late-summer visitant beginning in the early 1930s in the extreme southern part of the state. It wasn't until the 1950s that it became a regular spring and fall migrant and summer resident in southern Minnesota. Great egrets have gradually spread northward, and nesting was first observed at Agassiz National Wildlife Refuge in 1980 when three nests were found.

There is another part to the great egret story. In the late 1800s it became fashionable for ladies in places like New York City to adorn their hats with flowing plumes from wild birds. But as the popularity of plumed hats grew, so did the outcry against them from alarmed citizens, some of whom saw egrets and other species being shot on their breeding grounds. All the same, by 1900 the great egret population had been devastated by hunting. Their recovery was largely thanks to efforts by the Audubon Society, newly formed at that time.

The diet of the great egret is made up of insects, fish, frogs, and other animals. Nests are platforms of sticks in a shrub or tree, usually 20 to 40 feet above ground or water. Eggs, 3 to 4 in number, are incubated for about 25 days by both sexes. (The sexes look alike.) The young leave the nest 6 to 7 weeks after hatching. Wintering areas include southern states, Mexico, and Central America.

A Closer Look:
Thinking About Spiders

Spiders become more noticeable in August. We become aware of their great diversity and encounter more webs, although we know that not all spiders construct webs. Those that do not build webs include wolf spiders—large, hairy swift nocturnal hunters that chase down their prey; crab spiders, which ambush pollinating insects on flowers, usually in the daytime; and jumping spiders, which, as their name suggests, leap onto prey, usually during daylight.

Most familiar to the majority of people are the orb web spiders of which the common garden spider is an example. These spiders weave large, vertical, conspicuous open webs with distinctive spokes. However, money spiders are probably more significant in control of insect populations. These small and inconspicuous creatures weave dense, often gossamer-like webs of many shapes in nooks and crannies of rock formations, in brush piles, around branches of plants, and in our homes. The cobwebs we see are most often those of money spiders.

When young spiders emerge from their eggs, they already are adults in miniature. The mother spider cares for her eggs and watches over her young with as much diligence as the more sophisticated mammals.

It might appear that there are more spiders in August than in early summer because they become much larger and more noticeable after going through several molts.

Spiders energetically pursue, seize, and consume large numbers of insects. I often think about the numbers of tiny animals that become food for other tiny animals in our backyard. It's not a peaceful scene. But, without spiders, we would be overrun by insects. It is estimated that each year spiders eat enough insects to outweigh the entire human population. If you think about how many mosquitoes it would take to equal your own weight (about 200,000 mosquitoes per pound), perhaps you would be a little friendlier to spiders.

A Closer Look:

Passage of the Nighthawks

Anytime after mid-August and into early September, naturalists and birders are aware that it's nighthawk migration time. In afternoons and early evenings, flocks of these blue jay-size, dark-colored birds with long pointed, white patched wings can be seen gliding, diving, and circling, feeding on insects in the air and definitely heading south. Having been summer residents throughout Minnesota, the common nighthawks are on their way to winter in South America.

FIRST MIGRATING COMMON NIGHTHAWKS (TWIN CITIES)	
2007 - August 16	2002 - August 21
2006 - August 16	2001 - August 23
2005 - August 16	2000 - August 18
2004 - August 24	1999 - August 24
2003 - August 17	1998 - August 19

During fall migration, sometimes as many as a thousand common nighthawks are seen in a flock. Large migration flights have been recorded in Duluth where in late afternoons a thousand birds per hour could be observed between August 18 and 25.

The common nighthawk is a wide-ranging aerial forager that is found regularly over many habitat types including prairie, cropland, woodlands, wetlands, and residential and business districts of towns and cities.

Nighthawks have a tiny bill but wide, gaping mouth. The birds sweep up in their large mouths all types of flying insects from large moths and beetles to the tiniest of flies and mosquitoes. The remains of 34 May beetles were found in one nighthawk stomach.

The magical date we look into the sky and spot the first loose flock of nighthawks wheeling by for me marks the beginning of autumn. It's true that in our social community, Labor Day, about 2 weeks away, marks the official end of summer. It's is also true that the autumnal equinox in the third week of September marks the end of celestial summer. But, August slowly cools toward September and autumn. The time after the first common nighthawks move through is one of the best times to be out of doors, enjoying the cool fresh weather fronts as they pass by, giving us crystalline late-summer weather. The lakes are still warm enough for refreshing swims, the insect chorus is great, and there is plenty of food for wild creatures.

A Closer Look:
Spotted Touch-me-not, Jewel of Wet Places

The spotted touch-me-not or jewelweed (*Impatiens capensis*), is a native annual wildflower of moist, shaded areas from Saskatchewan to Newfoundland, south to Oklahoma and Alabama. It is an important nectar plant for hummingbirds and insects. The three-foot plant with succulent, watery stems grows in wetlands, along streams, lakes, and other wet shady spots throughout Minnesota.

Spotted touch-me-not is known for its bright orange flowers, spotted with reddish-brown, that can be described as pendent jewels that hang at the ends of slender stalks. Each flower has a forward-pointing spur that makes it nicely balanced. The plant is also called jewelweed because water droplets on its fragile, oval, toothed leaves shine like tiny jewels. If leaves are submerged in water, they will take on a silvery sheen.

A mature banana-shaped seed capsule will explode to discharge its seeds when touched, hence the source of one of the common names, touch-me-not. What is left is a curly spring-like appendage in its place.

A fun plant to grow in wildflower gardens, the jewelweed requires a moist soil and some shade. Propagation is by seeds sown as soon as they are ripe. Plants will self-sow once they are established, so volunteer seedlings will keep the planting going if conditions are right. The plant blooms from July to frost.

Young shoots of jewelweed, up to about 6 inches, can be boiled for 10 to 15 minutes in two changes of water and served as a cooked green. Do not drink the cooking water. Washing with the raw juice from the crushed stems and leaves should sooth the sting of nettles and help prevent the rash from poison ivy.

Week four (Aug 24-31)

Vegetable gardeners are harvesting beans, beets, carrots, eggplants, ground cherries, leeks, muskmelons, watermelons, summer squash, potatoes, winter squash, cabbages, tomatoes, sweet corn, and more. Beacon, State Fair, and Paula Red apples are ripe. Concord grapes ripe or nearly so. Beekeepers extract honey. Dahlias, glads, and garden roses bloom nicely.

With very few young birds and fewer eggs around, striped skunks eat grasshoppers and beetles and larvae of insects, and whatever else they can find. The young ones, born this spring, must disperse now to make it on their own. They have never been taught not to cross highways at night.

Juvenile male wood ducks have begun taking on adult plumage. Barn swallows line up on wires in family groups. White-tailed deer fawns have grown quite large and are losing their spots. Tiny, newly-hatched snapping turtles head for ponds or lakes.

Indian-pipe is showy white in forests. Giant puffball mushrooms, some basketball-size, can be found. Touches of red fall color now noticed on Virginia creeper vine and sumac shrub foliage. Native basswood tree leaves are showing some yellow autumn color. Wild plums are ripe and good eating. Jack-in-the-pulpit and prickly ash berries have become bright red.

Migrating monarch butterflies can be seen flying south, one by one. Honey bees, bumble bees, and ruby-throated hummingbirds feed on spotted touch-me-not flowers in wetlands.

In southern Minnesota, many soybean fields show some yellow as plants mature, and the chopping of field corn for silage begins. Asters, goldenrods, and tall sunflowers bloom nicely along northern Minnesota roadsides. Young loons have begun to take on some adult colors; their parents still watch over them.

scattered events

- **August 24, 1999** - Wild cucumber at bloom peak. Wild chokecherries at peak of ripeness in northwestern Minnesota.

- **August 25, 1996** - Many ripe wild grapes available. Statewide, 93 percent of the oats, 47 percent of spring wheat and 5 percent of the potato crop has been harvested.

- **August 25, 2007** - In Duluth, 20 warbler species are migrating through. An observer, sitting on a dock at Black Water Lake near Hackensack, counted 624 common nighthawks, migrating to the southeast, during one hour ending at 8:30 p.m.

- **August 27, 2005** - 3,310 common night-hawks were counted migrating over Hawk Ridge in Duluth.

- **August 27, 2007** - Lake Superior water level is 20 inches below normal.

- **August 28, 1998** - Orb spider webs with water droplets very showy this morning. Chestnut and Cranberry crabapples, and both Alderman and Mount Royal plums, now ripe. Monarch butterflies are on the move, heading south. Southern Minnesota farmers have begun cutting, raking, and baling the fourth crop of alfalfa.

A Closer Look:
Wild Plums

Photo: Arlene Gardinier

Now is the time to gather the ripe, red-and-yellow fruit from American wild plum trees. The plums can be eaten raw, cooked as sauce, or made into a jam or jelly. They were used extensively by Native Americans who often dried them for winter use by cutting them open, removing the center stones, and spreading them out in the sunlight.

Thickets of wild plum are common throughout southern Minnesota. The trees grow to a height of about 15 feet and have white flowers that bloom in the first half of May.

The American wild plum is native from Massachusetts to Manitoba and south to Florida and New Mexico. This species is the origin of many cultivated plums grown in Minnesota and other areas; in some cases directly by selection, and others by hybridization with other species.

A Closer Look:
Migrating Monarchs

Photo: Jim Gilbert

Of all the autumn migrants, maybe the most remarkable are the monarch butterflies, many of which are still emerging from the chrysalis stage at this time. For a few more weeks, up to about mid-October, we will see the black and orange beauty of their wings over prairies and meadows, and in our gardens. But for the next two weeks the monarch migration is at its peak. Incredible as it may seem, these fragile wisps of life are as successful at migration as most birds.

August is monarch butterfly month in Minnesota, where this insect was chosen to be our official state butterfly in the year 2000. We see them between May and October, but it's in later summer, when their population is the greatest, that we are most aware of this wonder of the insect world Monarchs are now seen roosting in groups, sometimes masses of them. These obvious aggregations tell us that their migration has begun.

The monarch is probably one of our most familiar insects. It can easily be seen because of its colors and large size; in addition, no butterfly is more widely distributed throughout the United States. Monarchs are bright orange and black, and have a four-inch wingspan. They travel individually, not in flocks. When hundreds or thousands are seen flying together, it's probably because of the sudden departure from a roosting location, where they had spent the night during migration—or perhaps several days and nights due to stormy weather.

Monarchs will fly anywhere from ground level up to seven thousand feet, the cruising altitude of many light airplanes. In migration, they save energy by riding thermals—rising air masses that lift them to favorable altitudes. Their soaring skills are so efficient that many arrive in Mexico fat and healthy, having gained, not lost, weight on the trip.

Traces of the mineral magnetite, the same material used in compass needles, are found in monarch butterflies. The magnetite might explain some of the monarch's navigational abilities. Essentially, they have little compasses in their bodies and may find their destination by using the Earth's magnetic fields.

Migrant monarchs can live up to 11 months; non-migrants live for about 30 days. During the summer there may be two or three generations of new monarchs, thus increasing the population of the final migrating monarchs.

I have been tagging monarchs since the 1970s. One individual monarch butterfly tagged by two junior high school students and me on September 6, 1975, on the Minnesota Landscape Arboretum prairie, was found on January 18, 1976, by Dr. Fred Urquhart, in an over-wintering colony in the volcanic mountains of Mexico; a straight line distance of about 1,750 miles. Ever since that time I have been concerned about the protection of the wintering monarchs. Fred and his wife, Norah, researchers from the Zoology Department, University of Toronto, Canada, are credited with locating the overwintering sites of the monarch butterfly in a remote area of Mexico. Each year about 100 million monarch butterflies make the journey from the eastern United States and southeastern Canada to the fir forests in the mountains northwest of Mexico City to take shelter for the winter.

A Closer Look:
Minnesota Apples

Between late July and October, more than a hundred Minnesota-grown varieties of apples ripen. Apple connoisseurs now begin to take notice of these numerous varieties, each with its own special flavor and texture. It's time for picking Beacon and State Fair apples; and soon Red Baron and Wealthy apples will be at their peak of ripeness, followed by other such favorites as McIntosh, Sweet Sixteen, Honeycrisp, Haralson, and Regent.

The apple provides a sweet touch that also is healthy and does not hurt the teeth. A medium-sized apple about 3 inches in diameter, besides being 85 percent water, has about 70 food energy calories, 20 grams of carbohydrate, and traces of many vitamins and minerals. In addition, the mild acid of the apple is effective in cleaning tooth surfaces and leaving a pleasant taste in the mouth.

Scientists believe the earliest apples to

be cultivated grew wild in the mountains of southwestern Asia—probably in the area between the Black and Caspian seas. The first Minnesota full-sized apple variety to withstand cold winters, bear fruit regularly, and have good keeping qualities and flavor was developed in the 1860s by Peter Gideon, who lived near the south shore of Lake Minnetonka. He was a self-educated horticulturist who moved to Minnesota in 1853.

Gideon's apple, named Wealthy after his wife, Wealthy Hull, ripens in late August and is still widely grown throughout Minnesota. This variety is good for fresh eating, pies, sauces, freezing, and baking. Since then, he and other horticulturists have developed many varieties of apples suitable to our climate and the taste of apple eaters.

A Closer Look:
Wild Rice Ripening

Wild rice is the only cereal grain native to North America, and was an important food to Native Americans in the Upper Midwest long before the arrival of European immigrants. It is estimated to have provided 25 percent of the total calories in their diet. This water-loving grass produces a nutty-flavored seed that ducks also love to eat. The Native Ojibwe moved to ricing camps along the shorelines of lakes and rivers in late August. They looked at the wild rice harvest as a ritual of both social and religious significance, symbolizing the peak of the natural cycles of earth, air, water, and sun, as well as providing food.

Traditional ricing is still being done today. It takes two people. One sits in the back of the canoe and pushes it through the rice stalks with a long pole. The other sits in the front facing the stern, with two rounded sticks, each about 3 feet long. With one stick the ricer in the bow gathers and bends the rice stalks over the middle of the canoe, before knocking the rice kernels into the bottom of the canoe with the other one.

Ricers return to the same stand several times over the course of time, because wild rice ripens gradually, and only 10 percent of the fruit head is mature at any one time.

Once rice was gathered it was dried on sheets of birch bark, then parched over a fire to loosen the kernels from the husks. Then someone would "dance" lightly on the rice. Finally the rice was winnowed—tossed into the wind, which would blow the lighter husks away while the heavier kernels fell to the ground.

It's important to dry the rice thoroughly (parch) after harvest, and rub it gently to break up hunks before winnowing. Wash the rice in cold water to remove the smoky flavor, and then prepare like brown rice.

Photo: Eli Sagor

The Minnesota DNR and various American Indian governments manage wild rice and regulate its harvest. Today it is Minnesota's official state grain and continues to be a popular food item. Personally, I enjoy wild rice soups. The seeds of wild rice contain an antioxidant that some people believe might help reduce the chances of getting cancer.

Wild rice, *Zizania aquatica*, grows in shallow water, usually less than 3 feet deep, and is found from Minnesota to Maine, north into southern Canada, and south into Missouri and Texas. In Minnesota it can be found in rivers and on sandy lake bottoms, mainly in the central and northern part of the state, but also down into the extreme southeast. Populations of wild rice have been declining for many years in Minnesota. Scientists are trying to learn more about how wild rice grows and why it's becoming less common.

Being an annual grass, wild rice has seed fall in the autumn and takes root under water in the spring. In summer the shoots grow up above the surface, and the plant takes on the appearance of green grass growing in the water—which is what it is. In late summer, when its seeds are mature and the plant stands several feet above the water surface, it resembles oats or wheat.

Starting in late August, the seeds ripen gradually from the top down and fall into the water. Because it is an annual, people who harvest the rice in the wild let some seeds fall into the water so wild rice populations can survive.

September

The green prime is passing, and we are coming up to the grand finale of the growing season. The first few days of the month may be summer-like, but the maples, sumacs, cottonwoods, and other trees will soon be showing their autumn splendor. The swimming season ends, steam rises from lakes on cold mornings, and frost can strike anytime now. Tomato plants must be covered if frost threatens.

Dozens of apple varieties become ripe. The last of the sweet corn is harvested. Chrysanthemum and garden rose flowers are superb. Black walnut and Ohio buckeye nuts drop. Mushroom watching is excellent. Baltimore orioles, ruby-throated hummingbirds, and monarch butterflies are among the migrants leaving.

READING THE LANDSCAPE

Week one (September 1–7)

Soybeans
Butternut Fruit
Baltimore Orioles Depart
Fields of Goldenrod

Week two (September 8–15)

Dahlias
Hummingbird Moths
First Frost
Duluth's Hawk Ridge

Week three (September 16–23)

The Ohio Buckeye Tree
Sumacs
Honeycrisp, the Minnesota State Apple
Yellow-rumped Warblers

Week four (September 24–30)

Minnesota's Native Cranberries
Why Garden or Feed Birds?
Dark-eyed Juncos
Sugar Maple Trees

first week in september

The commercial and garden grape harvest is underway. It's the peak time for beekeepers to extract honey. Wealthy apples and Chestnut crabapples are now ripe. Over-ripe apples attract red admiral and mourning cloak butterflies, and yellowjackets. New England asters begin to bloom, and the seven-foot Mexican sunflower garden plant has orange flowers. Both of these attract migrating monarch butterflies. A few late monarch caterpillars can be found on leaves of the common milkweed.

Giant puffballs can be found. The bright yellow-orange sulphur shelf fungus is seen on some stumps, logs and standing trees.

Acorns fall from red oaks and white oaks in numbers and become vital food for many animals, including wood ducks, wild turkeys, red-bellied woodpeckers, white-tailed deer, and black bears. Touches of red can be seen on sugar maple and sumac leaves. The mostly brown seeds of the boxelder give the impression of many dead leaves on the trees.

American crows can be seen in communal roosts again. Warbling vireos continue to be vocal. Male wood ducks have come into breeding plumage again. This is the last week that Baltimore orioles come to sugar water and grape jelly feeders in numbers; they are off to winter in Central America.

Woodchucks are busy foraging on plant

materials and storing up fat for hibernation. On September 1 in the Twin Cities, the normal high temperature is 77°F and the low is 56°F. Record high is 97°F, set in 1913, and the low is 36°F, recorded in 1974.

In the southern part of the state, many soybean fields are showing golden-yellow as the plants mature. The chopping of field corn for silage has begun, the sweet corn harvest continues, and alfalfa hay is being cut. Wild plums are at the peak of ripeness and good eating.

Along the North Shore of Lake Superior, flocks of cedar waxwings feed on the orange fruit from the mountain ash trees; warblers such as chestnut-sided and magnolia, and broad-winged and other hawks are moving through.

scattered events

- **September 2, 1998** - Virginia creeper vines are showing some red autumn foliage. Ripe wild grapes attract American crows. A steady stream of monarch butterflies is seen heading south over Gustavus Adolphus College in Saint Peter.

- **September 6, 1998** - Bur marigolds have showy yellow flowers. Swallows seen in long lines on utility wires. Statewide, 85 percent of the sweet corn is harvested, 29 percent of corn for silage has been cut, and 18 percent

of the potato crop is in.

- **September 6, 2001** - Wild plums at peak of ripeness. Jerusalem artichoke and Canada goldenrod are at overall bloom peak. Highbush cranberry shrubs have brilliant red fruit and European mountain ash fruit is radiant orange.

- **September 6, 2003** - First American coots are back on Lake Waconia for the fall season. Migrating shorebirds include semipalmated sandpipers and both lesser and greater yellowlegs.

- **September 7, 2002** - High of 92°F; first day above 90°F since July 31. Surface water temperatures of Twin Cities area lakes in the upper 70s and perfect for swimming. First raft of migrating American coots back on Lake Waconia.

A Closer Look:
Soybeans

It's September 4, 2007, and I drove from Waconia to St. Peter this morning. Fall semester classes began today at Gustavus Adolphus College, and I'm teaching two sections of ENV 101 (Environmental Studies, Interpreting the Autumn Landscape). From the car I noticed that Jerusalem artichoke is blooming and very showy, field corn chopping continues, lots of alfalfa hay is cut and waiting for baling, and soybean fields are in different stages of maturity. Some are still green, others show much golden-yellow foliage, and a few have plants that have lost most of their leaves.

My goal is to teach the Gustavus students to "read the landscape." The ENV 101 classes meet for two hours, Tuesdays and Thursdays, and most of our time will be spent out in the Linnaeus Arboretum, located on the south side of the campus, or in natural and agricultural areas around St. Peter. On this first day of class, the 26 students in each section learned that both great and common ragweeds were shedding pollen, Canada and other goldenrods are blooming but not shedding pollen, some barn swallows are still feeding their young, scissors-grinder and annual cicadas fill the air with distinctive sounds, and wild plum fruit tastes great. They also found out that a soybean field is located in the arboretum where someday we plan to have a fairly large restored tallgrass prairie. What I found out is that only two out of 52 students could identify a soybean plant, about the same number knew about ragweeds or cicadas or wild plums. Since a person sees what they are trained to see, or hears what they are trained to hear, the students soon became comfortable with the day and excited about what they were learning. This was a hot day with a high of 96° F in the afternoon.

In preparation for our next class meeting, the Gusties and I checked library resources and websites to learn more about soybeans so we could have a short discussion. What follows is a summary of what we learned.

Photo: John Toren

George Washington Carver and Henry Ford both called the soybean a miracle crop. That's still true today. Everything from lotions to cleaning products, ink, and plastics can be made with soy. Some city buses and government fleets run on soy biodiesel fuel. Farm animals are fed soybean meal. Many renewable products are made with soybeans, not to mention their importance as a reliable, abundant source of food for us. Soybeans aren't just tofu. There are breakfast shakes, baked goods, cooking oils, and salad dressings made using soy ingredients. Eating soy products may lead to a better diet low in saturated fat.

The soybean (*Glycine max*) is native to

China and Japan, belongs to the pea family, and is known in hundreds of varieties. Records five thousand years old mention its cultivation in eastern Asia, but there is no record of its first domestication. During the Chou Dynasty in China (1134–246 BC), the soybean was designated one of the five sacred grains, along with barley and others. Now it is one of the great agricultural crops of the world.

Cultivated soybeans are annual plants that may reach three feet or more in height. The leaves are trifoliate, and the small flowers are borne in clusters. The pods are hairy, about 2 inches long, and contain 2 to 4 seeds that have a delicious, slightly nutty flavor. Some varieties mature early; others require 150 days or more. Soil and climate requirements are about the same as for corn.

First introduced into the United States in 1804, it was not until the early 1900s that the soybean became a well-known farm plant. Now it's one our country's foremost crops, due to its adaptability to corn-belt agriculture, and also to vigorous research that has discovered more hidden values in the bean.

A Closer Look:
Butternut Fruit

Squirrels and humans are busy gathering falling butternuts. The seeds buried by the squirrels are sometimes forgotten or lost, thus facilitating reproduction. Butternut trees (*Juglans cinerea*, named and described by Linnaeus) are native from New Brunswick to Georgia and west to the Dakotas and Arkansas. In Minnesota the trees grow in rich forests and on the lower slopes of hills in the valleys of the Mississippi and St. Croix rivers. The tree seldom grows more than 40 feet tall. It has a thick trunk which branches into numerous limbs. The leaves are pinnately compound, each about 15 inches long with 11 to 17 leaflets.

What we notice about this southern Minnesota native is that by the first week in September many of the leaves are dingy-looking or have fallen or lost most of their leaflets. In fact, yellow fall color can be spotted on butternut trees by July 4.

Butternut's fruit, when it falls with the early autumn winds, is a little over 2 inches long, is oblong, pointed, greenish, and has sticky, rusty hairs on the husk that can leave a brown stain on our fingers. The husk contains an orange-yellow dye once used for coloring homespun clothing. The green outer husk of the nut is difficult to remove. It can be taken off with a hammer or by running a heavy object such as a car over it. After removing the husk, nuts should be dried for several months before cracking them to enjoy the edible kernels.

The butternut tree is an important member of the natural forest community, but we can also enjoy the sweet syrup or sugar made by boiling down its sap—though the yield is only a quarter that of the sugar maple. The wood is used in furniture, cabinet work, interior trim and wooden ware. It is still a favorite of the wood carver.

A Closer Look:

Baltimore Orioles Depart

The orioles are among the night-migrating birds. Like most temperate-zone birds, they begin their migrations because of the change in the length of daylight. For more than thirty years I have kept track of the spring arrival and the autumn departure of Baltimore orioles in the Lake Minnetonka and Twin Cities area. I have found that the first ones return on or close to May 1, and nearly all leave by the

photo: Rick Haley

end of the first week of September. At some feeding stations, dozens of Baltimore orioles will be coming for sugar water or grape jelly one early September day, and the next day, not a one. It seems quiet. We miss their orange and black colors but we also miss their songs—a rich melodic whistle, the pattern of which is extremely variable from one male to the next. Both sexes give a harsh scolding chatter when excited and the female's whistled call notes resemble the male's song in quality.

Baltimore orioles winter in areas from southern Mexico to northern South America. Observers in Central America report that the first ones arrive during the second week of September, but the large influx does not come until the end of the month. There is almost no other winter visitor so widely and uniformly distributed throughout its wintering range. It's an adaptable bird that makes itself at home almost anywhere that trees and shrubs provide fruit and insects. They winter in arid areas or rainforests, on mountain sides and plantations. I have seen them wintering in Costa Rica.

A Closer Look:
Fields of Goldenrod

About a dozen species of goldenrods bloom in Minnesota between July and October, but the peak of bloom comes in early to mid-September, when broad bands of goldenrod color are seen across the landscape. A variety of habitats—old fields, prairies, hardwood forests, sandy soil, moist places—are colonized by goldenrods. Goldenrod flowers are bright yellow and have considerable nectar, so they are visited by bees, flies, beetles, and butterflies. Their pollen, which is sticky and heavier than the typical windblown pollen, is carried by insects from flower to flower. Because very little goldenrod pollen gets into the air, these plants are not considered hay fever plants.

The use of goldenrods as summer and fall flowers in perennial gardens is becoming more popular. Also, some beekeepers locate their hives near fields of goldenrods, as the radiant flowers provide much nectar and remain conspicuous well into the twilight hours.

There are about 85 species of American goldenrods. Kentucky and Nebraska have each chosen one of the tall, handsome goldenrods as their state flower.

Among the showiest of the goldenrods at the present time is the stiff goldenrod, a common perennial of prairies and dry open thickets. Migrating monarch butterflies, hungry for nectar, are attracted to the dark yellow blossoms. These flat-topped clusters, several inches wide, are also visited by honey bees, wild bees, and Milbert's tortoise-shell butterflies.

Week two (Sept 8-15)

Pumpkins in fields and gardens have turned orange. Japanese silver grass is displaying its attractive silver-gray plume-like inflorescence. Annual flowers making a show include petunias, begonias, impatiens, marigolds and zinnias. Dahlias, chrysanthemums and roses have many-colored gorgeous blossoms in gardens. Ground cherries, a relative of the tomato, are ready to pick. McIntosh and Honeygold apples and Edelweiss grapes can be harvested. Black walnut and butternut trees are dropping their fruits. Migrating monarch butterflies stop to nectar on wild asters, and goldenrods, and also

Mexican sunflowers and Autumn Joy sedum in gardens.

Tiny snapping turtles continue to hatch out of clusters of eggs laid in late May or early June. Some of the loudest animal sounds at this time of year come from grasshoppers, crickets, and katydids. Green darner dragonflies migrate.

Rafts of American coots return for their autumn stay on Lake Minnetonka and other area lakes. American goldfinches and mourning doves continue nesting duties.

The first common milkweed pods open and start shedding seeds by means of "parachutes." Canada goldenrod is at bloom peak and taking the blame for allergies caused by ragweed pollen. In wetlands, cattail leaves look mostly green, but have turned about 20 percent tan-brown.

Most ruby-throated hummingbirds leave northern Minnesota by September 12 and the southern part of the state by September 25, but keep those sugar water feeders up until you are sure the hummers have all left. The wild rice harvest is well underway in the central and north. In the Red River Valley, it's harvest time for sugarbeets, potatoes, and sunflowers. Hazelnuts are ready for harvest in northern Minnesota forests.

scattered events

- **September 8, 1999** - First raft of American coots returns to Lake Waconia. Peak for monarch butterfly migration; thousands seen heading south. Some yellow fall color seen on elms and basswoods. Sugar maples show patches of burnt orange.

- **September 10, 2005** - We had a high temperature of 90°F. The surface temperature of Lake Waconia is 75°F and perfect for swimming. Garden roses are blooming nicely and at fall peak. Chrysanthemums of many varieties have begun blooming and telling us that summer is winding down. Field corn chopping has started in Carver County.

- **September 14, 2005** - Wood ducks eat acorns that have fallen to the ground. With clearing skies and a northwest wind, expect to see large numbers of migrating hawks passing over Hawk Ridge in Duluth. Today 13,761 hawks were counted.

- **September 14, 2006** - Red Baron and Honeycrisp apples are being picked. Ohio buckeye fruit is falling. Combining of soybeans begins in extreme southern Minnesota. From Baudette to the BWCA, deciduous tree and shrub foliage is more than 50 percent in fall color.

- **September 15, 1996** - Influx of Franklin's gulls. Statewide 23 percent of the potatoes are harvested, the sweet corn harvest is at 84 percent, and spring wheat at 85 percent.

- **September 15, 2000** - Third- or fourth-year needles of both white and red pines are showing much golden brown; this is natural.

- **September 15, 2003** - A remarkable 101,698 broad-winged hawks were tallied over Hawk Ridge in Duluth.

- **September 15, 2007** - First frost. Pumpkin vines killed. (By the next day, field corn plants in Carver County looked tan-brown). McIntosh, Wealthy, and Honeycrisp apples are being picked. A killing frost marked the end of the growing season over a large part of Minnesota. Ruffed grouse numbers peak about every ten years, and they are at peak now.

A Closer Look:
Dahlias

It's the morning of September 12, 2007, and I'm sitting in front of my amateur radio station, talking to friends in Bemidji and other parts of northern Minnesota with just 5 watts of power. Their voices, traveling at the speed of light over the 75-meter band, tell me of temperatures in the mid- to upper 20s and lots of frost. This first frost put an end to the growing season in portions of the north. In our Waconia neighborhood, steam fog was rising from the lake and nearby ponds but the thermometer read in the low 40s.

Later in the day I bought sweet corn and an orange pumpkin from a local grower, spotted the first raft of American coots on Lake Waconia, and saw migrating northern flickers. I also had the chance to walk through the garden rose collection and chrysanthemum and dahlia plantings at the University of Minnesota Landscape Arboretum. Alpine Sunset, an orange and pink hybrid tea, and Moondance, a fragrant white floribunda, were among hundreds of rose cultivars blooming nicely. Grape Glow, a purple-flowered 1988 University of Minnesota introduction, was one of dozens of mums in bloom. Dahlias at this time of year are at their best, and the photographers and painters, honey bees and monarch butterflies, zero in on them.

Dahlias bloom from mid-July until frost puts an end to their display. They are a tender, tuberous-rooted perennial from Mexico, first introduced into Britain in 1789 by Lord Bute. Belonging to the daisy family, *Compositae*, they commemorate Dr. Andreas Dahl, a Swedish botanist who was a student of Linnaeus. From a few species growing wild in some highlands of Mexico we now have thousands of varieties simply because dahlias are a cross-pollinated plant. This means that it is possible to produce unusual and original cultivars by raising plants from seed. Because of their origin, dahlias require well-drained soil and fairly sunny locations.

Nowadays, dahlias come in all flower colors except true blue. White, yellow, orange, red, pink, purple, maroon, and many combinations of these colors are seen in the arboretum gardens. Dahlias range in size from one-inch pompons to large dinner-plate-sized flowers; and there are also many forms, including daisy-like singles and fully double types.

A Closer Look:
Hummingbird Moths

Sphinx or hawk moths are insects with a wingspread of two to five inches. The fore wings are long, narrow, and usually pointed at the ends, and the hind wings are relatively small. The spindle-shaped hairy body is quite large to accommodate the powerful wing muscles required for hovering. We take notice of these large moths, with big eyes, when one

hovers in front of a flower with its long, uncoiled proboscis extended deep down to extract the nectar. They are excellent flyers, difficult to capture in a net, and are said to be capable of 35 miles per hour. Some are day flyers but most are active at dusk or after dark. Frequently they are mistaken for hummingbirds because of their large size and habit of hovering before flowers with wings vibrating so rapidly as to be invisible or a blur. Thus another common name for this member of the *Sphingidae* family of moths is "hummingbird moth."

Hummingbird moths are effective pollinators of plants, and in some instances have evolved a mutually beneficial relationship with certain flowers whose deep nectaries cannot be reached by other insects. Sphingid caterpillars are large, thick-bodied and usually have a conspicuous horn on their tip ends, and so are called "hornworms." This horn is not poisonous and is quite harmless. The caterpillars, mostly colored brown or green, often rest in a sphinx-like position for long periods of time. A few of these caterpillars are pests on cultivated plants such as tomato and tobacco, but some feed on harmful weeds and so are beneficial.

At this time of year, when people see a hummingbird-like animal hovering in front of a petunia or other garden flower during the day or in the evening, it's usually the white-lined sphinx moth, the most common of the hummingbird moths. On several occasions we have seen this moth species and a ruby-throated hummingbird working the same flowerbed. What a sight!

A Closer Look:
First Frost

The average date of the first frost for Minneapolis/St. Paul is October 3rd. This morning, September 15, 2007, just three days after the first widespread frost in northern Minnesota, it was frosty over much of the whole state right down to the Iowa border. Frost was glistening on rooftops and windshields, and our backyard on the northwest side of Lake Waconia was covered with a carpet of white. We quickly discovered that our tomato plants, which we had neglected to cover with old sheets or blankets, had been killed by the frost. Some

low temperatures mentioned on news reports included 18° at Embarrass, 21° in Hibbing, and a 27° reading at Lakeville.

In checking for further damage the next day we discovered that the frost had taken countless pepper and tomato plants, and damaged pumpkin leaves, impatiens, nasturtiums, and coleus. (Coleus are tender plants native to Java and tropical Africa). Thousands of acres of field corn plants in the area had turned from green to tan-brown overnight. On the other hand, there were localities in southern Minnesota that missed our first frost. And the native heath asters and blue wood asters, along with other native plants, had escaped with no damage even though they had been frost coated.

A Closer Look:
Duluth's Hawk Ridge

One of the fastest growing sports, indoors or outside, is bird watching. It can be very inexpensive, requires no special training, and can be enjoyed by almost anyone at any time and place. Bird watchers, or birders, just need to have an interest in seeing birds and learning differences in their individual characteristics. You may be happy observing birds out a window or in your neighborhood, but once in a while it's fun to head out to another location.

At this time in early autumn, one such

Photo: Linda Kahlbaugh

birding hot spot is Hawk Ridge in Duluth. If you arrive in layered clothing, equipped with binoculars and a bird identification book, you will find yourself surrounded by other friendly birders, many of whom are very knowledgeable and eager to share their observations.

Hawk Ridge runs along the crest of the hill at the east end of Duluth, about 800 feet above Lake Superior. It is one of the best places in the world to observe fall hawk migrations. Hawks, eagles, and other birds of prey moving south from Canada concentrate here because they're reluctant to cross a body of water as large as Lake Superior, and they've been enjoying the updrafts along the lakeshore on their way south. The North Shore acts as a funnel, and the ridge above Duluth is the spout.

Hawk-watching begins in mid-August and continues into December, with the biggest flights usually occurring September 8-23. The best time to observe the birds seems to be from about 10 a.m. to 2 p.m., but there is almost no migration on days with an easterly wind or precipitation. Clear skies and a northwest wind provide the best conditions. On one mid-September day, only 50 hawks were seen. The next day, after skies had cleared, 19,225 birds were counted. Fourteen species, including broad-winged hawks, turkey vultures, bald eagles, ospreys, and red-tailed hawks, are regular migrants over Hawk Ridge.

On September 15, 2003, a phenomenal 102,329 hawks were tallied as they flew and glided over Hawk Ridge; the most hawks ever counted in one day there. The weather in Duluth was warm and sunny, with a gentle west wind. About 99 percent of the migrants on that special day were broad-winged hawks. These birds often travel in huge wheeling flocks, known to hawk watchers as "kettles." The broad-winged hawk, about the size of a crow with a three-foot wingspread, nests in deciduous forests of the eastern United States and southern Canada. They winter in Central and South America.

Week three (Sept 16-23)

Monarch butterflies continue migrating through. They stop to nectar on New

England aster, butterfly-bush, and other flowers, but are heading south at an average speed of 11 miles per hour, and will reach their wintering sites in mountain forests west of Mexico City around the first of November. White-lined sphinx moths feed on the nectar of petunia, phlox, and hosta flowers.

The velvet on white-tailed deer antlers has disappeared. Gray squirrels are making leafy nests. Cedar waxwings and American robins feed on the ripe fruit on mountain ash and crabapple trees. Yellow-rumped warblers migrate through in large numbers. Loose flocks of blue jays wing their way south. We have banding records of some jays ending up in Texas, but others from Canada may winter in northern Minnesota.

Ohio buckeye nuts have begun falling; they are a beautiful chestnut-brown. Crocus and daffodil bulbs can be planted for bloom next spring. It's a perfect time to transplant peonies.

Showy along mucky lakeshores and in wetlands are the bright yellow flowers of the bur marigold. Other blooming, bright-colored, wildflowers include heath aster, blue wood aster, zigzag goldenrod, white snakeroot, and Jerusalem artichoke.

The combining of soybeans begins in southern Minnesota as farmers finish harvesting the fourth crop of alfalfa.

Splendid fall color blazes in the Boundary Waters Canoe Area Wilderness.

scattered events

- **September 20, 2006** - First ice on birdbaths. The first scattered frost nipped squash vines. First raft of American coots arrives on Lake Waconia. Grand fall colors can be seen on the hills above Tofte and Lutsen.

- **September 22, 2002** - It's the autumnal equinox and numerous furnaces are on for the first time this month. Lake Waconia had steam fog rising from its surface at 7 a.m. when the air temperature was only 42° F. Garden raspberry canes such as Autumn Bliss and Fall Red are producing delicious ripe fruit.

- **September 23, 2005** - Blue jays migrate through. First dark-eyed juncos arrive. Dahlia flowers are very showy in gardens. The low temperature at Embarrass was 19°F; it was 26° at Hibbing and 49° in the Twin Cities.

A Closer Look:
The Ohio Buckeye Tree

The fruits of the Ohio buckeye trees are now falling in southern Minnesota. These leathery three-part capsules each contain one, two, or three seeds. Each seed is roughly spherical and 1 to 1½ inches thick. The shiny, dark reddish-brown seeds are fun to collect and keep as special souvenirs of autumn, but are not to be eaten.

Native from Pennsylvania to Nebraska and south to Texas, Ohio buckeye (*Aesculus glabra*) trees have been planted in yards and parks throughout Minnesota for years. They form round-headed trees up to 40 feet tall. Their greenish-yellow 1½-inch flowers form upright 6-inch clustered stalks which are very showy in May, followed by fruit in blunt spiny cases. Leaves are palmately compound with 5 to 7 leaflets, arranged like fingers on a hand, and are normally light green. Just after the fruit falls, by September 20 or so, the foliage ranges in color from yellow to red.

The twigs, leaves, and blossoms all produce an unpleasant odor when crushed. Both buckeye leaves and seeds have a poisonous alkaloid and can cause serious reactions ranging from nausea to paralysis if eaten. The flowers are also poisonous. This otherwise attractive, long-lived tree was proudly chosen as the state tree of Ohio. It grows naturally there in fertile river-bottoms and on stream banks.

Although its use is quite restricted because of its relative rarity, the Ohio buckeye is a valuable timber tree. The wood is white, close-grained, lightweight, easy to carve, and resists splitting, so is ideal for use in the manufacture of artificial limbs and in woodenware, and has been used as paper pulp.

A Closer Look:
Sumacs

After driving from St. Peter to Waconia on September 18, 2007, I wrote in my field notes that fall colors were coming on fast for the sumacs. They were showing much red, in many beautiful tones, and some yellows. Between now and the end of the month, sumacs are truly in their autumn splendor.

Although the sumac's color display is impressive, the colonies within which it grows also tend to have a beautiful shape. Most are tall in the middle and slope off on the sides like a dome, because the younger, shorter plants grow out on every side from the "adult" plants in the middle. The process is called root suckering.

In Minnesota our two most common sumacs are staghorn (*Rhus typhina* L.) and smooth (*Rhus glabra* L.). Both grow as tall shrubs with crooked, branched stems that often look like antlers. Staghorn sumac has fuzzy twigs and is common in southern Minnesota in the deciduous forest areas, and infrequent northward to the Duluth region. (The leaves and fruits of staghom sumac are also noticeably more hairy than those of smooth sumac.) Smooth sumac is common throughout the state and has smooth twigs. Both sumacs have pinnate, feather-like, leaves with 11 to 31 leaflets and clusters of red fruit.

Photo: Jim Gilbert

Sumacs provide food for wild animals. Rabbits and deer browse the twigs and at least several dozen species of birds eat the fruit. The bright red clusters of fuzzy fruits remain on the plants far into winter and are widely available when other, more desirable foods are scarce. American robins, eastern bluebirds, wild turkeys, and ring-necked pheasants rely on sumac fruit as a winter or early spring food.

In summer to early fall, before rains wash out most of the acid, we can make a cold drink from the dense clusters of the small, dry, hairy, red fruits. Collect the entire fruit cluster, rub gently to bruise the acidic red hairs, and soak for about 15 minutes in cold water. Remove the cluster and pour the pink juice through cheese-cloth to strain out the hairs and any loose berries. Sweeten to taste and chill; the drink tastes like pink lemonade.

A Closer Look:
Honeycrisp, the Minnesota State Apple

Every few years scientists at the University of Minnesota Agricultural Experiment Station release a new fruit variety for northern gardens. While they are always good, sometimes an introduction is spectacular. Such was the case of the Honeycrisp apple released in 1991. Honeycrisp apple trees have been sold in local nurseries and garden centers and grown in commercial Minnesota orchards since then, so each year more apples are available. Yet the demand for this apple remains much greater than the supply. It's a mid-season cultivar recommended for both commercial or home garden production. The trees have demonstrated good hardiness under normal winter conditions in east central Minnesota. The Honeycrisp's sweet taste and vibrant red color are among the traits that made it popular. In fact, Minnesotans adore Honeycrisp apples, and this cultivar has been our official state apple since 2006.

Called "explosively" crisp, Honeycrisp apples have a pleasant balance of sweetness and tartness, a mildly aromatic flavor, and juicy texture. The fruit has shown excellent storage characteristics. The outstanding flavor and texture can be maintained for at least six months in refrigerated storage.

The University of Minnesota has a long history of breeding fruit trees. Although many of their apples aren't well known beyond the state's borders, they often have a lot going for them both in hardiness and flavor. For example, the Haralson apple, released in 1922, is known for its tart flavor and suitability for fresh eating, pies, sauce, and baking. Because Haralsons (and many other U of M apple introductions) are meant to be grown and consumed locally, plant breeders have not been required to sacrifice flavor, disease resistance, keeping quality, and other good traits, in order to produce skins tough enought to ship long distances.

The Honeycrisp itself resulted from a cross between Macoun and Honeygold in 1960, and has been evaluated since that time for its performance. The harvest season ranges from September 15 to October 10. Honeycrisps ripen evenly and hold well on the trees, so they can be harvested over an extended period or in a single picking.

A Closer Look:
Yellow-rumped Warblers

It's the peak time for fall migration of the yellow-rumped warbler, our most abundant warbler, and loose flocks are commonly seen along shores of lakes and in trees and shrubs on forest edges. These birds breed in the coniferous and mixed forests of northeastern Minnesota and Canada, placing their nests in pine, spruce, tamarack, and birch trees. They are now on their way to the southern United States for the winter.

One of the easiest warblers to identify, yellow-rumped warblers (formerly called myrtle warblers), get their name from a yellow patch on their rump, but they also carry yellow on their sides and on top of their heads. Berries and insects are the major food items. The bird's fondness for wax myrtle fruit gave rise to its earlier common name.

Week four (Sept 24-30)

It's time to enjoy the spectacular landscape. Virginia creeper vines are drapped through trees and on fences like red garlands. Sumac—mostly showing red—are very colorful along roadsides. Green ash trees have sunny-yellow foliage. Red maples have striking red leaves. Naturalist Beth Conant from the Minnesota Zoo wrote in late September of 2007: "From a distance the woods are like a rich tapestry of color—red, orange, rust, maroon—sewn together by the buttery-yellow grape vines."

In the garden, ever-bearing strawberries and fall-bearing raspberries continue producing ripe fruit. We do anticipate scattered frost and ice on birdbaths any day.

White-tailed deer are seen in their gray-brown winter coats. Muskrats build their mounded shelters in permanent ponds. More painted turtles are up sunning on logs now that the water temperatures are dropping. Woollybear caterpillars fatten-up on plantain leaves before looking for safe hibernating spots.

A few late migrating ruby-throated hummingbirds can still be expected at sugar water feeders in southern Minnesota. Dark-eyed juncos and white-throated sparrows arrive at our feeding stations, announcing that, whether we like it or not, cold weather is on its way.

Farmers in the western and southern parts of the state are busy combining soybeans and chopping field corn for silage. The combining of corn begins.

In northern Minnesota, stunning fall colors are seen. It's the peak of the fall color season at Isabella, Finland, and the Gunflint Trail; also from International Falls to Thief River Falls and from Grand Rapids to Park Rapids. Black bears begin to go into hibernation. Common loons assemble on larger lakes before migrating to the Gulf Coast or Atlantic seaboard. The rutting season for moose occurs from mid-September to mid-October.

scattered events

- **September 24, 2007** - Fall color peak at Oberg Mountain near Lutsen. The reds on the sugar maples are splendid.

- **September 26, 1999** - We can still pick and eat ripe wild grapes. Shaggymane mushrooms are popping up. Dahlias, chrysanthemums, and garden roses continue to bloom nicely. Fall colors are just great in the Grygla area (NW Minnesota) and at overall peak.

- **September 29, 2007** - In the Lutsen area, the first snow buntings arrived today. Large numbers of palm warblers, white-throated sparrows, and juncos are passing through. With 6 inches to as much as 20 inches of rain in Cook County this month, the drought is on hold and streams running into Lake Superior are roaring again.

- **September 30, 2006** - Many Asian ladybugs. The New England aster is at bloom peak.

A Closer Look:
Minnesota's Native Cranberries

In the Itasca State Park area, paper birches and quaking aspens are now showing golden-yellow leaves, sumacs and red oaks

add a bit of red, and along with the dark green on spruces and pines, it is a spectacular scene. This is a perfect time to visit a nearby northern bog and walk carefully on a sedge mat to become acquainted with a few of the plants.

At the end of September, tamarack tree foliage is turning a smoky-gold and bog birches show red and yellow leaves, but one of the biggest finds for those willing to explore a bog is the ripe cranberry fruit. The native cranberries are low creeping shrubs with small green leaves and many-seeded, juicy red berries, a bit less than one-half inch in diameter. Although some guidebooks say that the fruit is sour and nearly inedible when raw, many bog-walkers pick and enjoy eating the fresh fruit anyway. The berries are usually gathered while still firm, just before or just after the first frost, but those that are not picked will remain on the stems during the winter.

Wild cranberry fruit can be used in any recipe calling for commercial cranberries. The berries contain their own pectin. If you are able to gather enough cranberries, they would make good cooked fruit, jelly, or cold drinks.

The jack pine forest of Lake George, seven miles east of Itasca State Park, is known for its blueberry shrubs—low, woody plants with leaves showing mostly red fall color. Usually at this time of year, hikers are rewarded with a few ripe blueberries to eat for a snack.

A Closer Look:

Why Garden or Feed Birds?

Why is gardening the most popular hobby in the United States? Some people want to produce potatoes, tomatoes and carrots, to put more (or better tasting) food on the table. Others enjoy the beauty of petunia and chrysanthemum flowers, the foliage of coleus, and the yellow fruit capsules of the American bittersweet vine that burst open at this time to reveal spectacular orange-colored seed clusters. Our deep-rooted human kinship with the earth probably is nowhere more clearly seen than in the satisfaction we find in making a garden. Gardening gives us respect for rain, the soil, plants, and the whole magnificent ecosystem of which we are a part.

How many bird watchers do we have in this country? I have heard estimates as high as 60 million, depending on the definition of "bird watcher." The hard-core "birder" is probably the person who has observed most of the birds in our well-written and illustrated bird guidebooks. This person would travel many hours to a location like Grand Portage, on Lake Superior, or Hendricks, on the South Dakota border, to add a new species to their Minnesota list. Far more numerous, however, are the window-watchers and the garden birders. They may not travel to far places for rare bird sightings but their satisfaction comes from knowing a few familiar local species, and once-in-a-while spotting an unexpected visitor that may come through. They also have the comfort of knowing that their feeding station is helping out the local birds during stormy or very cold times.

John Bates, a gifted nature writer from Wisconsin, says, in his book, *A Northwoods Companion: Fall and Winter*, "Feeding birds and growing gardens put us in touch with natural beauty, giving us a consistent connection with the natural world—a connection that our technological society obliterates." I agree. We all need to interact with at least a few of the plants and animals that share planet Earth with us. Hopefully these experiences will make us better stewards.

Photo: David Brislance

A Closer Look:
Dark-eyed Juncos

Mary and Dave Brislance, friends from Lutsen, wrote to me on September 27, 2007. They said, "Large flocks of juncos flew into the county (Cook) this week." The two of them ended up scattering birdseed on their lawn for the migrating juncos, and for the many white-throated sparrows and white-crowned sparrows also passing through the area.

At the Minnesota Landscape Arboretum the first junco of the fall season was spotted on September 17, and on September 24, Ruth Krueger from rural Cologne noted the first junco at her feeding station. Between the end of September and through October we can count on seeing big influxes of dark-eyed juncos, also called "snowbirds" because they often arrive just in time to herald the first snow flurries or snowfall of the season. Their arrival signals the beginning of winter for many people. After being abundant fall migrants throughout the state, usually only a few birds will be found around feeding stations during the winter in the southern part of the state. A rare bird may be seen in northern regions.

Some observers have been confused by the several names attached to this species, such as "slate-colored junco," "Oregon junco," and "white-winged junco." These are geographic races and are combined under the name "dark-eyed junco" (*Junco hyemalis*). All of these types have white outer tail feathers and are similar in behavior and trilling calls, and will mate with one another freely.

The "slate-colored" race is the only form usually seen in the eastern United States. They have solid gray on their heads, backs and sides, with white abdomens. Females are slightly browner and lighter colored than adult males.

The dark-eyed junco ranges from Alaska and Newfoundland south to Georgia and Mexico. They winter south to the Gulf Coast and northern Mexico. Winter habitat includes fields, thickets, gardens, and city parks. Nesting habitat is coniferous or mixed forests, which for Minnesota would be in the northeast and north-central regions. Huge numbers nest in Canada. The nest is a cup of twigs and grass on the ground, containing 3 to 6 eggs incubated only by the female for about 12 days.

Food for juncos consists of insects, berries, and seeds. In fall and winter at our feeding station on the edge of Lake Waconia, the dark-eyed juncos like generous portions of millet or cracked corn spread on the ground. During the autumn and winter months juncos are social birds, gathering in flocks of a dozen or two, and they often associate with American tree sparrows. The two species can be seen together at feeding stations or foraging about in fields, fencerows, and edges of forests.

A Closer Look:
Sugar Maple Trees

Just as the sap of the sugar maple, *Acer saccharum*, is a valued item in the early spring, so its autumn foliage splendor is valued as it contributes to the beauty of our landscape. Many observers believe that the most magnificent display of color in all the kingdom of plants is the autumnal foliage of the trees of North America. The foliage of the sugar maples —now showing clear yellow pigments, the richest crimson, and brilliant burnt-oranges—outdoes all the other trees.

This tall, handsome tree is among the best known trees in eastern North America. Sugar maples are native from Nova Scotia to Minnesota, and south to northern Georgia and Arkansas. They grow in a variety of soil types, but do best in deep, rich, well-drained soils. They could live for 300 years, and are the main component of the eastern deciduous forest. In Minnesota they grow in association with basswood, ironwood, red oak, white oak, and bitternut hickory. The seedlings and young trees prefer shaded conditions.

Sugar maples are valuable to wildlife. Birds feed on their buds and flowers. The fruits in paired wings, mature in fall with the seeds providing food for birds and other small animals. Squirrels eat the seeds, frequently storing them in caches after removing each hull and wing. Birds often use the leaves and seed stalks in nest building. Deer browse the twigs in winter. Birds, squirrels, and others use the trunk and multitude of branches for nest sites. Countless insects, spiders, and other tiny animals use the sugar maple for food and shelter.

The sugar maple is a 50- to 70-foot-tall tree with a relatively short trunk when growing out in the open, and a large crown spreading some 35 to 45 feet. Male and female flowers are produced in separate clusters in spring as the first small leaves emerge; flowers are yellow, minute, clustered in groups near the ends of twigs, and borne on slender drooping stalks. Seen from a distance, the trees have a yellow glow when the flower clusters are out.

Leaves of the sugar maple, well-known symbols for Canada and the maple syrup industry, are broad, long-stalked, and 3 to 6 inches long. They are quite thin, dark green above, paler green beneath, 3-lobed or 5-lobed, with a main vein running to the tip of each lobe. The full spread of a sugar maple's foliage in summer gives deep, cool shade.

Sugar maples are commonly planted as shade trees. However, they suffer in urban areas because of their intolerance to road salt and air pollution. If you have one in your yard and it needs trimming, remember to delay pruning until the leaves are fully open in spring. Sugar maples "bleed" sap badly when pruned in late winter.

This maple species is the principal source of maple syrup and sugar; trees are tapped in very early spring. Native Americans who lived near the Great Lakes and the St. Lawrence River produced maple sugar and syrup long before Europeans arrived in North America.

Sugar maple wood is heavy, hard, strong, durable, and close-grained. It has a high fuel value and is much used as firewood. It is also used for furniture, flooring, cabinet work, tool handles, and in making violins and other musical instruments.

October

The first two weeks of October is the time of the illuminated woods as many deciduous tree species around the state reach their fall color peaks. Waves of American robins and other migrating birds move through. More dark-eyed juncos arrive at our feeding stations. Eastern chipmunks gather seeds in their cheek pouches to take into their underground burrows. Leopard frogs head for lakes where they will hibernate. Garden chrysanthemum flowers are very showy. Apple varieties being picked include Haralson, Connell Red, Sweet Sixteen, Keepsake, Regent, and Fireside. Nearly all of the soybean and field corn harvest is completed in October.

READING THE LANDSCAPE

Week one (October 1–7)

Aurora Borealis
Daylight Amount is Shrinking
Why Leaves Change Color
Leaf Watching

Week two (October 8–15)

Fall Color Peak in Twin Cities
Quaking Aspens
Migrating Turkey Vultures
Amur Maples Display Red

Week three (October 16–23)

White-throated Sparrows
Indian Summer
Blackbird Roosts
Coyotes Howling

Week four (October 24–31)

Backyard Bird Feeding
White-breasted Nuthatches
What to Call Animals in Groups
Boston Ivy

first week in october

The normal high temperature for October 1 in the Twin Cities area is 66°F, and the low is 45°. A high of 86° on this date in 1897 is the record, and the record low is 24° set in 1974.

Fall color is coming on fast. Woodlands are illuminated with vivid colors. Sumac and poison ivy shrubs are in tones of red; green ash, bitternut hickory, quaking aspen, and paper birch in shades of golden-yellow; and sugar maples display glorious mixtures of yellow, red, and orange. Lindens and honeylocust trees glow in golden-yellow. Three-year-old red pine needles are golden brown and falling.

Both great and common ragweeds end their pollen-shedding season. Shaggymane mushrooms are up.

Muskrats continue building their dome-shaped winter lodges in marshes and ponds with cattails and other vegetation. White-tailed deer are in their gray-brown winter coats. Woodchucks can be seen carrying mouthfuls of dried leaves into underground dens as hibernation begins soon. American toads are still above ground.

There is a big influx of American coots and dark-eyed juncos. Flocks of American robins, cedar waxwings, and yellow-rumped warblers pass through; some stop to feed on red cedar berries. Huge flocks of migrating red-winged blackbirds and common grackles stream overhead in undulating swarms. Eastern phoebes and white-throated sparrows eat wild grapes.

Statewide, farmers continue combining corn and soybeans. Fall color is peaking in Alexandria, Brainerd, Sandstone, and most of the rest of central Minnesota, and also along the North Shore of Lake Superior. Most numerous of the North Shore bird migrants are the golden-crowned and ruby-crowned kinglets, white-throated sparrows, juncos, and sharp-shinned hawks.

scattered events

▪ **October 2, 1995** - Virginia creeper vines, also called woodbine, at height of fall color with their bright red foliage. This rainy afternoon we enjoyed the watery, muted fall colors on sumacs, green ashes, and others. Several thousand Franklin's gulls spent the night on Lake Waconia; they'll be here well into November.

▪ **October 3, 2004** - White-lined sphinx moths, also called hummingbird moths, are seen during daylight hours nectaring on flowers of such garden plants as hostas and petunias.

▪ **October 4, 1998** - Green ash trees show much golden-yellow and are at fall color peak. Statewide, the soybean harvest is complete

on an estimated 68 percent of the acreage, compared to the 5-year average of 24 percent.

▪ October 7, 2007 - Humid and hot, with a temperature in the low 80s, for the 26th annual Twin Cities Marathon. Runners and spectators treated to beautiful fall colors, especially from sugar maples now showing bright red foliage. Some swimmers enjoyed a last of the season dip in a lake.

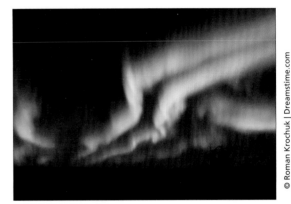

© Roman Krochuk | Dreamstime.com

A Closer Look:
Aurora Borealis

When I have the opportunity to see the northern lights flame and shimmer across the sky, it always inspires in me a sense of beauty, wonder, and awe. During the years from 1970 to 1998, when I was an outdoor education teacher for the Hopkins School District, I was able to point out nature's light show to several hundred students. It would have been great to have interpreted the swirling and pulsating lights to an even greater number of students during night hikes or camping trips, but most often we were satisfied to see several constellations, a couple of planets, and maybe the moon.

Perhaps the fact that the northern lights do not show themselves on most nights makes the moving curtains and streamers of light even more impressive when they do appear. The best time of year to see them is in March and April or September and October, when the earth's magnetic field is most closely aligned with the sun's. The best hour is just before midnight, especially during the time of month when the moon is new and skies are darker. The finest displays seem to light up the whole sky, but even then they seldom exceed the light of the moon during its first quarter.

It's when charged particles from the sun hit our planet at a particular angle that we are likely to see an aurora. Northern lights are visible about 200 nights a year at the latitude of Fairbanks, Alaska, about 100 times a year in Edmonton, Alberta. Minneapolis/St. Paul can expect the natural light show about 30 times a year, Chicago and Seattle about 25 times a year. The lights only appear about 5 times a year over San Francisco and once every 10 years above central Mexico. Since the north magnetic pole is located in Canada, just about due north of Minnesota, we have a much higher incidence of auroras than other locations around the Earth at our latitude. Such displays are almost as frequent in Minnesota as in Sweden, which is much further north, though only in the darker rural areas of the state can auroras be seen thirty times a year. In metropolitan areas, they are visible much less often since they must compete with city lights.

The more formal phrase for the northern lights here in the Northern Hemisphere is *aurora borealis*. In the Southern Hemisphere the lights are called *aurora australis*. Scientists have studied the aurora for centuries. Italian Renaissance astronomer Galileo first named the lights for Aurora, the Roman goddess of dawn, to which he added a reference to Boreas, the Greek god of the north wind. Putting the two together, Galileo came up with *aurora borealis* or "northern dawn."

Benjamin Franklin was among the earliest to attribute the aurora to electricity. In 1950, Swedish physicist Hannes Alfven, a Nobel laureate, discovered that solar winds blowing across the Earth's geomagnetic field produce an electric current responsible for the aurora.

What we know now is that the aurora is caused by high energy charged particles, electrons and protons, streaming from the sun at speeds up to three million mph. This flow of charged particles is known as the solar winds. Solar wind gusts, captured and concentrated by the Earth's magnetic field near the poles, can interact with gases high up in our planet's atmosphere, causing them to glow like gases in a fluorescent light bulb. If the sun is near its peak of activity in its eleven-year sunspot cycle, as in 1990, there are more solar flares and more displays of the aurora on Earth.

The aurora appears in many forms—as arcs of light, as bands that fold across the heavens like curtains up to two-hundred miles wide and a couple of thousand miles long, as patches like glowing clouds, or as rays like searchlight beams. The light can also flicker like a flame. Auroras come in many colors. We most often see pale green, red, or white lights. The most conspicuous auroras occur at heights of fifty to a hundred miles.

The aurora is visual evidence that the Earth's magnetic field is being disturbed. Stories of the swish, whistle, crackle, howl, and roar of the aurora are only legends. According to our knowledge of sound, noise from the aurora could not reach the Earth. But the severe magnetic storms that sometimes accompany exceptionally bright auroras can effect radio communication and telephone and power lines.

photo: Jim Gilbert

A Closer Look:
Daylight Amount is Shrinking

The days quickly grow shorter during October, with each day here in Minnesota losing about three minutes of light. The sun is still strong enough to push the mercury into the lower 90s early in the month with highs in the low 80s possible all the way up to Halloween.

In the greater Twin Cities area we will start out on October 1 with 11 hours and 41 minutes of daylight. Sunrise is 7:11 a.m. and sunset at 6:52 p.m. on this date in 2008; that could vary a minute or two in other years. By October 31, when the sunrise is 7:51 a.m. and sunset is 6:02 p.m., we are down to 10 hours and 11 minutes of daylight. So our loss for the month is 90 minutes of daylight. Meanwhile, the normal high temperature is dropping from 66° to 50°, and the low from 45° to 32°.

Some people say there is a sadness in the air in autumn, but we adjust by moving some activities indoors, dressing in layers, and making plans for the near future. To survive, wild animals must migrate, hibernate, or adapt to the colder days and longer nights while remaining active. Short-lived species may die, leaving their offspring in eggs or some other form to take over in the spring.

Plants likewise prepare for winter by going into dormancy and/or producing seeds or spores that will insure the survival of each species.

Photo: John Toren

A Closer Look:

Why Leaves Change Color

Throughout the spring and summer, most of the foods necessary for growth of a tree are made in the leaves. This food-making process takes place in the cells containing the pigment chlorophyll, which gives the leaf its green color. The chlorophyll absorbs energy from sunlight and uses it in transforming carbon dioxide and water to carbohydrates such as sugars and starches. But in fall, because of shorter periods of daylight and cooler temperatures, the leaves stop their food-making process. The chlorophyll breaks down and the green color disappears. Two underlying chemicals, xanthophyll and carotene, are unmasked, leaving yellow and orange. Familiar trees which show yellows in the fall include paper birch, green ash, and American elm.

Red coloration appears only in those woody plants with leaves that contain certain sugars or tannins. Fall weather conditions favoring formation of brilliant red autumn color are warm sunny days followed by cool nights with temperatures below 45° F. Much sugar is made in the leaves during the daytime, but cool nights prevent movement of sugar from the leaves. From the sugars trapped in the leaves the red pigment called anthocyanin is formed. Anthocyanins produce the brilliant reds and purples we see in apples and grapes as well as in leaves and stems of red-osier dogwoods and maples. Familiar trees with red or scarlet leaves in autumn are red maple, sugar maple, and northern red oak. The foliage of the staghorn sumac shrub and Virginia creeper vine also turns red.

Within the same species, the degree of color may vary from tree to tree or branch to branch. For example, leaves directly exposed to sunlight may turn red, while those on the shady side of the same tree may be yellow. The foliage of some tree and shrub species just turns dull brown from death and decay and never shows bright colors.

Fallen leaves fertilize the forest floor. They contain valuable elements, particularly calcium and potassium, which were originally a part of the soil. Decomposition of the leaves enriches the top layers of the soil by returning part of the elements borrowed by the tree, and at the same time provides for more water-absorbing humus.

A Closer Look:
Leaf Watching

John Burroughs, a well-known nineteenth-century American naturalist and writer, described October as "the time of the illuminated woods." There may not be an illuminated woods where you live but all throughout Minnesota and the Upper Midwest, during this first week in October there are illuminated trees and pockets with fall colors. Some sumacs are still displaying beautiful reds

and many sugar maples glow in burnt-oranges, reds, and golden-yellows. Some willows, silver maples, and wild grape vines have sunny-yellow leaves.

There are people who take long road trips to catch the panoramic views, and others simply walk a neighborhood sidewalk or stand in their own backyard to enjoy the fleeting colors. Our son Christian, who teaches kayaking, schedules his fall semester classes so paddlers can take in fall color views while gaining new skills and exercising their muscles.

Some people feel a sense of urgency to the task of getting out into the country before the colors fade and the deciduous trees drop their foliage. In recent years fall color tours, self-guided or in groups, have attracted tourists and travelers by the millions to wooded regions in the Midwest and Northeast, and eastern Canada. Each fall in these areas the campgrounds and lodging establishments are filled, buses are chartered, cars crowd certain highways, and bikers and hikers hit the trails. People want to experience nature's extravaganza. It's part of our culture to admire northern fall colors.

In the Twin Cities area, the drive on Highway 95 from Stillwater to Taylors Falls, or Highway 7 from Hopkins to St. Bonifacius, or simply a drive through the University of Minnesota Landscape Arboretum will provide great views of autumn hues.

Out of Minneapolis or St. Paul, a drive on Highway 61 from Hastings to Winona and beyond, or from Northfield to Faribault, can provide nice vistas of fall colors. Farther afield, a drive in the Mille Lacs Lake or Walker area, and the special fall color drives out of Tofte and Lutsen all offer the splendors of autumn.

Ask a dozen people from various parts of the state and they'll probably give you a dozen more places to view spectacular fall foliage. How about Fort Ridgley State Park; or Maplewood and Banning and Savanna Portage and Bear Head Lake state parks? All these and many other Minnesota state parks are favorite areas to admire the turning leaves.

Week two (Oct 8-15)

The fall color season goes on, but look for massive leaf drops. The leaves of silver maples, hackberry trees, and wild grape vines are a bright sunny-yellow, those of eastern cottonwoods and American elms are golden-yellow, and sugar maples are showing reds to yellows. Even on gray, overcast days the Amur maples seem to be illuminated from within, like nature's stained glass.

Boston ivy vines are showing splendid tones of red on the sides of schools and other buildings. New England asters and Mexican sunflowers continue to bloom in gardens, inviting the late-season butterflies such as clouded sulphurs, red admirals, painted ladies, and monarchs. Brussels sprouts, broccoli, cabbage, cauliflower, and leaf lettuce keep on growing in cool weather. There is still time to plant daffodil, tulip, and crocus bulbs in gardens for flowers next spring.

A few very late-to-migrate ruby-throated hummingbirds come to southern Minnesota feeders. In the northern part of the state, black bears usually head for their winter dens between September 24 and October 24. Along the North Shore of Lake Superior, fall color persists with the golden yellow leaves of paper birches and quaking aspens, and the bright red leaves of pin cherries and bush honeysuckles.

scattered events

- **October 8, 1998** - The big mature native sugar maples are showing much color. Gardens still yield tomatoes. Large numbers of white-throated sparrows have returned to the Chisago City area, where they and the juncos and warblers make good use of birdbaths. Fall color peak from Brainerd to Taylors Falls, and to Prairie Farm, WI.

- **October 9, 1996** - Big leaf drop today—

basswoods, sugar maples, cottonwoods, and bur oaks have leaves falling in numbers. In the Brainerd area, tamaracks are smoky-gold.

- **October 12, 2006** - Low of 23° F. Hard freeze ends the growing season. Plants killed include tomato, impatiens, begonias, and morning glories. Forest areas are looking quite bare. There was a late sighting of a ruby-throated hummingbird coming to a sugar water feeder in Red Wing.

- **October 13, 1998** - Red oaks are showing deep reds, and sugar maples have foliage in the yellows and reds. The first tundra swans return to the Alma, Wisconsin, area.

- **October 13, 2007** - At the end of the Gunflint Trail, lake trout are spawning in the shallows of Saganaga Lake, aspen trees still show golden yellow foliage, and tamarack trees have the stunning smoky-gold needles.

A Closer Look:
Fall Color Peak in Twin Cities

There is a date for each area when there truly is an overall peak of autumn foliage colors. To phenologists and naturalists, that special date is when the fall leaf colors are spectacular considering the many trees, shrubs, and vines that give us the fantastic show. For weeks before and after the height of fall color

PEAK DAY FOR AUTUMN FOLIAGE COLORS IN THE WACONIA, LAKE MINNETONKA AND TWIN CITIES AREA	
2007 October 19	2002 October 13
2006 October 3	2001 October 8
2005 October 15	2000 October 7
2004 October 12	1999 October 9
2003 October 7	1998 October 11

we can see patches, pockets, and even whole groves of trees with striking fall color. For each date listed I was the judge, so at least that part is consistent.

Some fall seasons are more colorful than others because an early frost can kill the foliage. Dry conditions or a cloudy autumn can also produce dull colors. The splendid color changes that take place as deciduous woody plants prepare to drop their leaves are triggered by shortening days and cooler weather.

A Closer Look:
Quaking Aspens

Of all the tree species in North America, quaking aspen has the widest distribution. It is found from northern Alaska to Labrador, and south to Pennsylvania on into the alpine reaches of Mexico. It's the long, flattened, and

© Ron Chapple Studios | Dreamstime.com

flexible leafstalks that make the round, silver dollar-sized leaves flutter in the slightest breeze. This creates a rustling sound that serenades our ears, and a restless, quivering appearance like that of a tree viewed through hot shimmering air. From this arose the two popular names for *Populus tremuloides*, "quaking" and "trembling" aspen. The leaves are dark green in summer and turn an attractive golden yellow in the fall.

Aspens are often found growing near paper birches, and the two trees are similar in appearance, but aspen bark does not naturally peel. It's trunk is smooth and graceful, with bark that can be creamy and powdery to green on younger trees, becoming fissured and dark on mature trees. The bark is easily scratched, exposing the inner green tissue where photosynthesis occurs even in winter. Unfortunately, it is also easily scarred and can be effaced for decades by people carving initials and other signs.

Aspens commmonly rise to a height of 40 to 50 feet and seldom live more than a century. These rapidly growing trees are one of the most aggressive of the pioneer species, moving quickly into bare areas and soon establishing dense stands of young trees by sending out suckers that create a wide-ranging and extensive root systems. When aspens are damaged by fire, logging, or heavy browsing by deer, fast-growing stems emerge from their roots, creating thickets of "suckers." The suckers from the root system of one single tree constitute a clone, a group of genetically identical individuals that can live for hundreds of years and spread across many acres by producing successive generations of new suckers. All members of a clone will be of the same sex, have bark of the same color, and leaves that turn the same shade of yellow in the fall—at the same time.

For us humans, the quaking aspen is a major pulpwood species, and it also plays an important role in the lives of many other organisms. It has seen estimated that some five hundred species of animals and plants, from bears to the lowly fungi, utilize them. The bark is a favorite food of the beaver, and branches and trunks help form the main structural elements of beaver dams. Ruffed grouse eat quaking aspen buds in winter, snowshoe hares and white-tailed deer dine on the twigs, and moose and porcupines feast on the foliage.

photo: Greg Gillson

A Closer Look:
Migrating Turkey Vultures

Master birder Oscar Johnson, from Brooklyn Park, told me on October 13, 2007, that he was seeing many migrating American robins this week. Also waterfowl migrants such as American wigeons, blue-winged teal, and northern pintails have arrived in Hennepin County. On the same day I heard from Mary and Dave Brislance, residents of Lutsen, who said, "The headline in the Arrowhead could be that the migration of the turkey vultures and American crows has started." We're also seeing turkey vultures in southern Minnesota. Lately I've seen them soaring over the Lake Waconia area and over the Minnesota River Valley at LeSueur, and birders from St. Peter tell me about many turkey vultures roosting together in tall trees.

High daily counts of more than seven hundred turkey vultures have been made at Hawk Ridge, Duluth, in fall seasons. In summer they are residents and nesters in the forested part of Minnesota's northeastern region and along the St. Croix and lower Mississippi, and adjacent river valleys. Their range is from southern Canada, all across the 48 United States to South America. In the Bahamas I heard the residents call them "crows." And in Ohio and other areas they are sometimes called "buzzards."

Turkey vultures weigh four to five pounds, have red skin on their heads and dark body feathers resembling those of a turkey. The six-foot wingspan is held in a shallow V when soaring. There is a two-toned look to the underwings, black wing linings against gray flight feathers. This apt soarer travels wide circles, tilting from side to side, and sustains itself with only occasional slow flaps of its wings. What they are doing is patrolling the area for food.

Turkey vultures seldom kill their own prey. They are on the lookout for road-killed rabbits, raccoons, and skunks, dead fish on river banks, or any other carrion such as dead livestock. An old carcass can be a messy meal, but the vulture's unfeathered head is beautifully suited to making the most of such a diet, which is how this "nature's cleaner upper" keeps alive.

A Closer Look:
Amur Maples Display Red

Native to central and northeastern China and Japan, the Amur maple, *Acer ginnala*, was first introduced into North America in 1860, and is now grown throughout Minnesota. It's an extremely cold-hardy maple with small toothed-edged leaves about three inches long with two basal lobes and a longer terminal lobe. Fragrant yellow flowers, in clusters, appear in May. The handsome winged fruits turn red in late summer while the leaves are still a rich dark green, making an interesting color combination. In autumn, the leaves turn mostly bright red before they fall, and this is when many people really take note of the Amur maple. Yes, its vivid scarlet autumn color is probably the tree's most conspicuous characteristic.

Amur maples grow 15 to 25 feet high. They have excellent tolerance to dry soils, can withstand partial shade, and are fine plants for raised planters and difficult sites. This maple in some areas can be a problem weed tree, but most often is thought of as a versatile small tree that can be grown as a single trunk tree, in groupings, or as a large shrub or large hedge. Because they can stand heavy pruning, Amur maples can quite easily be used as a hedge or screen.

Week three (Oct 16-23)

Leaf watching is great! Both red and white oaks continue to show deep red and brown foliage. Sugar maples are still wearing red, yellow, and burnt-orange leaves. Tamarack trees are at their fall color best and the needles exhibit spectacular smoky-gold. Falling clusters of golden brown, scale-like leaves pile up artistically under arborvitae trees. The winged euonymus, or burning bush, a native of Asia, has bold, rose-red leafage.

Loon migration, which began in late August, reaches its peak in mid-October and continues into December. Apple growers are picking late-season varieties such as Haralson, Regent, Fireside, and Keepsake. Rutabagas, having been sweetened-up from the frosts, can be dug for excellent eating. Since garden roses are damaged when the temperature drops below 20° F, the best and safest method for protecting them is complete soil cover.

Both common and narrow-leaved cattails

are shedding millions and millions of fluffy seeds to the winds. Duckweeds look green on pond surfaces.

Migrating birds that are on the move include both golden-crowned and ruby-crowned kinglets, fox sparrows, white-throated sparrows, and yellow-rumped warblers. Waterfowl watchers keep an eye out for redheads, canvasbacks, lesser scaup (also called bluebills) and northern shovelers. During October and into November, thousands of Franklin's gulls return to Lake Waconia and some other southern Minnesota lakes around sunset to roost on the water and leave again at sunrise.

Beavers are busy cutting trees to store for winter food, which consists of bark from aspens, alders, birches, maples, willows, plus other vegetation. Nearly all 13-lined ground squirrels are now in hibernation in underground burrows. Short-tailed weasels have begun turning from brown to white. American toads must cover their bodies with soil, digging down more than a foot to stay below the frost level. We look for the height of the fall color season in the southern one-fourth of the state. Statewide, farmers try to finish the harvest of potatoes, sugarbeets, soybeans, field corn, and sunflowers.

Minnesota lakes have begun turning over. Each lake is circulating, is approximately 50°F

throughout, and oxygen is again returned to the depths and nutrients to the surface during this fall overturn.

In the bogs of northern Minnesota, wild cranberries are bright red and tamarack trees radiate their impressive golden yellow. The first flocks of snow buntings return to Grygla and other parts of the state's northern tier.

scattered events

- **October 17, 1995** - Ginkgo trees have ornate golden-yellow leaves. At the Minnesota Landscape Arboretum, common witch-hazel is in full-bloom with small spider-like flowers. The garden roses have just been put underground for the winter, and 75 varieties of mums are in bloom.

- **October 19, 2007** - It's overall fall color peak day, from the Twin Cities to Spicer and south to Lake City and St Peter, considering the many deciduous trees, shrubs and vines that provide the captivating display. Lawns look lush green.

- **October 22, 1995** - Harvest statewide includes 85% of potatoes, 82% of soybeans, 81% of sugarbeets, 72% of sunflowers, and 59% of the field corn.

Photo: David Brislance

A Closer Look:
White-throated Sparrows

The whistling of the white-throated sparrows is a favorite song of many outdoor enthusiasts. Their song is often translated as "oh, sweet Canada, Canada, Canada," which is appropriate since most of them nest in Canada. We find them passing through in large numbers during spring and fall migrations.

In the course of migration they come to feeding stations located near woods or shrubbery. They're ground feeders and like millet seeds, but their main foods the rest of the year are seeds of grasses and other low-growing plants, plus insects.

White-throated sparrows are one of the easiest to identify. First listen for its clear whistled song; then look for a sparrow with a gray breast, a white throat patch, a yellow spot between the eye and bill, with black and white head stripes.

A Closer Look:
Indian Summer

Minnesota summers are short, but even shorter are our Indian summers, which may last as little as a day or perhaps for several days, and a frequently made up of days scattered intermittently across the calendar. An Indian summer day is one with an above-normal temperature and little or no wind. These warm, sunny, hazy days always follow autumn's first frost and occur when a high pressure system is passing through.

The origin of the phrase Indian Summer is as hazy as the brief "season" it refers to. Some sources say it was born in New England and referred to the period when Native Americans made their final preparations for winter. They often burned grassy areas in late fall to flush out game for one final hunt before winter. The burning grasses would give the still autumn air its extra hazy appearance.

Indian summer is rare and that's why people relish it. Golfers and bikers, picnickers and hikers will be out in numbers. The added lure of autumn colors will bring photographers and landscape painters out. In addition, banded woollybears and leopard frogs cross roads and paths, garter snakes and painted turtles sun themselves, honey bees visit the remaining aster and chrysanthemum flowers, and several species of butterflies will be on the wing. An Indian summer day seems for a few hours to hold back the coming of winter.

A Closer Look:
Blackbird Roosts

At sunrise, an interested observer might see several thousand blackbirds leaving their roosting area, usually a low wetland area, in the space of five minutes, flying in a narrow band like a fast moving stream. About a half-hour before sunset the same event takes place in reverse, as a steady stream of blackbirds moves back to the roost.

Soon after adults stop caring for the young, blackbirds begin to flock together. Each night in summer, until they move farther south later in fall, huge congregations of common grackles, red-winged blackbirds, and brown-headed cowbirds, all members of the blackbird family, will fly from their feeding grounds to their roosts, creating the largest and most commonly observed groups of land birds in North America. Assemblies of red-wings reach

a peak in about mid-October and grackle flocks are at their peak a bit later. Slowly, as the season progresses, the enormous flights drift south.

© Darksidephotos | Dreamstime.com"

A Closer Look:
Coyotes Howling

Our family lives in a rural area of Waconia, so once in a while on cool crisp autumn nights, we have the chance to hear coyotes yelping. Or is it "howling," "barking," or maybe "singing?"

In Minnesota there are two wild species of the dog genus (Canis), the wolf and the coyote. The coyote is a medium-sized, slender dog with a bushy tail and pointed ears and nose, weighing less that half that of a wolf. In the field a coyote–often referred to as a "brush wolf"—can be distinguished from a wolf by its longer tail, which it holds between its legs when running.

Coyotes are chiefly carnivorous but, like most dogs, they eat a variety of fruits when available. In Minnesota their diet includes birds, small mammals such as mice and rabbits, and carrion. Corralled and well-cared-for domestic animals probably suffer little from the coyote. It gets the blame, however, for much damage done by its tame relation, the domestic dog. Coyotes play an important role in the regulation of natural populations, and they are a clever and colorful part of the Minnesota countryside. Our state would be poorer without them.

Week four (Oct 24-31)

The crunching and aroma of fall leaves makes walking in the woods special at this time of year. Most deciduous forests are quite bare, but pockets of fall color remain, especially in oak woods. Red oaks, pin oaks, and white oaks are showing dark red and rich brown foliage.

Marshes look mostly brown from a distance because cattail plants have turned brown. Tamarack trees—conifers that shed their needles each fall—are still glowing a smoky gold in wetlands. Bittersweet vines have dropped their leaves, leaving bright orange fruit.

Lawns are still nice and green. This week marks the normal peak of the leaf raking season. Leaves can be shredded with a power mower and then left on the lawn, or put in flower beds and vegetable gardens to enrich the soil and help hold moisture. Chrysanthemums keep on blooming and adding color to fall gardens. They can withstand some frost and a temperature as low as 28°F for several hours and keep flowering.

Rubs and scrapes made by white-tailed deer can be found in the woods now because the rut, or mating season, has begun. A few eastern chipmunks remain above ground but the majority have begun hibernating. On sunny days, expect late sightings of painted turtles on logs in ponds, basking in the warm light. Leopard frogs are moving back to lakes, ponds, and slow-moving streams where they will hibernate.

Rafts of American coots on area lakes may contain more than a thousand individual birds. American goldfinches are in their somber winter dress looking mostly brownish. In southern Minnesota, Franklin's gulls and ring-billed gulls follow farmers doing fall plowing to pick up worms and other small animals in the soil.

Statewide, nearly all soybeans and sugarbeets have been harvested. Watch for steam fog rising from ponds, lakes, and rivers on cold mornings.

scattered events

- **October 25, 2003** - First snow flurries. Tamarack trees have the beautiful golden yellow foliage. Migrating flocks of American robins feed on crabapple fruit. Juncos, white-throated sparrows, and fox sparrows are numerous at feeding stations. They feed on the ground.

- **October 26, 2007** - The fall color season continues with browns on oaks and golden yellow foliage on eastern cottonwoods, quaking aspens, paper birches, and American elms. At the University of Minnesota Landscape Arboretum, ginkgo trees display bright yellow and golden yellow leaves, serviceberry shrubs are showing reds and golden yellows, and eastern redbud leaves are bright yellow. Also in the Arboretum, seventy-five varieties of chrysanthemums are blooming.

- **October 30, 1996** - Cold temperatures marked the end of the growing season by killing the blooming geraniums, petunias, and marigolds. Snow is being made at Afton Alps Ski Area. Close to a hundred thousand Canada geese congregate at Lac Qui Parle Wildlife Area. The weather system today ushered tens of thousands of ducks out of Minnesota.

- **October 31, 2002** - Thin ice on ponds this morning. A flock of about 40 snow buntings

Photo: Frank Leung

was spotted in an open field near Northfield.

- **October 31, 2006** - The first flocks of migrating tundra swans were heard and seen over the Lake Waconia area, flying southeast.

A Closer Look:
Backyard Bird Feeding

The end of October is a perfect time to begin feeding wild birds. Now is when birds are establishing their feeding patterns for winter. With proper cover—trees, shrubs, or brush piles—birds will congregate in numbers at feeding stations. On snowy winter days I have recorded as many as 15 different species and several hundred individual birds at the Lowry Nature Center feeding station in Carver Park, near Victoria. We also see good numbers of birds at our home feeding station on the northwest side of Lake Waconia.

Setting up a feeding station is easy. All one needs is some food and a feeder or two. But knowing what type of food to put out, where to put it, and how to make it easy for the birds to find can be the difference between an active, successful feeding station and one that is only occasionally visited.

You can place the seeds for the birds on the ground in sheltered places, and in a variety of feeders. Ideally the feeders should be in spots where there is shelter, but also where you can see the visitors from a window. Shelter includes woody plants like trees, especially evergreens, and brush piles; all places to get away from wind, rain, snow, and enemies. The feeders themselves could be simple open trays, hopper feeders, or hanging feeders. Having several feeders of various designs and at different levels would be the best, then no one bird species can dominate.

To simplify wildlife feeding at our home I like to put black oil sunflower seeds in the feeders and scatter millet or cracked corn on the ground below the feeders. Yes, the northern cardinals will join the juncos, American tree sparrows, mourning doves, and blue jays on the ground to eat millet and cracked corn with gusto. The large-beaked seed eaters, including northern cardinals, blue jays, and grosbeaks, readily eat sunflower seeds. Black-capped chickadees, both white-breasted and red-breasted nuthatches, and American goldfinches also head for the sunflower seeds as their staple food of choice.

More than twenty species of birdfeeder birds relish both black oil and striped sunflower seeds. Black oil sunflower seed is the more economical choice because the smaller seeds go farther than the bigger, plump striped variety, which has fewer seeds per pound. Black oilers also have a higher oil content, so they give the birds more calories. The other advantage to black oil sunflower seed is that smaller birds can crack it readily.

Under the feeders the hulls of sunflower seeds cracked by the birds soon build up. You might think these hulls would make good mulching for the garden or around trees, but like the black walnut tree and sumac shrubs, sunflowers are allelopathic. The hulls of sunflower seeds contain chemicals that inhibit the growth of plant competitors. It's best to rake up the hulls and put them in a corner of the yard where worms and other natural decomposers can turn them back into soil.

Another very popular bird food is beef suet—the white, hard beef fat available at most meat counters or in suet cake mixes. Suet is a good energy source for birds. It's a favorite of the woodpecker clan, but is also eaten by nuthatches, chickadees, blue jays, and others. Suet is just as popular during the summer months as in winter. Place in mesh bags, such as an onion bag, or in wire mesh suet holders. Suet feeders need to be placed out of the reach of dogs. Secure chunks of suet so that they cannot be removed by mammals or bird guests.

Sunflower seed, millet, and cracked corn are highly preferred seeds for attracting birds, and suet is important too. But these foods also attract shrews and rabbits, squirrels and opossums, raccoons and deer. Why not share some food with these mammals and call your feeding station a *wildlife* feeding station. You can derive as much pleasure from feeding wild mammals as the wild birds. Try it!

A Closer Look:
White-breasted Nuthatches

White-breasted nuthatches are found throughout the United States and parts of southern Canada wherever deciduous forests grow. Although they are classified as permanent residents in Minnesota, at least a portion of the population will migrate southward in some years. Pairs typically remain together year-round. We see them nearly every day at our feeding station. Now, in late October, as well as at other times, whenever chickadees and downy woodpeckers appear at the feeders there is a good chance the white-

photo: Greg Gillson

breasted nuthatches will be there too.

They can perch upside down on a tree trunk and walk on the undersides of horizontal branches. The sexes have similar plumage, blue-gray above with a white face and belly, but can be separated by the color of the cap, which is black on males and blue-gray on females. White-breasted nuthatches are small, sparrow-sized, stocky birds with short legs, a stubby tail, and long toes for clinging to the sides of trees. Their incredible climbing ability is aided by an extra long hind toe nail, nearly twice as long as the front toe claws. The nuthatch's habit of hopping head first down tree trunks helps it see insects and their eggs that birds climbing up the trunk might miss. Their long, chisel-like bills are suited for probing and digging out insects from bark as well as for opening seeds.

At feeding stations, a nuthatch will take a sunflower seed, fly to a nearby tree and wedge it into the bark of the trunk. With the seed tightly locked, as in a vice, the nuthatch will then strike the shell with its long bill until the nut inside is extracted. This "nut-hatching," as it is sometimes called, has given the bird its name. The word "hatch" is a corruption of the old English word "hack." The white-breasted nuthatches we see in our yard are certainly "nuthackers."

A Closer Look:
What to Call Animals in Groups

At this time of year we are seeing flotillas of American coots called rafts, kettles of hawks high overhead, and braces of ducks. When we happen to see bunches of birds of various species, especially now during migrations, we sometimes are uncertain about whether to call them "flocks" or "bands" or something else. "Flocks" in most cases is fine but it's also fun to be more imaginative.

I have found several lists that include group names for some types of birds as well as for other animals. The correct terms may seem archaic but they are certainly descriptive and may add a bit of spice to our vocabularies.

Collective nouns are words that identify a collection of individuals. Instead of having to

---

A FEW ACCEPTED BIRD GROUP NAMES

Charm of hummingbirds or goldfinches

Staring of owls

Covey of quail

Chattering of starlings

Unkindness of ravens

Party or **band** of jays

Wedge of swans

Rafter of turkeys

Raft of ducks (when large groups on an open lake appear as a solid body)

Puddle of ducks

Fall of woodcocks

Host of sparrows

Flight of swallows

Exaltation of larks

SOME OTHER ANIMAL GROUP NAMES TO THINK ABOUT:

Swarm or **hive** of bees

Colony of ants or beavers

Rabble of butterflies

Bed of clams

School of fish

Pack of wolves

Band of coyotes

Cloud of gnats

say "Look at the 137 geese!" a simple "Look at the flock!" works better. In researching the correct group name for the many Canada geese I see daily in the Twin Cities area, I found that "flock" is correct, but only if the geese are standing around, grazing on grasses in a park or on a golf course. If the group is flying, it becomes a "skein," and if the group is on water, it's a "gaggle."

A Closer Look:
Boston Ivy

The so-called "Boston ivy" is not native to North America at all, but to Japan and central China. Here in the Upper Midwest we see Boston ivy on schools, churches, places of business, and even on some homes. At this time, in late October, the vines on Olin Hall and Johnson Union at Gustavus Adolphus College in St. Peter, and growing up on buildings on Summit Avenue in St. Paul, are showing brilliant shades of red on the leaves that were lustrus green during the growing season. The leaves are simple and generally three-lobed, sugar maple-shaped, and average four to eight inches in width.

Boston ivy (*parthenocissus tricuspidata*), also called Japanese creeper, forms long, slender stems and ascends very high walls by means of its sucker-like tendrils. It can grow to the top of a three-story building within a few years. This is the best vine for clinging to stone or brick walls; the green leaves cover the wall in summer, in fall we enjoy the vivid scarlet foliage, and the branching pattern against the wall is attractive in winter. Some pruning may be required in the summer to keep the vine from covering windows. The tiny flowers in spring are not showy but the ripe bluish-black fruits, mostly hidden by the foliage, are very much sought after by birds. Boston ivy is hardy in zone 4b which just includes extreme southern Minnesota, but don't be afraid to plant it even a bit north of the Twin Cities. Dieback sometimes occurs after a severe winter, but new growth from the base will soon cover a wall again.

Photo: Jim Gilbert

November

November often starts out like autumn but ends up wintery. There are fewer thunderstorms but the liklihood of sleet, freezing rain, and snow increases. Trees are silhouetted against blue skies and cloud formations, dried grasses and herbs stand tall, there is plenty of natural food for the wild animals, winter birds are colorful, and new ice appears. This is the month of clouds, so we often end up with some of the best sunsets of the year. Fall colors linger, honey bees visit surviving flowers, and there are big migrations of waterfowl across the state. The rutting (mating) season of the white-tailed deer reaches its peak the last two weeks of November. Lakes steam on cold mornings and many freeze over. Raccoons enter their winter sleeping dens.

READING THE LANDSCAPE

Week one (November 1–7)

Flying in V-shaped Wedges
Ginkgo Trees
Nature's Voice to Humans
Snowshoe Hares

Week two (November 8–15)

Snow Buntings, Arctic Visitors
Russian Olive Trees
Hibernation
A Beautiful Fog

Week three (November 16–23)

Flying Squirrels
Opossums
White-tailed Deer
Ice Forms on Ponds and Lakes

Week four (November 24–30)

Talking Turkey
Blueprint for a Muskrat House
The Great American Crow
Lake Waconia, Freeze-up History

first week in november

Indian summer days result in open golf courses, fishing boats on lakes, and picnickers and walkers enjoying the sunshine. The normal high temperature in Minneapolis/ St. Paul for November 1 is 50°F, but by November 30 it's only 32°. Also for November 1 the normal low is 31°, the record high temperature is 77° set in 1933 and record low is 10° recorded in 1951. The November 1 record of 18.5 inches of snow came during the famous Halloween snowstorm of 1991, which dumped a total of 26.7 inches of snow on the Twin Cities overnight.

The native pin oaks and northern red oaks still show some attractive red and brown foliage. Red cedar trees have begun taking on the brownish-red look of winter. Common witch-hazel shrubs have lost most of their leaves, making the clusters of yellow spider-like flowers easy to see.

The stunning rose-red foliage remains on winged euonymus shrubs. Norway maples and Lombardy poplars display beautiful golden-yellow leaves. European larch trees have vivid smoky-gold needles. The silver and green leaves of the Russian olive are dropping. Weeping willows have about 30 percent sunny-yellow foliage; the rest is still green.

It's possible to still be picking ripe fruit from Regent, Haralson, and other late-producing apple trees, though the leaves have fallen. Asparagus plants appear golden-yellow. Some years, dozens of chrysanthemum varieties, and also alyssum, pansies, and geraniums, keep blooming in outside gardens. Lawn mowing is about done for the year, but sod continues to be cut and put down for new lawns.

Tundra swans are seen overhead and we hear their muffled musical whistles—a wonderful sign of fall. They are coming from their summer range which is mainly north of the Arctic Circle and heading for their wintering range along the Atlantic coast. A good area to see hundreds, sometimes thousands, of tundra swans is the Mississippi River and its backwaters between Minneiska and Brownsville. The last flocks of migrating red-winged blackbirds, common grackles, and American robins move through. Both white-throated and fox sparrows forage beneath backyard feeders.

Statewide, farmers labor to finish up the combining of corn and other field work. Southern Minnesota farmers harvest the last crop of lush green alfalfa. Gray squirrels collect fallen leaves and strips of bark from branches to add to their winter nests. Snowshoe hares in northern Minnesota are changing from brown to their white winter coats.

scattered events

- **November 1, 2001** - Deciduous forests of native trees are nearly bare, and have been for about a week. The non-native weeping willows, Lombardy poplars, and Norway maples have very attractive golden-yellow foliage. Flocks of Bohemian waxwings feed on mountain ash fruit in Grand Marais and area.

- **November 3, 2002** - Huge flocks of common grackles and other blackbirds, in long black "rivers of life," travel from roosts to feeding areas in the morning and back before sunset.

- **November 3, 2006** - Low of only 12°F. Ice formed on ponds. Several thousand migrating tundra swans have gathered on the Mississippi River in the Brownsville area.

- **November 7, 2000** - Weeping willows have golden-yellow foliage. Big rafts of American coots can be seen on some lakes. The first one-inch snowfall descended on evergreen boughs and inspired the season's first snow sculptures.

A Closer Look:
Flying in V-shaped Wedges

As a bird flaps its wings it disturbs the air and leaves whirling eddies behind. Some gregarious species, such as the Canada goose, have learned to take advantage of the upward

photo: Helen M. Roman

disturbed air created off the wings of others in the flock by flying in a V-formation. Each bird thus adds the lift lost by the bird ahead to its own. This "drafting" allows the geese to travel at an easier pace through their long flights. Researchers have found that geese flying in Vs can fly as much as 70 percent further than they would otherwise have been able to.

When traveling long distances, tundra swans fly in the same V-shaped formations as geese and for the same reason. The resistance of the air is less as each bird flies in the widening wake of its predecessor. The leader has the hardest work to do as he or she "breaks the trail" but is relieved at intervals and drops back into the flock to rest.

Besides the many flocks of Canada geese and tundra swans we observe traveling in V or wedge-shaped formations, many other species of swans, geese, ducks, cormorants, shorebirds, and gulls also regularly arrange themselves in that pattern. Throughout

October and well into November, I'm filled with awe each evening at sunset, as one V-formation after another of Franklin's gulls makes its way to Lake Waconia, where these social birds will spend the night as a huge surface water flock.

A Closer Look:
Ginkgo Trees

On November 7, 2007, I wrote in my field notes that the ginkgo tree next door, in Dave and Peggy Philp's yard on the shore of Lake Waconia, had a beautiful layer of bright yellow leaves within a circle directly under the tree. About 99 percent of the leaves were down. This was at 7:30 am, with very light south winds, 27°F, and a mostly cloudy sky. Later that morning, Sandy and I drove into downtown Minneapolis, and on the way we noticed that other ginkgo trees were also in the process of losing huge numbers of their leaves. Once again I was reminded that this widely planted street and ornamental tree, with outstanding yellow fall color, has a unique feature—the fan-shaped leaves often fall to the ground during a single day or overnight.

The leaves had emerged in clusters on branch spurs in May. They look like long-stemmed fans, have parallel veins, and are more or less notched or divided at the broad summit.

In the world of trees, the ginkgo is a living relic. It is the sole survivor of an extensive family of trees that was distributed over all the temperate regions of the world when dinosaurs roamed the Earth about 190 million years ago. The ginkgo tree has not changed its design in all these years. We should feel a special respect for a living species that has adapted so well it feels no need to evolve further. During the last Ice Age, glaciers wiped out the ginkgo everywhere except the mountain forests of eastern China. It is not certain if any ginkgo trees exist there in a natural state today, but its re-emergence is due to the priestly planting of it in temple gardens, first in China, and then in Japan. Surviving as a living fossil, the ginkgo is popular in many parts of the world today for planting along busy streets. Its ability to live through millions of years of change seems to help it withstand urban pollution.

The name is the Japanese version of the Chinese "yin-kuo," meaning silver fruit. Female trees produce fruits with a fleshy covering that rots with an unpleasant smell, although the kernels can be roasted and eaten and are prized in oriental cuisine.

Europeans first heard of the ginkgo when a surgeon named Kaempfer, an employee of the Dutch East India Company, wrote of his visit to Japan in 1690. Ginkgoes were first introduced into Europe in 1730 and to the United States in 1784. There are specimens growing in China which are more than one thousand years old.

The ginkgo tree (*Ginkgo biloba L.*) will do well in zone 4—southern Minnesota and along the North Shore of Lake Superior. Full sun is best but it can tolerate some shade. These trees will grow in any soil that isn't too alkaline or doesn't have poor drainage. Most often male trees are planted.

A Closer Look:
Nature's Voice to Humans

Birds are animals with feathers. They see in color. In addition they are warm blooded with high constant body temperatures, have skin covered with feathers, and their forelimbs are modified as wings. However, not all birds fly; think of penguins and the ostrich.

© Marlena Zagajewska | Dreamstime.com

At this time about 9,700 species of birds live on our planet Earth. About 650 species are found in North America. Of the 427 bird species sighted in Minnesota, 60 species or so stay all winter and about 15 of these species visit feeding stations.

About a hundred billion birds live on Earth; that's 15.5 times the human population. The fossil record shows us that the highly diversified array of birds we see today are descendants of dinosaurs that went extinct about 65 million years ago. Birds range in size from the ostrich, which may stand 8 feet tall and weigh 300 pounds, to the tiny bee hummingbird of Cuba, with a length of only 2.25 inches.

Birds are nature's voice to humans. They are also the "litmus paper" of our environment—indicators of the health of our land, air, and water.

Roger Tory Peterson, no doubt the best-known twentieth-century American ornithologist and bird artist, once said, "Birds, not rooted to the Earth are among the most eloquent expressions of life."

In the Twin Cities area, we usually have spotted our first brown creepers of the season by this time, and dark-eyed juncos (also called snowbirds and known as the harbingers of winter) are numerous at feeding stations. A few rafts of American coots can still be seen on local lakes and a few flocks of American robins and eastern bluebirds are still migrating through. Huge flocks of blackbirds (mostly red-winged blackbirds and common grackles) fly in narrow bands like fast-moving streams to and from roosting and feeding areas. The assemblies of red-wings and grackles create the largest and most commonly observed groups of land birds in North America. Slowly, as the autumn season progresses, the huge flights drift south. Also, flocks of those gregarious and sleek crested birds called cedar waxwings are commonly seen devouring crabapple and mountain ash fruit. Flocks of tundra swans, known for their muffled musical whistles, stop to rest on Lake Minnetonka and other area lakes.

A Closer Look:

Snowshoe Hares

Sometimes known as the "rabbits" of northern Minnesota's cedar swamps and spruce forests, snowshoe hares are changing from brown to their white winter coats. By mid-November they will be nearly white except for the black tips of their ears, and will stay that way until April. The unusually large feet, which are covered with long dense fur, enable the hare to travel on or near the top of deep snow, much like humans on snowshoes.

© Alain | Dreamstime.com

They are found in the northern half of the state. Many times I have taken students on hikes at Wolf Ridge Environmental Learning Center, located near Finland and the North Shore of Lake Superior, to study snowshoe hare ecology. Against a background of snow the white pelage of this "ghost" is tough to detect but most often we saw at least one bounding off in a wooded area.

Snowshoe hares prefer dense cover during the day but come out into open areas to feed at night. Their food consists mainly of green vegetation during the summer months and twigs, buds, and the bark of shrubs and small trees during the winter. Home range is about ten acres.

Hare tracks can be confusing because when a hare hops, its hind feet plunk down in front of the front feet so that the rear, big prints are forward, indicating the direction of the hare's movement.

Female hares begin breeding when they are about a year old, and have two to three litters of four to six young annually. Foxes, wolves, owls, and the Canada lynx take advantage of this fruitfulness. All rely on the non-hibernating hares as a reliable source of winter food. The first young hares appear in May, and others may be born as late as August. The gestation period is about 36 days. The two-ounce babies, called "leverets," are born fully furred and with their eyes open, and are able to walk by the time their fur has dried, unlike rabbits, who are born helpless, hairless, and blind. No nest is built to receive the young hares. They come into the world in the shelter of a shrub or in a brush pile. The young begin eating green vegetation in about eight days.

It is well-known that populations of snowshoe hares fluctuate wildly. In a period of ten or eleven years it may increase from a single hare to several hundred in a square mile. Then, within a few months, it may decrease again to low ebb through disease and the stress brought on by overcrowding, dwindling food supplies, predation, and other factors.

Week two (Nov 8-15)

Weeping willow trees, which are native to Europe and Asia, are exhibiting golden-yellow fall color. Winterberry fruit is bright red and bittersweet fruit is glowing orange. Wooded areas are quite open but the green leaves of the common buckthorn are very noticeable, revealing how invasive this small tree has become.

Common milkweed is as distinctive now as when it was blooming in July; the large warty seedpods have split open and are shedding dark-brown seeds on silver-white parachutes across windswept meadows.

Photo: Barbara Jane Carter

Truckloads of newly cut Christmas trees—firs, pines, and spruces—are seen on highways heading for retail sales lots. It's time to wrap young tree trunks, especially those of fruit trees and maples, for winter protection from both sun and rodent damage. Rutabagas and parsnips sweetened by the frosts can be dug for delicious eating or stored for winter use.

Gossamers—single strands of spider silk—hang from tree and shrub branches, glistening silver-white in the sunshine. Short-tailed weasels are now white except for the tips of their tails, which remain black. Having turned white, they are looking for snow cover. Weasels in white are called ermines.

Heated birdbaths and crabapple fruit invite flocks of cedar waxwings. Lingering flocks of eastern bluebirds remain. About fifteen species of birds, including dark-eyed juncos and white-throated sparrows, can be observed at feeding stations. Migrating waterfowl include American wigeons, common pintails, canvasbacks, lesser scaup, buffleheads, ruddy ducks, and tundra swans. We notice a big influx of Canada geese on harvested soybean and corn stubble fields.

Flocks of snow buntings, migrants from the arctic, are visitors along the North Shore of Lake Superior.

- **November 8, 1995** - About 14,000 tundra swans are on the Mississippi River and backwaters between Wabasha and the Iowa border. Thousands of Canada geese and some snow geese have assembled at Silver Lake in Rochester. Freeze-up date for Caribou Lake near Lutsen, and both Cannon Lake and Wells Lake at Faribault.

- **November 8, 2006** - Last of the Regent apples were picked. Summer-like afternoon with a high of 72 degrees in the Twin Cities, and 82 degrees at Mankato and Redwood F alls.

- **November 9, 2006** - Last flock of common grackles seen. About 7,000 moose live in Minnesota; one came from the north into the Lake Minnetonka area today.

- **November 10, 1990** - The number of migrating tundra swans gathered at the Weaver Marshes and thereabouts is now about 8,000. This represents the largest concentration of tundra swans in the central United States.

- **November 10, 1998** - The wild rose hips and American bittersweet berries are attractive on this wet day. It's easy to count a hundred bald eagles while driving along the Mississippi River between Red Wing and Wabasha.

- **November 10, 2004** - Some gardeners still picking ripe raspberries.

- **November 10, 2005** - A killing frost ended the 229-day growing season, the longest on record going back to 1891.

- **November 11, 1996** - Last night this season the thousand-plus Franklin's gulls spent on Lake Waconia. Freeze-up date for Lake Ocheda near Worthington, Winsted Lake in McLeod County, and both Portage Lake and Upper Bottle Lake in Hubbard County.

- **November 11, 2004** - About six thousand tundra swans are congregated on the Mississippi River and backwaters near LaCrescent.

- **November 12, 2001** - Record high temperature of 65° marks sixteenth straight day with above-normal temperatures in the Twin Cities. Lawn mowing continues. A few Connell Red, Haralson, and Regent apples are still being picked. Thousands of Franklin's gulls spend the night on Lake Waconia, but they'll be leaving soon.

A Closer Look:
Snow Buntings, Arctic Visitors

The second weekend in November, 2007, Sandra and I, together with our dog Gilbey, spent much of our time walking trails in the Lutsen area. Water was rushing

photo: David Brislance

in the Poplar River, common ravens and red-breasted nuthatches were vocal, mosses looked lush green, red-osier dogwood twigs glowed red, and there were a few patches of snow in protected spots. But one of the most outstanding natural features was the presence of snow buntings. We encountered many flocks of a dozen to twenty birds in open areas and along roads.

These migrants from the Arctic are a bit larger than juncos. They looked quite brown on the ground but when they circled over us their flashing white wing patches identified them. In fact, overhead the snow buntings looked almost entirely white. We often heard their wild twittering before spotting a flock.

Friends Dave and Mary Brislance, who live on the ridge above Lake Superior in Lutsen, wrote to me October 24, 2007, saying they had seen snow buntings the previous three days on a gravel road leading to their house. Dave walked out to photograph them but of course they flew off in their chirping magnificent spiral. Then, to quote Dave: "I had my camo jacket on, so pulled up my hood and stood between two small six-foot spruce trees and waited. Sure enough, they wound their way back, making two passes overhead and the flock of sixteen politely landed ten feet in front of me. I stayed there for an hour and took almost a hundred photos of them, and managed to get many shots of them feeding on the weed seeds in the rocks and gravel."

By November 17, 2007, a birder spotted a snow bunting flock near Faribault. On February 28, 2008, large flocks of snow buntings were seen in Polk County.

These few observations give some indication of snow bunting activity for a single season here in Minnesota. They are considered to be common to abundant winter visitants throughout much of the state each year. They are uncommon to absent in the heavily wooded areas of the north-central and northeastern regions. Snow buntings are most numerous in December and January, when flocks numbering in the thousands are occasionally encountered. Fall migration into Minnesota peaks in early November, and the spring migration north peaks in late March as flocks of snow buntings head to their summer nesting sites in the Arctic tundra.

This circumpolar bird, often called "snowflake," breeds farther north than any other songbird. They even nest on Ellesmere Island and in northern Greenland. Their nests are at the very edge of the icy land. So long as the winds or weak Arctic sunshine expose patches of bare earth and the seeds of hardy plants, the snow bunting is content. Insects and spiders are also consumed. During the summer breeding time a male has black on its back, a white head, and mostly white on underparts, wings and tail. Females are similar but duller.

A Closer Look:
Russian Olive Trees

Russian olive leaves don't change into fall color, but they have a very long leaf-dropping period beginning in early November and lasting close to three weeks. Now is the time we see their unique silver and green leaves falling to the ground.

Native from southern Europe to western and central Asia, the Russian olive (*Elaeagnus angustifolia L.*) has been planted and grows throughout Minnesota as a large shrub or small tree, usually to a height of about 22 feet with a 16 foot width. It is known for its small fragrant yellow flowers which appear in June,

and for its long narrow leaves that are dull green above with a silvery underside. The fruit is yellowish and coated with silvery scales, about .4 inch long, and has a sweet mealy flesh. It is edible, and ripe in September and October. In parts of Asia the fruit is made into a sherbet-like drink.

For landscape use, Russian olive requires a well-drained soil and grows best in full sun. It is somewhat drought resistant. It is used as a background small tree or accent in a border, or sometimes as an ornamental clump specimen. In many parts of North America it is considered an invasive tree, but Russian olive is useful in the plains in shelterbelts as it withstands alkaline soils and exposed locations.

A Closer Look:
Hibernation

In November we become aware that the numbers and species of animals in the wild have greatly dwindled. Winter strategies for wild Minnesota animals include migration, hibernation, and coping. For example, multitudes of our Minnesota barn swallows head for South America in winter, while honey bees beat their wings furiously to keep warm in their hives. The Minnesota gopher escapes winter by hibernating from October to March or April.

During the winter untold millions of reptiles, amphibians, many insects, and some mammals hibernate in Minnesota.

The physiology of this "sleep" is amazing. The animal's pulse slows to a few beats per minute, breathing nearly stops, the blood thickens, the internal temperature drops down close to freezing, the metabolism slows, and the kidneys and digestive system almost stop functioning. Hibernating animals can "sleep" through almost any disturbance. A few are able to wake up if their body temperatures approach freezing, but this seldom happens as many animals hibernate below the frost line on land or below the ice under water.

A Closer Look:
A Beautiful Fog

On bitterly cold late-fall days, when there is still open water on lakes and streams, we can see a rolling, moving fog—we call it evaporation or steam fog—rising like smoke or steam from the water surfaces. It's caused by cold air moving over the water and picking up moisture which then condenses. This advective-type fog is responsible for the beautiful layers of rime frost that often build up on trees and shrubs on the windward side of a body of water. Many photographers and painters enjoy catching the soft beauty of such a fog.

Week three (Nov 16-23)

We are deep into November, the month of clouds, and with that comes some of the most colorful sunrises and sunsets. November 19 is the average date for permanent snow cover in the Twin Cities.

Weeping willows and European larches keep showing golden-yellow leaves. A few dandelions still bloom, but on short stems. Avid gardeners cover rows of carrots with straw so fresh carrots can be dug when they are needed throughout winter.

Bald eagles can be seen patrolling Lake Minnetonka and other area lakes. They come each year about this time to feed on fish and wounded waterfowl. European starlings are in their winter dress, with speckled feathers and black bills. Hairy, downy and red-bellied woodpeckers come to feeding stations for suet, but will also take seeds. Juncos are the most numerous birds at many feeding stations. The last rafts of American coots and flocks of Franklin's gulls on southern Minnesota lakes will soon be leaving as the water temperature of lakes drops to a uniform 39°F throughout.

On the first calm, freezing day or night after a particular pond or lake reaches 39° in all parts, an ice cover will form.

- **November 16, 2005** - High temperature of 27° and a low of 13°F at the Minneapolis/ St. Paul International Airport. Below freezing all day for the first time this season. Ice formed on ponds. Many flocks of tundra swans were seen over the Twin Cities and south to Trempealeau, Wisconsin.

- **November 18, 2003** - Flocks of cedar waxwings feed on crabapple fruit. European larch trees have smoky-gold foliage. Russian olive leaves still green and silver, but now are falling in numbers.

- November 19, 1989 - About 100 bald eagles are in the Reads Landing area in the Mississippi River valley.

- **November 19, 1996** - Freeze-up date for Mille Lacs Lake and Leech Lake, and Lake Florida near Spicer.

- **November 21, 2007** - Small ponds froze over. Lawns still look green. Late osprey sighting.

- **November 22, 2005** - Franklin's gulls follow plow in field just outside of Waconia. Near Rice, MN, at Little Rock Lake, 42 bald eagles were spotted out on the ice next to an open water spot where they were catching fish.

- **November 23, 1999** - Thousands of Canada geese are gathered on the south side of Lac qui Parle Lake.

Photo: David Brislance

A Closer Look:
Flying Squirrels

Flying squirrels don't hibernate, although during an extreme cold spell they may huddle together in groups in a state of light, transitory hibernation known as torpor. Because they are strictly nocturnal, we rarely see these restless little squirrels. However, they are common woodland creatures and readily come to wildlife feeding stations for seeds and suet. A spotlight aimed on your feeders will not keep them away, but will give you an opportunity to watch them feed.

The southern flying squirrel prefers deciduous forests and is found throughout the eastern United States but seldom where coniferous trees dominate. Northern flying squirrels are found in mixed coniferous and deciduous forests from Alaska across Canada and into the United States. Both species live in Minnesota. In the southern part of the state we have the southern flying squirrel, which is about ten inches long, including the tail, and weighs about two ounces. The northern species weighs an ounce or two more and is an inch or so longer. Both species have thick soft fur that is brown on the upper body and white below.

The two forms of the flying squirrel have similar behavior and are the only truly nocturnal members of the squirrel family in Minnesota. Flying squirrels don't really fly but they are super gliders. They have a folded layer of loose skin along each side of their bodies that extends between their wrists and ankles, and with front and hind legs spread wide, they can sail through the air for distances of up to 150 feet. On the downward gliding approach to a tree trunk landing, a squirrel will raise its tail so as to slow down. Upon grabbing the tree the squirrel immediately scampers to the other side of the trunk to foil any hungry owl that may be following too closely.

Flying squirrels make their nests in old woodpecker holes or some other cavity in a tree. They also build leafy nests in the branches of trees and in the attics of houses and outbuildings. Flying squirrels are gregarious and live together in communities where good habitats may support five or more per acre.

Flying squirrels commonly eat seeds, buds, nuts, fruits, mushrooms, insects, bird's eggs and birds.

A Closer Look:
Opossums

In the last 20 years the opossum has expanded its range to the point where folks in central and even northwestern Minnesota can now turn on a yard light and catch sight of one eating from a dog dish or feasting on sunflower seeds from an easily-accessible birdfeeder. Although opossums are now quite common in the Twin Cities area and throughout southern Minnesota, they are almost entirely nocturnal in their habits and are therefore seldom seen.

Adult opossums are the size of house cats, have short legs, are grayish-white in color, and have long naked tails. The leaf-like ears are thin and naked. Some people may say that the opossum is not very intelligent. I disagree. It has succeeded as a species where other forms have become extinct. It has also followed the progress of civilization even into regions of severe winters, where it remains active throughout the year. So don't be surprised to see one at your wildlife feeding station one of these November evenings or even in February or March.

The opossum is special. It's our only North American marsupial. Yes, the female carries the young in a pouch on her abdomen like a kangaroo. Opossums also have prehensile tails, which makes it easy for them to climb trees.

The 3 to 14 young are born just 13 days after mating. Each is about half an inch long, naked and grub-like in appearance. They are cared for in their mother's pouch for 4 to 5 weeks, at which point they begin to venture forth for short periods. By 8 weeks of age each must shift for itself.

The natural habitat for the opossum is a wooded area along a stream, near a lake, or in a swamp. They are found from Minnesota to New York and as far south as central Mexico, and have been introduced into Washington, Oregon, and California. You might find them living in a hole in a tree, a deserted den of another mammal, or a brush pile. A true opportunist among wild mammals, the opossum might make its home in almost *any* shelter in which it can be dry and safe from enemies—even under or in an old building.

© Teekaygee | Dreamstime.com

By the same token, opossums will eat almost anything organic, including carrion, spoiled fruits, fresh fruits, eggs, nuts, and insects.

Opossums are slow-moving, so if you or your dog chase one it will seek safety up a tree, in a brush pile, or, if a retreat cannot be reached it may play "possum," that is, pretend death. These animals are relatively harmless to people, but do treat them with respect, as they have more teeth than any other mammal found in Minnesota. They are enjoyed as food by some people.

A Closer Look:
White-tailed Deer

For nearly forty years I have been observing deer in their natural surroundings and photographing their actions. During much of that time I worked as an interpretive naturalist helping school children and also many adults search for signs of deer to learn more about their interesting lives. A fresh snowfall in mid- to late November always presents us with an opportunity to study these animals.

Deer tracks in the snow mark the daily routines of animals adjusting to the seasonal changes in their environment The tracks often lead to deer trails, and along deer trails we could find scat, urine markings, and woody plants that have been browsed. From mid-morning to mid-afternoon, deer often bed down to rest, so if we were lucky we might come around a wooded hillside just as several deer were jumping out of their beds, or at least we often found recently used deer beds. All these years I have told people we could learn more about deer by observing their signs than by actually seeing them. I think they believed me, but still most were hoping to see a deer. That really happened many times on our trail hikes.

Photo: David Brislance

The white-tailed deer is the largest wild animal in southern Minnesota. They are found throughout the state in border areas between forests and openings. Adult deer average three feet tall in shoulder height and weigh 100 to 300 pounds. When seen at a distance or when bounding through the woods the deer appear to be much larger.

The most conspicuous part of this

magnificent animal is the large white tail. When fleeing, whitetails send up the danger flag; their white tails stand tall and alert others of possible trouble. Bucks often exceed 36 inches at the shoulders by a few inches and can top 250 pounds in weight. A possible Minnesota record buck taken in Cook County weighed 400 pounds dressed out, and alive could have exceeded 500 pounds. Does rarely weigh more than 150 pounds. A reddish summer coat gives way in autumn to the thick, gray-brown, hollow-haired insulating winter coat.

When active, deer prefer the hours of subdued light. On moonlit nights they may feed all night. They are munchers, rarely remaining in one place to feed until full. Instead, they eat a few leaves here, a green shoot there, or a fungus somewhere else. Their diet changes with the seasons. During the fall, over much of Minnesota, they may subsist almost entirely on acorns while this food source lasts. With the coming of winter they become browsers, eating small twigs from a variety of trees and shrubs, and will eat mosses and the tips of white cedars. We think of deer as plant eaters but on occasion they have been known to eat fish and even insects, rather unusual items in their diet.

The white-tailed deer's running speed is about 30 miles per hour to a maximum speed of 50 miles per hour. Still, a deer depends on camouflage and its keen senses to survive. Deer can jump exceedingly well, clearing objects 7 to 8 feet high from a standing position. Whitetails also can swim but enter deep water only when pressed.

Deer are color blind, seeing the world in monochromatic tones and shades of gray. They do not appear to see an object that does not move; however, the slightest movement will be seen immediately.

The sense of smell plays a very important role in a deer's world. Observations show that a distance of about one-third mile is the maximum range that a scent can be detected by a deer. Their hearing is also excellent. Ears are constantly in motion, picking up sounds of possible danger. Alarm calls of the blue jay, American crow, or red squirrel can send deer bounding away.

A Closer Look:

Ice Forms on Ponds and Lakes

Freezing and the formation of ice covers on lakes or other waters is a process controlled in large part by a unique characteristic of water. Most materials, for example mercury in a thermometer, shrink as they cool. Water also shrinks as it cools from summer temperatures to 39°F. As the cool water sinks it mixes with the rising warmer water until the lake becomes a uniform 39°. However, as water drops below 39° it begins to swell. For this reason, water cooler than 39° is lighter than water at 39° and will float on the surface. Ice forms at 32°, so on the first calm, freezing day or night after the lakes and ponds reach 39° throughout, ice covers will form. The temperature of the water just in contact with the ice sheet in winter is 32°, but a few feet below the ice the temperature is 35° to 38°, and 39° on the bottom.

If water cooler than 39° continued to shrink and to become more dense and sink, ice would form from the bottom of a pond, lake or stream, rather than the top. Just think, our lakes and other bodies of water would have permanent ice covered by a layer of water in the summer.

Listed below are 2007 freeze-up dates for ten Minnesota lakes. The freeze-up date is the first day when at least 90 percent of the lake is frozen over and stays frozen over.

✲ FREEZE~UP DATES ✲

Date	Name of Lake	Location
November 22	Wolf Lake	Lake County, near Finland
November 22	Lake Hendricks	Lincoln County
November 22	Moosehead Lake	Carlton County, at Moose Lake
November 27	Lake George	Hubbard County
November 28	Round Lake	Crow Wing, near Nisswa
November 28	Forest Lake	Washington County
December 1	Lake Minnewashta	Carver County, near Excelsior
December 2	Green Lake	Kandiyohi County, at Spicer
December 3	Lake Calhoun	Minneapolis
December 3	Lake Minnetonka	Hennepin County

Week four (Nov 24-30)

Evergreens such as pines, spruces, firs, yews, and arborvitae add much interest to the late November landscape. In low angle sunlight, the silvery dandelion seedheads and clusters of common milkweed seeds on silver carriers are a splendid sight. The low sun angle now makes driving more difficult in mornings and afternoons.

It's freeze-up time for Minnesota lakes. Remember, it takes at least 4 inches of new solid ice in contact with stationary freshwater for safe skating and ice fishing. A snowmobile takes 6 inches of ice, 8 to 12 inches are needed for a car or small truck, and 12 to 15 inches for a medium-size pickup. You don't want to fall through the ice as cold water saps body heat 25 times faster than air of the same temperature. In 32° water, you have about 15 minutes before going unconscious.

As long as most days remain above 27° F, raccoons will be active about the landscape. Muskrats can be observed up on the ice of ponds, eating water plants they have gathered below.

The brown creeper—a five-inch, camouflaged tree-climbing bird—can be seen going up and around tree trunks. A heated birdbath is very popular with birds and other wildlife at this time. Flying squirrels visit some feeding stations after dark, where they relish sunflower seeds and suet.

Down-hill ski and snowboard areas hope to be open with many runs by now. It's time for the Upper Mississippi River shipping season, above Lock and Dam Number 2 at Hastings, to end for the season.

In the southern part of the state Jack rabbits have turned from brown to white. Thousands of migrant Canada geese gather at Silver Lake in Rochester.

Look for pine grosbeaks and pine siskins at northern and central Minnesota feeding stations. In the same area, black bears are sleeping—not hibernating. They go into torpor, a very reduced state of activity and metabolism, from which they can easily be awakened.

scattered events

- **November 24, 2004** - Freeze-up date for Wolf Lake near Finland and Portage Lake near Park Rapids.

- **November 25, 1996** - At 4 p.m., hundreds of American crows assemble in tall trees to roost in the vicinity of Summit Avenue in St. Paul.

- **November 25, 2001** - A few pansies, chrysanthemums, and alyssum are still blooming. Last big flocks of Franklin's gulls come in the late afternoon to spend the night on Lake Waconia. We picked and ate the last Regent apples fresh off our tree.

- **November 27, 1999** - Parsley is green and growing, and ornamental kale is showy in gardens. Near St. Peter, several hundred red-winged blackbirds foraged in a corn-stubble field. Nine species of waterfowl, including canvasbacks and ring-necked ducks, seen on Loon Lake at Waseca.

- **November 28, 2006** - High temperature of 56°. Thunderstorms moved across the Twin Cities area. Sod is still being cut for new lawns. The last tug and barges of the season, coming from St Paul, went through Hastings.

- **November 30, 2006** - Ponds and small lakes froze over. The low temperature was 7° and the high only 18° F in the Twin Cities.

Photo: Mike Lentz

A Closer Look:
Talking Turkey

Although they feed on the ground, wild turkeys roost in trees at night. Seeing these large birds, which stand three to four feet tall and usually weigh from 8 to 18 pounds, spring off the ground and fly nearly straight up into a tall tree is quite a sight. I have watched wild turkeys head up to their tree roosts in the Waconia area on several occasions. They are brown and bronze, each with a striking blue and red featherless head.

The home range of the wild turkey is the eastern, southern, and southwestern United States, and down into Mexico. There is no positive evidence that this species had ever existed in Minnesota before European settlement, but they were introduced into the southern part of the state as far back as 1936. Now, after a series of introductions during the 1960s and '70s, they are seen year-round in open woodlands, along forest edges, and in wooded swamps scattered across the southern one-third of the state. Many of us enjoy observing flocks containing a half-dozen to forty of these largest of game birds, scavenging along country roads near wooded edges or even coming to wildlife feeding stations. The state's wild turkey population grew from a few small flocks in the 1970s to about 60,000 birds by 2006.

The domestic turkey is a subspecies that had been tamed, and was taken from Mexico to Europe by the Spaniards in the sixteenth century. There was confusion from the start regarding the origin of this great bird. It was initially thought that it had originated in the country of Turkey. Hence, the name we use today. History tells us that English settlers brought the domestic turkey back to North America.

Wild turkeys prefer acorns but will eat any kind of seed, plus fruits, insects, frogs, and other small animals. They spend the winter in same-sex or mixed-sex flocks. At any time of year wild turkeys may gobble but it is in the spring that each tom reigns over his own small clearing, gobbling in earnest with tail fanned. Males may mate with many females, but it is the hens that raise the young. The 6 to 20 eggs hatch after an incubation period of about 28 days. Nests are a leaf-lined depression on the forest floor. The chicks, also called poults,

are able to run soon after hatching and can make short flights when just two weeks old. The young birds remain with the mother hen through the following winter.

In 1782, the turkey lost by a single vote to the bald eagle to become our national bird or national symbol.

A Closer Look:

Blueprint for a Muskrat House

Muskrats are taking advantage of new ice sheets, using them as platforms on which to rest and eat. They are largely vegetarians, and we can see them bring various aquatic plant parts, like tubers, up for their picnics on ice. Muskrats, found in most parts of the United States and Canada, are more active at night than during the day. Although they do not hibernate, they build houses shaped like miniature beaver lodges in preparation for winter.

Muskrat houses are about four feet high and eight feet in diameter. They are made of cattail plants, mud, and small water plants that are built into mounds. Then, like beavers, the muskrats dig out a chamber inside these mounds and create an underwater entrance where they can enter and leave unobserved from shore.

We usually spot muskrats on ponds and the marshy shores of lakes. Sometimes they burrow into banks and have their tunnels above high water. The entrance, however, always is sufficiently below water lever so that it is difficult to observe and is below the winter ice level.

A Closer Look:
The Great American Crow

American crows are omnivorous, consuming great numbers of grasshoppers, cutworms, and other insects. In late fall and through winter they eat the kernels of corn in fields after harvest, and also weed seeds, wild fruits, animal matter collected near water, traffic-killed animals, and garbage.

In the southern half of Minnesota, American crows are seen regularly in winter. These stocky birds have a wingspread of about three feet and weigh about a pound. They are an all-black bird, including the bill, legs, and feet.

American crows are resourceful and mischievous. They are one of the most recognizable birds in Minnesota and are also among the most intelligent When several are feeding together, one stands by as a sentinel to warn of approaching danger. They feed on roadkill but are rarely hit by cars. Unmated birds known as helpers help raise the young. A crow often entertains itself by provoking chases with other birds.

Another example of intelligence is their well-developed system of communication. Variations of the basic "caw" convey vital information to all other American crows within hearing distance. They "caw" to keep fellow crows on alert, to warn of hunters, and to pass the word on about new sources of food. Crows also announce to neighbors that a stranger is walking through "their" forest.

A Closer Look:
Lake Waconia, Freeze-up History

Our family lives along the northwest side of Lake Waconia. Since we arrived in 1970, I have recorded ice-out and freeze-up dates for the lake, the second largest in the metro area, using these criteria: ice-out—first day when at least 90 percent of the lake is free of ice; Freeze-up—first day when at least 90 percent of the lake is frozen over, and stays frozen over. Mary and Stan Giesen and Butch Wollum kept track of freeze-ups and ice-outs before we arrived, so the Lake Waconia record goes back to 1940. This isn't a long enough record to draw any conclusions except to say that the amount of days the lake is ice free is quite variable from year to year. I'm including 40 years of freeze-ups in this entry.

Photo: Jim Gilbert

LAKE WACONIA FREEZE-UP HISTORY

1968 • November 23	1978 • November 21	1988 • November 21	1998 • December 21
1969 • November 30	1979 • November 30	1989 • November 23	1999 • December 16
1970 • November 24	1980 • December 3	1990 • December 2	2000 • November 21
1971 • November 30	1981 • December 5	1991 • November 7	2001 • December 20
1972 • November 29	1982 • December 8	1992 • November 27	2002 • December 3
1973 • December 6	1983 • November 29	1993 • November 26	2003 • November 29
1974 • December 1	1984 • December 3	1994 • December 7	2004 • December 14
1975 • November 27	1985 • November 21	1995 • November 22	2005 • November 30
1976 • November 15	1986 • November 15	1996 • November 19	2006 • December 3
1977 • November 25	1987 • December 4	1997 • November 21	2007 • December 1

277

December

With new snow and ice, and maybe a surprise white frost, December can provide some of the year's most dramatic landscapes. The darkness of night now exceeds fifteen hours, and many people miss the vanished daylight. Lakes continue to freeze over. Beavers are active inside their lodges, feeding on bark from tree branches they stored underwater earlier in the fall. White-tailed deer begin dropping their antlers. Cattail heads look like hotdogs on sticks in frozen marshes. Pheasants feed in corn stubble and pick up roadside gravel to help with digestion. Blue jays, cardinals, pine grosbeaks, and other winter birds provide welcome color as they perch on snow-covered evergreen boughs.

Reading the Landscape

Week one (December 1–7)

Lake Minnetonka, 25 Years
  of Freeze-up Data
Stargazing, a First Look
Stargazing in the December Sky
Rime and White Frost

Week two (December 8–15)

Red Squirrels
Gray Squirrels
Animal Tracking in the Snow
Snowfall Amounts

Week three (December 16–23)

What Deer are Eating
Bohemian Waxwings
Astronomical Winter
Northern Cardinals

Week four (December 24–31)

Audubon Christmas Bird Counts
Wind Chill
Walking in the Moonlight
Wintering Robins

first week in december

The normal high temperature for December first in the Twin Cities is 32° and the low is 17° F. The record high for December 1 is 68°, set in 1998, and the record low of -15° was recorded in 1893. With sunrise at 7:31 a.m. and sunset at 4:33 p.m., a good share of us are now leaving for work in the dark and coming home from work in the dark. According to meteorologists and climatologists, December 1 is the first day of winter here in the Upper Midwest.

Bald eagles hunt fish where open water prevails. Flocks of cedar waxwings feed on the fruit of junipers, mountain ashes, and crabapple trees. Mourning doves, northern cardinals, and juncos consume the cracked corn spread on the ground below feeders. Immersion heaters (available commercially) keep birdbaths or bird drinkers ice-free. Birds need the water year-round, and other wildlife will come for water too. As Mary and Dave Brislance of Lutsen remarked to me in a letter during the winter of 2008: "We empty two ice cream buckets of water into our heated birdbath each day. The deer, red squirrels, gray fox, and all the birds drink it dry. Thirsty critters we have."

A majority of raccoons have retreated to

their winter quarters. They will be slumbering in sheltered places such as hollow trees and abandoned buildings until well into January or February. Raccoons are not true hibernators as their body temperatures do not decrease.

scattered events

- **December 1, 1999** - Nearly all Minnesota lakes are ice-free. Several fishing boats were out on Lake Minnetonka. A Belle Plaine truck farmer harvested late cabbage, broccoli, and spinach.

- **December 1, 2006** - No snow on the Twin Cities landscape; also true for most of the state. Still a few late eastern chipmunks out and about. Freeze-up date for Pelican Lake at Breezy Point.

- **December 4, 1997** - Up to 5 inches of ice covers Lake Waconia. Walleyes and northerns are biting. Lake ice was cracking and booming with dropping evening temperatures.

- **December 4, 2007** - The second snowstorm for December. There was a feeding frenzy at our feeding station during the snowfall, with Northern cardinals, juncos, American goldfinches, and gray squirrels among the active animals. About eight inches to a foot of snow covers the Twin Cities area; twice that amount in Duluth and along the North Shore of Lake Superior.

- **December 5, 1998** - High of 54° as the warm spell continues. Lawns are still nice and green, gardeners planted tulip bulbs, earthworms worked close to the surface, spiders ballooned, and forest mosses looked lush green.

A Closer Look:
Lake Minnetonka, 25 Years of Freeze-up Data

The tenth largest of Minnesota's 15,291 lakes and the largest in the metropolitan area, Lake Minnetonka covers an area of 14,500 acres (22 square miles) and has approximately 110 miles of shoreline. The word "Minnetonka" is Dakota for "Big Water" ("minnie" for water, "tonka" for big) and was officially named by Governor Ramsey in 1852.

Minnetonka is more of a meeting of waters than it is a single lake. In addition to the Upper Lake and Lower Lake, there are 23 named bays and areas. The complex of 16 interconnecting lakes was largely formed by melting blocks of ice that fell off the retreating glaciers about 11,000 years ago.

Lake Minnetonka is old, large, and a bit cumbersome to study. It's even difficult to determine the exact freeze-up time year after year. We have to be satisfied with a freeze-up *day* rather than a freeze-up minute or

FREEZE-UP DATES FOR LAKE MINNETONKA					
2007	December 3	1998	December 25	1989	December 3
2006	December 5	1997	December 26	1988	December 1
2005	December 7	1996	November 25	1987	December 17
2004	December 19	1995	November 28	1986	December 5
2003	December 12	1994	December 11	1985	November 27
2002	December 3	1993	December 11	1984	December 6
2001	January 2 (2002)	1992	December 18	1983	December 2
2000	December 5	1991	November 25		
1999	December 21	1990	December 18		

hour. I define freeze-up as the first day when at least 90 percent of a lake freezes over and stays frozen over. With the help of long-time Lake Minnetonka observers such as Dick Gray, Millard Skarp and Jim Wyer, I have been recording freeze-ups for this beautiful lake for a quarter of a century. Jim has been observing Lake Minnetonka happenings for eighty years, and the other two close to that.

Listed in the sidebar above are the results of our observations.

A Closer Look:
Stargazing, a First Look

Try stargazing. It's a way of being part of nature on the grandest scale. Nothing can stretch the mind like study of the night sky. The light reaching our eyes tonight from many stars has been traveling through space since the Ice Age, or even since the time of the earth's dinosaurs.

Stargazing is the art and science of observing the objects and events in the nighttime sky. It doesn't have to be a complicated, expensive activity. What you need is an inquiring mind and discerning eye. To begin with, you will want to become familiar with the sky. This can be done by following the moon's phases, noting the positions of the planets, looking for the northern lights, and finding out where constellations such as Orion and Cygnus are located. Bookstores and museums sell books for beginners, and the Minnesota Weatherguide Environment Calendars

Photo: NASA

good books available to help viewers locate hundreds of deep sky objects with binoculars, a spotting scope, or the naked eye.

Since 1989, Rod Nerdahl has been the astronomy consultant to the Freshwater Society, creating the sky charts and astronomical data published in the Minnesota Weatherguide Environment Calendars. As an educator he has been involved in public astronomy education for more than thirty years. Rod once remarked: "Somewhere along the way, you will discover an amazing fact about stargazing. It's one of the ways that human beings have learned to appreciate the awesome universe in which they live, and their equally awesome place in it."

A Closer Look:

Stargazing in the December Sky

Stretching around the sky in a complete circle is the Milky Way, a band of light composed of millions of stars in our galaxy. You can easily see this band of light arching across the heavens provided you can get far away from bright city lights.

The nearest star visible to the naked eye from most parts of the United States is also the brightest in appearance, Sirius. Sirius is about eight light years away. It is interesting to note that light reaches us from the sun (which is a star, of course,) in just eight minutes, and

have star maps and information on planet locations and moon rise and set times. Plan to visit a nearby nature center, museum, or planetarium to find out how to get in touch with astronomy enthusiasts in your area.

You probably don't need a telescope, at least for your first year or so of observing. For a deeper look into the oceans of space you can achieve greater success and satisfaction with a pair of binoculars or small spotting scope, the tools used by birdwatchers. They offer wide fields of view and make things easier to find, require little maintenance, and can easily be taken to rural areas where the nights are filled with starlight rather than light pollution from streetlights and neon signs. There are yet it takes eight *years* for the light leaving the surface of Sirius to reach our eyes.

The North Star, Polaris, is not terribly bright, but it is fairly easy to find at the end of the handle of the Little Dipper. It is 432 light years away.

Orion the Hunter serves as the hub of the winter constellations and, along with the Big Dipper, is undoubtedly the most recognizable star pattern. It's one of the few constellations that looks somewhat like its namesake. Most people can imagine it as the figure of a big person with a club in one hand and a shield in the other. In the right shoulder of Orion is the star called Betelgeuse (pronounced "beetle-juice"). This red super giant is about 429 light years away, and it fluctuates in diameter from about 300 million miles to around 1 billion miles. It's the largest star within 1,000 light years of the Earth. To quote Mike Lynch, WCCO Radio meteorologist and popular Minnesota amateur astronomer: "The next time you see Betelgeuse, keep in mind that it's the biggest single thing you've ever seen!"

A galaxy is a large assemblage of stars, and a typical galaxy contains millions to hundreds of billions of them. The Whirlpool Galaxy (M51) is located just below the star at the end of the handle of the Big Dipper. It is 37 million light years away, and is a spiral galaxy that may contain 100 billion stars. With a small telescope you can see its spiral arms.

The Andromeda Galaxy, 2.5 million light years away and the next-door neighbor to the Milky Way, is the most distant object the human eye can see. If you're stargazing in the dark countryside, you can see it with the naked eye as a tiny fuzzy spot. Astronomers think that there could be over 100 billion other galaxies besides our own in the universe, some of them possibly more than 13 billion light years away.

Photo: Nataraj Hauser / eyeDance

A Closer Look:
Rime and White Frost

A white granular deposit of ice crystals on the windward side of objects, rime forms during foggy weather on cold days of fall and winter. Rime is light, white, flaky, and often thick. It is easily shattered. Examined up close, these white ice crystals on crabapple fruit, twigs, grasses, wires, or any sub-freezing object are examples of fragile beauty. A line of trees and shrubs covered with white rime is a spectacular sight.

Fog is a cloud on the ground. It too is made up of tiny water droplets. These droplets change into rime when they hit cold objects. In our area, rime can be especially thick along rivers or open lakes where steam fog is able to feed off warm waters. It is thicker on hilltop trees as opposed to valley areas. This happens because air is slightly chilled as it rises and expands.

Rime is not the same as the ice coating called glaze, which forms on trees and other objects when drizzle or rain falls. It is also not the same as white frost, also called hoar frost, which is formed when water in its gaseous, invisible vapor form clings to objects colder than the dew point. Rime is more dense and harder than white frost.

White frost is the result of water vapor passing from a gas to a solid form. The solid ice crystals form on objects exposed to the air such as tree branches, plant stems, wires, and poles. White frost forms when nights are clear and calm, and air next to the surface is relatively moist. If the surface temperatures of objects stay above freezing under these general conditions, dew is likely to form. White frost, with its interlocking crystals, can transform a landscape of trees, shrubs, fences, and utility wires into a splendid winter scene. The clear blue morning sky and white frost-covered countryside or cityscape really brings out the photographers and others who appreciate nature's beauty.

Week two (Dec 8-15)

Fresh snow is nature's best reflector, mirroring back close to 95 percent of the sun's radiation that hits its surface. Lake ice can be heard cracking, groaning, booming, and thundering as it expands and contracts in response to the changing temperatures.

House finches, mourning doves, chickadees, and nuthatches are some of the birds that come to heated birdbaths to drink the water. About a dozen species of birds, plus gray squirrels and red squirrels are numerous and active at feeders. Just before and during a snowstorm there is a feeding frenzy at wildlife feeding stations. Each individual downy and hairy woodpecker roosts at night in a separate tree cavity and will retreat there during daylight hours if the weather is threatening.

We have reached the time when we begin to understand the winter environment of the north, where all life is judged by its ability to adapt to cold, snow, and limited sunlight. One adaptation is hibernation. Right now there are millions and millions of animals in deep sleep across Minnesota, including woodchucks, thirteen-lined ground squirrels, turtles, snakes, lizards, frogs, toads, salamanders, spiders, ticks, and insects.

scattered events

- **December 11, 1993** - 178 bald eagles were counted by one birder while standing in a single spot overlooking the lower end of Lake Pepin, which froze over today.

- **December 13, 1998** - We are still in a warm spell. Dandelions bloom on short stems, flowering kale and parsley continue growing in gardens, mosses at tree bases are bright green, and people continue to play tennis outdoors.

- **December 14, 2004** - Flocks of wintering American robins relish crabapples. Official freeze-up date for Leech Lake at Walker, Green Lake at Spicer, and both Lake Waconia and Lotus Lake in Carver County. A low of -25° F was recorded at Embarrass this morning.

- **December 14, 2005** - Winter wonderland! Six inches of new snow. The wet snow stuck to deciduous trees and evergreens. At Two Harbors, 26.3 inches of Lake Superior-enhanced snow fell, and Tofte received 13 inches.

- **December 15, 1993** - About 600 bald eagles have congregated at the Reads Landing area where the Chippewa River flows into the Mississippi.

A Closer Look: Red Squirrels

From Alaska and Canada, the red squirrel's range extends southward in the Rocky Mountains to New Mexico, and in the Appalachians to South Carolina. They lend charm and color largely within the conifer belt, are active all winter, and are boisterous in work or play.

Because red squirrels prefer evergreen forests they aren't as abundant in southern Minnesota as in the north. Cones, seeds,

Photo: David Brislance

acorns and other nuts are stored under tree roots or in underground burrows. Also, they'll tunnel through snow to search for food. Generally they're vegetarians, but may eat eggs, young birds, and even baby cottontails. Many mushroom species are eaten, fresh or after drying, including poisonous ones ingested with no ill effects. The red squirrels seem to be able to detoxify such substances.

Where fir, pine, and spruce cones are in ample supply, the red squirrel often gathers them together and shucks them all while sitting on a favorite log, stump, or rock. The seeds are eaten or stored, but the piles of cone scales built up with time to become conspicuous middens, sometimes accumulating over the years to depths of many feet. It takes approximately two minutes for a red squirrel to strip a cone.

Red squirrels, the smallest of the tree squirrels, measure a foot in total length and weigh about one-half pound. This woodland sentinel wears a rusty red coat with grayish-white beneath. Their eyes are ringed with white fur.

The territory of a red squirrel is small—seldom more than four hundred feet in diameter. But if anything unusual is going on within its territory, the squirrel responds with a loud chattering and scolding. The nests of these squirrels may be placed on branches or in holes in trees. Outside nests are more common in regions where tree trunks are small and few cavities are available. Nests are usually bulky structures made up of twigs, fibers, lichens, mosses, and strips of bark, with the inside chamber impervious to the weather.

A Closer Look:
Gray Squirrels

The grays are the squirrels of the hardwood deciduous forests. The eastern gray squirrel, with its long, bushy tail and a general gray coloration, is the species we see in Minnesota. They are most common in the south but can also inhabit the mixed coniferous/deciduous forests in the northern part of the state. From extreme southern Canada to the Gulf of Mexico the range of the eastern gray squirrel covers most of the eastern half of the United States, from eastern North Dakota to eastern Texas to the Atlantic Coast. They are highly arboreal and usually associated with nut-bearing trees such as hickory and oak. The casual observer knows that these squirrels can become quite tame, and are the ones that people feed in our city parks.

Black (melanin) and white (albino) phases of the species are not rare. Sometimes these mutations, either partial or complete, are so common that they become the dominant color phase in an area.

© tim elliott | Dreamstime.com

Gray squirrels are 18 to 20 inches long, including the tail, and weigh about one pound. In winter the soft gray fur grows long and dense, allowing these animals to be out and about except during very stormy or extremely cold days.

Acorns, hickory nuts, walnuts, and butternuts supply much of the gray squirrels' diet from late summer to the following spring. Wild berries and other fruits are also eaten.

Individual squirrels consume about 2 pounds of food a week, or 100 pounds a year. Bark and twigs can often keep squirrels alive when food stores run out in winter. Even better would be sunflower seeds or corn from some kind person's feeding station. Early spring produces sweet sap to lick and swelling buds to eat.

A Closer Look:
Animal Tracking in the Snow

For every creature seen or heard, at least a hundred pass by unobserved. Only when we see tracks in the snow do we begin to realize all of the activity going on around us.

For more than 25 winters, starting in 1970, it was my privilege to be the Hopkins School District naturalist and have the opportunity to take hundreds of groups animal tracking each winter. Mostly we hiked the trails at Lowry Nature Center, located in Carver Park near Victoria.

On these excursions looking for signs of deer was always a favorite, and we would often find deer tracks and beds in the snow. Fox tracks also created much excitement among the students, as did raccoon tracks that we could count on seeing during warm winter spells. Tracks for both red and gray squirrels often led to and from the base of trees, and eastern cottontail rabbit tracks were almost always quite numerous. Mouse and shrew tunnels and tracks, and the footprints of ring-necked pheasants and small birds, were eagerly recorded by the students on their data sheets.

Probably the most memorable tracking experience for me took place one bright morning when several inches of snow had fallen in the night. A class of sixth-graders were scheduled for a walk, and I was helping them get into their snowshoes. A few managed to get the snowshoes on themselves and I told them they could walk around a bit to get their "snowshoe legs."

A few minutes later several students rushed over to me as I was bent over putting snowshoes on some student's boots, to say they had seen the best track ever in the snow and I had to come immediately to see it. Several sixth graders on their snowshoes were in a large circle around the special track when I arrived. They were anxious for me to photograph the track. I did, and have used the image hundreds of times in my nature talks. What was it? It was the perfect imprint of the wings and body of a great horned owl as it hit the snow trying to catch a mouse or other small animal. To me the best part of the whole situation was the excitement of discovery for the students, and the fact that they wanted to preserve this outstanding track for many others to see.

A grouse track

If you would like to experience the sense of discovery, the day after a light dusting of snow is a good time to track wildlife. Wet snow best preserves details of tracks. Look on sidewalks and driveways, paths in parks, or beneath bird feeders for prints of squirrels, mice and deer.

A Closer Look:
Snowfall Amounts

Each snowflake has fragile beauty, one of the most transient of natural forms. Myriads of snowflakes nourish and protect the farmer's alfalfa, keep the frost from moving too deep, and help insulate house foundations.

In cities and suburbs, snow can become a cold, slushy, and often costly nuisance. To travelers, snow can be a slippery blinding hazard whether on foot or in a vehicle. Yet a fresh snowcover also brings us a brand-new landscape with rounded corners and freshened surfaces. A snowfall can transform a forest into an enchanting kingdom, a meadow into a shimmering wonderland.

The Minnesota state record for a 24-hour snowfall is 36 inches on January 7, 1994, at Wolf Ridge Environmental Learning Center located near Finland in Lake County, about 800 feet above Lake Superior and a mile or two from the shore. The seasonal average for Minneapolis/St. Paul snowfall is 56 inches.

With that in mind, here are some national extremes: The winter of 1971–72 brought 1,122 inches (93.5 feet) of snow to the Paradise Ranger Station on Mount Rainier in Washington.

The greatest 24-hour snowfall was 76 inches at Silver Lake, Colorado, during April 14–15, 1921.

A single storm, from February 13–19,1959, covered Mount Shasta Ski Bowl in northern California with a 189-inch snowfall.

Week three (Dec 16-23)

Snow on boughs of white pines and other evergreen trees is a stunning sight. The day after a light dusting of snow is a good time to try animal tracking.

Pairs of great horned owls can be heard duet hooting, probably establishing nesting territories or at least keeping in touch. American tree sparrows, dark-eyed juncos, and northern cardinals are the first and last birds at feeding stations each day. They begin coming to feeders about 25 minutes before sunrise and continue to come until about 25 minutes after sunset. All three species prefer to eat on the ground.

Flying squirrels come nightly to a good number of wildlife feeding stations. They typically arrive about five p.m. to dine on sunflower seeds and suet. Floodlights don't scare the squirrels, nor does the presence of someone sitting quietly outside watching them.

Thousands of Canada geese spend the winter at Silver Lake in Rochester; the giants migrate to Rochester from Manitoba.

In parts of northern Minnesota, ruffed grouse dive down into powdery snow to keep warm at night. Even on cold days, porcupines can be seen high up in trees feeding on the inner bark and twigs of aspens, basswoods, pines, and other trees. Moose have begun dropping their antlers.

scattered events

- **December 16, 1995** - On the Audubon Christmas Bird Count for the Faribault/ Northfield area of Rice County, 39 people today saw 47 species and 6,352 individual birds, including 895 mallard ducks, 694 dark-eyed juncos, 266 snow buntings, 99 northern cardinals, 32 red-breasted nuthatches, 20 brown creepers and 1 American robin.

- **December 16, 2006** - On the Audubon Christmas Bird Count for Mankato, 42 species were observed. Highlights included 20 bald eagles and 134 American robins.

- **December 17, 2004** - Last ocean-going ship of the year left the Duluth Harbor. Common redpolls, pine grosbeaks, and great gray owls numerous in the Finland area, where snow is knee-deep and perfect for snowshoeing and cross-country skiing. Still no snow on the Twin Cities landscape.

- **December 17, 2005** - Sixty people observed and recorded 66 bird species and thousands of individual birds on this clear but cold (high of only 11° F) day for the 37th annual Bloomington Audubon Christmas Bird Count. Highlights included thousands of mallard ducks and hundreds of Canada geese at Black Dog Lake, a snowy owl seen at the airport, dozens of wild turkeys and American robins, plus two pied-billed grebes and one Carolina wren.

- **December 17, 2006** - The 61st Cedar Creek Christmas Bird Count (northern Anoka County) resulted in 43 species observed and recorded. Species that surpassed the high

count of individuals seen in the previous 60 years include (with numbers for this year): 142 wild turkeys, 11 bald eagles, 31 red-tailed hawks, 20 rough-legged hawks, 54 mourning doves, 50 northern cardinals, and 13 pileated woodpeckers.

- **December 21, 1999** - Freeze-up date for Lake Minnetonka, Lake Harriet and Lake Calhoun in Minneapolis, Lake Sylvia near Annandale, and Grindstone Lake in Pine County.

A Closer Look:
What Deer are Eating

Deer are primarily browsing animals. They will eat fungi, acorns, grasses, and herbs in season. In winter they browse twigs of sugar maple, basswood, bur oak, ironwood, red-osier dogwood, staghorn sumac, and other trees and shrubs, eating mostly woody parts that are pencil-size or smaller. Deer don't have front teeth on the upper jawbone, so it's easy for the trained observer to differentiate between the rough-chewed twigs nipped off by deer and the "knife-cut" twigs removed by rabbits or snowshoe hares.

Wildlife biologists have found that a two-hundred-pound buck white-tailed deer needs ten pounds of nutritious woody browse each day to stay healthy. On average deer need six to twelve pounds of twigs per day consistently through winter. But finding food is difficult so deer commonly lose 10 to 30 percent of their body weight in the winter.

White-tailed deer are not strict vegetarians. They can catch and eat fish in shallow streams, eat birds, and dig through six inches of snow to feed on wintering colonies of ladybug beetles.

A Closer Look:
Bohemian Waxwings

Bohemian waxwings are erratic winter visitors to Minnesota, varying widely in numbers and distribution from year to year. They are present most often in the northern and central regions of the state, but in years of abundance, as flocks move about searching for food supplies, they can also be encountered in the south. They are often seen in flocks of fifty to a hundred birds but in the Duluth area and along the North Shore sometimes the flocks can contain more than five hundred birds.

On December 17, 2007, Dave and Mary Brislance, from Lutsen, spotted a flock of well over a hundred Bohemian waxwings while on a shopping trip in Grand Marais. The birds had been shopping too and came upon a big crop of native mountain ash tree fruit right in the city. They were in the middle of a feast. Dave was able to get dozens of fantastic photos of the

Photo: David Brislance

birds while they fed.

The Bohemian waxwing is a bird of the coniferous forests of Eurasia, western Canada, and the Rocky Mountains. They sometimes wander in large flocks far to the east and south of their normal range. Their food consists of insects and berries.

Bohemian waxwings are larger than the closely related cedar waxwings, and they also have strong white markings on their wings and a deep rusty color under their tails. Like the cedar waxwings, they have a sleek crest and yellow tips at the ends of their tails. Beginning in the third year the tips of their wings look as if they have been dipped in red wax.

A Closer Look:
Astronomical Winter

For meteorologists in the Upper Midwest, winter runs from December 1 to the end of February. On the first day of meteorological winter in 2007 we had our first snowstorm and many lakes froze over, including Lake Minnewashta and Pierson Lake in Carver County and Green Lake in Chisago County.

By coincidence we also had a good snowfall on the first astronomical day of winter, December 22, 2007. On that day, according to astronomical calculation, winter arrived at 12:08 a.m., as the Earth reached the point in its revolution about the Sun when the North Pole was inclined 23½ degrees away from the Sun, giving those of us who live in the Northern Hemisphere our longest night and shortest day. We call this the winter solstice.

Astronomical winter begins on December 21 or 22 each year, and at noon on the first day of winter the sun is 21½ degrees above the horizon in the Twin Cities and only 18 degrees at International Falls. The Twin Cities receives 8 hours and 46 minutes of sunlight and people in International Falls must get by with a half-hour less.

Even though our daylight begins to increase again following the winter solstice, things typically continue to get colder for five more weeks, with our coldest days often arriving in late January. It takes that long before radiation from the slowly-returning sun can have a positive effect on the frozen snow-covered ground and chilly air. Statistically, January 25 is our coldest day of the year.

A Closer Look:
Northern Cardinals

The northern cardinal is a non-migrator, and is one of the common year-round birdfeeder birds in the Twin Cities area and throughout the southern half of Minnesota. Its name comes from the Latin word "cardinalis," which means "important." The bright red males with black faces are unmistakable, though many consider the greenish-red females, who have the same conical beak and crest, to be equally beautiful. Both male and female are typically eight inches long, have a twelve-inch wingspan, and weigh 1.5 ounces.

Cardinals are usually the earliest birds at the feeders in the morning and the last to leave at dusk, sometimes feeding so late during the winter days that we have trouble seeing them. They never tire of sunflower seeds but like cracked corn and other seeds too. Always they

Photo: Mike Lentz

prefer to feed on the ground or on a tray feeder. This bird more than any other has come to symbolize wild bird feeding.

The current range of the northern cardinal includes all of the eastern United States, west into the central plains, and extreme southern Canada. It also occurs locally in the southwestern states and Mexico. This is an expanded distribution from a century ago, as our landscape changes have provided more habitat opportunities for cardinals.

Northern cardinals are fairly new to Minnesota. They first arrived in the southeastern part in the late 1800s, and it was not until the mid-1930s that they were established as permanent residents in the Twin Cities. Planted and native evergreens help provide shelter and may encourage range expansion, along with food offered at feeding stations. Insects, wild fruits, and seeds are their natural foods.

Cardinals can live in different kinds of shrubby areas, away from people or right in our backyards. Look for them in edges of deciduous forests, farm windbreaks, and urban woodlots. During the past few years observers have seen a few cardinals in the Brainerd and Mille Lacs Lake areas, along the North Shore, and at other northern Minnesota locations.

Studies show that northern cardinals not only mate for life, but they remain together the whole year. As winter approaches, the residents of an area often associate together in loose flocks, especially in locales where food is plentiful. Flocks usually disband by early March as pairs move into their breeding territories.

Week four (Dec 24-31)

The sun no longer creeps southward, but each sunset moves a little to the north. We can all take comfort in that. Below zero temperatures, or close to that, bring elegant frost designs to the insides of some clear glass windowpanes. The patterns come in swirls and feathers, fronds and trees.

Showy fruit on highbush cranberry shrubs, bittersweet vines, and crabapple trees is available to birds and other wildlife. The Christmas cactus, which is native to the tropical parts of Brazil, blooms nicely in our homes. Its cherry-red flowers vary in color intensity depending on various growing conditions.

With a heartbeat of seven-hundred pumps a minute, black-capped chickadees need to eat the equivalent of their own weight every day during the winter. Chickadees sometimes take seeds from human hands.

Chipmunks awake but stay in and eat from the supply of food stored in their underground burrows.

Instead of worrying about squirrels raiding what you set out on a birdfeeder, it would be better to protect the birds from predation by house cats left to roam outdoors.

Heavy snow can be tough on trees and shrubs. The native spruces, both back and white, and balsam firs of northern Minnesota have a spire-shaped growth form that acts like a steep-pitched roof, allowing the snow to slide off. Yet snow still gets caught on the boughs. It's beautiful to us, but research shows that a single forty-foot balsam could end up holding more than six-thousand pounds of snow.

scattered events

- **December 25, 1922** - Dr. Thomas S. Roberts reported that veteran golfers enjoyed the novelty of playing their game on Christmas Day. On this spring-like day there was no snow on the ground in the Twin Cities and the temperature was 51° F at noon.

- **December 25, 2005** - White Bear Lake has 6 to 8 inches of ice. About 99 percent of Minnesota is having a white Christmas. Only the extreme southwest part of the state has no snow. Three to five inches of snow covers the Twin Cities and area, with close to twenty inches at Lutsen.

- **December 25, 2006** - Brown Christmas in the Twin Cities, Duluth, and most of Minnesota.

- **December 30, 2004** - Record high of 51° in the Twin Cities. Not a trace of snow left. A coating of water is seen on top of lake ice. Black-capped chickadees sang spring "fee-bee" songs over and over. Worthington and Redwood Falls both had a high of 57° F.

- **December 31, 2006** - The biggest storm of the new winter season hit on this last day of the year. Ten inches of snow fell on Waconia and Mankato. Birdfeeder birds such as juncos and chickadees were numerous and active.

A Closer Look:
Audubon Christmas Bird Counts

The weekend of December 15/16, 2007, marked the beginning of the 108th annual National Audubon Society's Christmas Bird Count. Dr. Frank Chapman, a pioneer ornithologist, began the count in Englewood, New Jersey, in 1900 as a substitute for heavy

Christmas-time bird shooting. For the first count, 25 reports were filed by 27 participants. This year tens of thousands of observers took part in more than a thousand bird counts across the United States. There are also bird counts made in other countries. The count is unquestionably the world's greatest cooperative survey of wildlife. The Audubon Society regards the counts as very successful these past hundred plus years. They have steadily grown in popularity and importance.

In 2007–2008, a record 73 locations across Minnesota held a Christmas Bird Count. A count is done within a 15-mile-diameter circle, and all took place in an 18-day period between mid-December and early January. Each count lasts one day. Among the locations participating were Bloomington, Excelsior, Red Wing, Rochester, Bluestem Prairie/Buffalo River State Park, Walker, Duluth, Two Harbors, and Bemidji. A total of about 120 species and hundreds of thousands of birds were counted all in all. The most frequently counted bird was the Canada goose, followed by mallard duck, black-capped chickadee, house sparrow, European starling, rock pigeon, American crow, and dark-eyed junco.

A summary of one count: December 15, 2007. Today on the Bloomington Audubon Christmas Bird Count, 67 people observed 62 species and 15,948 individual birds. No new species were added to the count which is in its 39th year. However, record numbers were observed for seven species: 130 wild turkeys, 93 red-tailed hawks, 573 rock pigeons, 66 red-bellied woodpeckers, 19 pileated woodpeckers, 290 cedar waxwings, and 4 fox sparrows.

The bird count data is published in the Audubon Society's journal *American Birds*, and scientists use the mass of data accumulated over the years to keep track of the increase or decline of various species, to learn more about life cycles, and to add to our knowledge of birds' migratory habits.

A Closer Look:
Wind Chill

We can't let wind chill keep us from enjoying winter activities, so we need to be aware of what it tells us and dress accordingly. The wind chill temperature is based on how the average person loses heat off his or her bare skin. Our bodies produce heat and generate a thin layer of warm air that insulates our skin. Wind, when combined with cold air temperatures, eats away at the thin layer of warm air over our skin, accelerating heat loss. The faster the wind, the faster the heat leaves our skin.

The wind chill temperature is based on a complicated equation that calculates the temperature that our skin feels because of heat

Wind Chill Chart

Wind (mph)	\ Temperature (°F)	40	35	30	25	20	15	10	5	0	-5	-10	-15	-20	-25	-30	-35	-40	-45
5		36	31	25	19	13	7	1	-5	-11	-16	-22	-28	-34	-40	-46	-52	-57	-63
10		34	27	21	15	9	3	-4	-10	-16	-22	-28	-35	-41	-47	-53	-59	-66	-72
15		32	25	19	13	6	0	-7	-13	-19	-26	-32	-39	-45	-51	-58	-64	-71	-77
20		30	24	17	11	4	-2	-9	-15	-22	-29	-35	-42	-48	-55	-61	-68	-74	-81
25		29	23	16	9	3	-4	-11	-17	-24	-31	-37	-44	-51	-58	-64	-71	-78	-84
30		28	22	15	8	1	-5	-12	-19	-26	-33	-39	-46	-53	-60	-67	-73	-80	-87
35		28	21	14	7	0	-7	-14	-21	-27	-34	-41	-48	-55	-62	-69	-76	-82	-89
40		27	20	13	6	-1	-8	-15	-22	-29	-36	-43	-50	-57	-64	-71	-78	-84	-91
45		26	19	12	5	-2	-9	-16	-23	-30	-37	-44	-51	-58	-65	-72	-79	-86	-93
50		26	19	12	4	-3	-10	-17	-24	-31	-38	-45	-52	-60	-67	-74	-81	-88	-95
55		25	18	11	4	-3	-11	-18	-25	-32	-39	-46	-54	-61	-68	-75	-82	-89	-97
60		25	17	10	3	-4	-11	-19	-26	-33	-40	-48	-55	-62	-69	-76	-84	-91	-98

Frostbite Times: 30 minutes   10 minutes   5 minutes

On November 1, 2001 the National Weather Service (NWS) implemented a replacement Wind Chill Temperature (WCT) index. The new formula uses advances in science, technology, and computer modeling to provide a more accurate, understandable, and useful formula for calculating the dangers from winter winds and freezing temperatures. The new formula requires stronger winds or colder temperatures to reach the wind chill levels of the past. To calculate the wind chill using the chart above, find the row for the current wind speed, then locate the place where the row intersects the column for the current temperature.

loss from the combined effect of the actual temperature and the wind speed. The numbers are subjective because it assumes everyone loses heat from their bodies at the same rate.

Because heat loss due to wind chill can cause hypothermia and frostbite to set in quicker, each of us needs to be covered with insulating clothing when conditions warrant.

Our car engines won't drop to the wind chill value because they aren't bare human skin, but increased winds in winter cold will cause the cars or any object outside to cool off faster.

The wind chill formula and resulting chart was adjusted in 2001 to make the perceived temperature a little more realistic. The old formula exaggerated the wind chill values.

To calculate the wind chill using the chart, find the row for the current wind speed, then locate the place where the row intersects the column for the current air temperature.

© Odysseyf22 | Dreamstime.com

A Closer Look:

Walking in the Moonlight

If you have the opportunity, take a walk in the woods or in a park, or even around a city block on a December night when the moon is full, or nearly so, and there is a good covering of snow on the ground. A walk under the full moon is worth the discomfort of the cold, but remember there is no such thing as bad weather, only bad clothing. Always dress in layers during a Minnesota winter. Once you are outside your eyes adjust to the moonlit landscape quickly and you notice the sparkling light on the snow and the wondrous silhouettes of the trees, and those dark tree shadows. Most anyone doing this adventure mini-trek, with or without snowshoes, with or without a companion, hopes to hear the hoot of a great horned owl. But it's the cold silence and the light from the moon that gets us thinking and restores our minds.

Just thinking about the moon is fun. Probably no other celestial object is held in greater affection than the moon, unless it's our closest star, the sun, which is the source of the moonlight. The moon is linked to romance in our culture. During a full moon we see face-like features in the light and dark patterns of its disk. We watch it go through all of its phases during the month and find beauty in all of them. Both the words "month" and "moon" derive from the same root, which means "to measure," and our most important tool for measuring time, the calendar, was designed around the moon's phases.

The average month of thirty days coincides closely (though not exactly) with the 29 days, 12 hours, and 44 minutes it takes for the moon to make a complete circuit around the earth. And the period between phases—from one full moon to next, for example—is close to 29½ days.

Agricultural people for many centuries have used the phases of the moon to guide planting and harvesting. Ocean tides are the result of lunar gravitational force. The same force causes our atmosphere to bulge slightly in the direction of the moon. There is even evidence that tidal effects, in a small way, make changes in air pressure which then affect the fluids in living creatures, which may, in some cases, be enough to cause subtle changes in behavior. Perhaps there is such a thing as lunar-generated mood changes in humans.

The distance to the moon is about 239,000 miles and the reflected sunlight it emits takes about 1.3 seconds to reach us. Full moonlight is so bright that it obliterates four-fifths of the stars we might otherwise see on a moonless night, reducing the number from two thousand to four hundred.

The amount of light we receive from the moon varies immensely with its phase. When the moon is full, its light is nearly bright enough to read by, but a quarter moon emits only one tenth as much. Despite the brilliance of the full moon, it shines with less than 1/400,000 the light of the sun.

A Closer Look:
Wintering Robins

The robin is our most familiar thrush and songbird, seen regularly in our yards and parks from early spring through fall, tugging earthworms from the ground. Being super adapters, it's not too surprising that a small percentage of Minnesota's robins don't migrate to states south of us, but spend the winter in low swampy areas and valleys where they can escape the cold winds. In winter they search for remaining wild fruit and insect eggs. Many of the non-migrators will perish before spring.

Hundreds of American robins winter among ornamental plantings, especially crabapple trees, in the residential areas of Minneapolis, St Paul, and other cities. They winter by the dozens in clumps of red cedar trees when the berry crop is good. Some robins are even known to overwinter successfully along the North Shore of Lake Superior where fruit from native mountain ash trees no doubt sustains them.

You can help robins through tough times by using a low tray feeder or clearing an area on the ground and providing berries, chopped apples, raisins, moistened dog food, and bits of hamburger or other raw meat.

153 YEARS OF LAKE MINNETONKA ICE-OUT HISTORY

(1855 – 2008. 129 years known, 24 years missing)

March Ice-out dates: 11th - 1878; 18th - 2000; 21st – 1987; 27th – 1910, 1981; 30th – 1858, 1945

April Ice-out Dates

1	**2**	**3**	**4**	**5**	**6**	**7**	**8**
1899 1902 1911 1968	1905 1946 1999	1921 1976 1995 1998 2007	1942 1966 1973 1990	1896 1930	1919 1931 2004	1925 1929 1935 1988	1907 1953 1986 1991
9	**10**	**11**	**12**	**13**	**14**	**15**	**16**
1894 1938 1967 2005 2006	1934 1959 1963 1977 1992	1892 1948 1958 1994	1908 1955 1927 2003 1943 1954	1903 1984 1912 1985 1949 1964	1877 1941 1887 1961 1918 1932		1890 1900 1906 1960 2002
17	**18**	**19**	**20**	**21**	**22**	**23**	**24**
1914 1989 1971 1922 1915 1939 1978 1969 1920	1855 1997 1928 1913 1897 1917 1933 1926 1989	1916 1993 1980 1970 1937 2001 1982 1974 1947	1936 1957	1891 1956	1952 1983	1901 1923 1944 1979 2008	1899 1924 1996
25	**26**	**27**	**28**	**29**	**30**		
1888 1904 1940 1962	1909 1972		1893 1951 1975				

May Ice-out dates: 1st – 1965; 2nd – 1950; 4th – 1859; 5th – 1857; 8th – 1856